Transnational Corporations and Uneven Development:

THE INTERNATIONALIZATION OF CAPITAL AND THE THIRD WORLD

Rhys Jenkins

Methuen

LONDON and NEW YORK

First published in 1987 by
Methuen & Co. Ltd
11 New Fetter Lane, London EC4P 4EE

Published in the USA by
Methuen & Co.
in association with Methuen, Inc.
29 West 35th Street, New York, NY 10001

Typeset by Scarborough Typesetting Services
and printed in Great Britain by
Richard Clay (The Chaucer Press) Ltd
Bungay, Suffolk

British Library Cataloguing in Publication Data
Jenkins, Rhys, 1948–
   Transnational corporations and uneven development:
   the internationalization of capital and the Third
   World. – (Development and underdevelopment).
   1. International business enterprises –
   Developing countries   2. Developing countries
   – Economic conditions
   I. Title   II. Series
   338.8'881724   HD2755.5

   ISBN 0–416–73340–9
   ISBN 0–416–73350–6 Pbk

Library of Congress Cataloging in Publication Data
Jenkins, Rhys Owen, 1948–
   Transnational corporations and uneven development.
   Bibliography: p.
   Includes index.
   1. International business enterprises – Developing
   countries.   2. Finance – Developing countries.   I. Title.
   HD2932.J45   1987   338.8'83   87–12351

   ISBN 0–416–73340–9
   ISBN 0–416–73350–6 (pbk.)

Contents

List of Tables

List of Figures

Series editors' preface

Development studies is a complex and diverse field of academic research and policy analysis. Concerned with the development process in all the comparatively poor nations of the world, it covers an enormous geographical area and a large part of the modern history of the world. Such a large subject area has generated a varied body of literature in a growing number of journals and other specialist publications, encompassing such diverse issues as the nature and feasibility of industrialization, the problem of small-scale agriculture and rural development in the Third World, the trade and other links between developed and developing countries and their effects on the development prospects of the poor, the nature and causes of poverty and inequality, and the record and future prospects of 'development planning' as a method of accelerating development. The nature of the subject matter has forced both scholars and practitioners to transcend the boundaries of their own disciplines whether these be social sciences, like economics, human geography or sociology, or applied sciences such as agronomy, plant biology or civil engineering. It is now a conventional wisdom of development studies that development problems are so multi-faceted and complex that *no* single discipline can hope to encompass them, let alone offer solutions.

This large and interdisciplinary area and the complex and rapidly changing literature pose particular problems for students, practitioners and specialists seeking a simple introduction to the field or some part of the field with which they are unfamiliar. The Development and Underdevelopment series attempts to rectify these problems by providing a number of brief, readable introductions to important issues in development studies written by an international range of specialists. All the texts are designed to be readily comprehensible to students meeting the issues for the first time, as well as to practitioners in developing countries, international agencies and voluntary bodies. We hope that, taken together, these books will bring to the reader a sense of the main preoccupations and problems in this rich and stimulating field of study and practice.   RAY BROMLEY
GAVIN KITCHING

Preface

This book is the result of a long period of research and teaching on the impact of transnational corporations on the Third World. Although my research has concentrated mainly on Latin America and on the manufacturing sector, teaching students forced me to broaden my horizons to take in other regions and sectors. As a result I hope that this book is not too biased in one direction.

Although the main impetus to writing this book was teaching about TNCs on a course on International Economic Relations at the School of Development Studies, I have tried to avoid excessive use of technical terms in an effort to make it accessible to non-economists and lay readers. Where technical terms have inevitably slipped in, I have tried to explain them in a short glossary. Particularly with students in mind, I have also included a guide to further reading at the end of each chapter.

The emphasis throughout the book is on the different theoretical perspectives which underlie contrasting assessments of the impact of TNCs on the Third World. Although I am aware of the dangers of such an approach, it is one that I have found useful in teaching students in this field. However I have not attempted to achieve a spurious objectivity and I make no secret of my own sympathies. Indeed part of the purpose of the book is to argue the case for an internationalization of capital approach to the TNCs, as opposed to the more common neoclassical or institutionalist approaches. I hope however that in doing so I have also managed to bring out the merits of other approaches.

In terms of the development of this book my foremost debt is to the students who at different times were the guinea pigs on whom the ideas presented here were first worked out and who I can only hope learnt as much as I did in the process. I am also heavily indebted to Chris Edwards, Gavin Kitching, Sol Picciotto and John Thoburn who read and commented extensively on an earlier draft of the text, although they should be absolved of any responsibility for the inadequacies of the finished product. Last but not least, my thanks to Ruth, Megan and Sam for putting up with me while the book was being written.

1

Transnational corporations: significance and growth

INTRODUCTION

Few economic institutions give rise to such passionate feelings as the transnational corporation (TNC). This is particularly true in the context of its impact in the Third World. It has been portrayed both as an engine of growth capable of eliminating international economic inequality and as a major obstacle to development. It is seen both as a force capable of revolutionizing the productive forces in the economically backward areas of the world and as a major cause of underdevelopment through a massive drain of surplus to the advanced capitalist countries.

These debates have not been confined to academic students of development but have also been fought in national and international political fora, business and trade union circles, the media and even in the arts. The aim of this book is to provide the reader with an understanding of the different positions in this continuing debate and the underlying analytical frameworks of the participants. Its focus is the impact of TNCs in the Third World and as such its scope is relatively narrow. Nevertheless a number of issues will need to be considered in order to obtain an overall perspective on this question.

DEFINITIONS AND TERMINOLOGY

Before embarking on a discussion of the impact of TNCs it will be as well to clarify a few points concerning definitions and terminology. There is no universally accepted definition of a transnational corporation. Indeed after over a decade in operation the United Nations Centre on Transnational Corporations has not been able to arrive at a definition. The broadest definition put forward by the UN Economic and Social Council refers to 'all enterprises which control assets – factories, mines, sales offices and the like – in two or more countries' (UNCTC 1978, 158). Usually, however, the term is limited to firms that control *production* in at least one foreign country (Hood and Young 1979, 3). The term is sometimes qualified by specifying that firms should have a certain minimum level of overseas activities, either in terms of the number of countries in which they operate or the proportion of production, assets or employment overseas, and that they should be of a certain minimum size. Thus, for example, the Harvard Business School Multinational Enterprise Project defined a US firm as a multinational if it was listed in the Fortune 500 largest US corporations and had subsidiaries in six or more countries. Another issue which has been debated within the United Nations is whether the term should only be applied to privately owned firms or whether it should also extend to state corporations, some of which, such as Renault, are indistinguishable from privately owned TNCs.

In a book of this kind which seeks to examine recent debates and which draws on a variety of sources for its empirical material it would be undesirable and probably impossible to adopt a single, rigid definition of transnational corporations. In other words an author is obliged to take on board the definitions which are employed by other writers. Having said this, it seems desirable to exclude from the definition firms that supply foreign markets entirely through exports and to concentrate on those which engage in international production. It is also important to bear in mind that different writers may be working with different definitions and to seek to avoid unnecessary confusion. Often empirical evidence from both home and host countries is available only on direct foreign investment and not on the operations of TNCs. The extent to which this constitutes a major problem will depend on the proportion of foreign investment which is accounted for by non-TNCs. The degree to which a relatively small number of TNCs dominate overseas investment (see below) limits the distortion involved in using such data.

It should also be noted that the book is primarily concerned with the internationalization of industrial capital. As such it does not seek to examine the operations of transnational banks or services, such as advertising, accounting, etc., except in so far as these are related to the international expansion of industrial capital.

In writing this book I have tried consistently to use the term 'transnational corporation' as opposed to alternatives such as 'multinational corporation', 'multinational enterprise', 'international firm' and so on. This is the term used in United Nations publications and institutionalized with the creation of the UN Centre on Transnational Corporations in 1974. The UN adopted the term 'transnational' in preference to 'multinational' at the insistence of certain Latin American and Caribbean states who wished to distinguish between foreign-owned TNCs and joint-ventures of two or more participating countries established as part of regional integration schemes (UNCTC 1978, 159). This term emphasizes that such corporations are usually national firms (in the sense of having a clearly identifiable home base) which operate across national boundaries.

The second term that requires definition is 'Third World'. Fashions come and go in development studies to describe groups of countries. In this book the term Third World is the main one used as a shorthand for the countries of Latin America, Africa (excluding South Africa) and Asia (excluding Japan). To avoid undue repetition the term 'less developed country' (LDC) is also used from time to time.

A word of caution is in order here, as much to the author as to the reader. The use of the term Third World suggests an unified entity which has many common features. However the Third World is in fact extremely heterogeneous and in the process of becoming more so. The states which make up the Third World range from Brazil to Botswana, Saudi Arabia to Surinam, and Taiwan to Tanzania. In talking of the impact of TNCs in the Third World there is a real danger of losing sight of this heterogeneity and presenting it as though their impact is the same everywhere irrespective of local class structures, levels of development or state forms.

The danger is all the more real because most studies of TNCs in the Third World have tended to be concentrated on a few countries which have been the main hosts for foreign investment. These have tended to be either middle-income countries, or countries with substantial natural resources. The reader should therefore always try to bear in mind the heterogeneous nature of the Third World and ask him/herself, what kind of Third World country does this point apply to? What would be the situation in a different kind of country?

ORIGINS AND GROWTH OF THE TRANSNATIONAL CORPORATION

Capital has operated internationally from the earliest days of capitalism. Merchant capital, engaged in long-distance trade, pre-dated the emergence of the capitalist mode of production in Europe. Later trade played a major role in the emergence of industrial capitalism in eighteenth-century Britain. In the nineteenth century finance also became increasingly internationalized as Britain, and to a lesser degree France and

Germany, invested abroad in government and municipal bonds, and shares in railways, trams and public utilities. In contrast to the direct foreign investment associated with TNCs, this was primarily *portfolio* investment[1] and at the outbreak of World War I 90 per cent of all foreign investment was portfolio investment. The late nineteenth century how-ever also saw the beginnings of the internationalization of productive capital and the origins of some of today's major TNCs. This was the outcome of a number of developments in the capitalist mode of pro-duction. From the middle of the nineteenth century certain develop-ments in transport, storage and communications had paved the way towards the creation of a more integrated international economy. These included the development of the railways, iron steam shipping, refriger-ation and temperature-controlling techniques, and the invention of the telegraph.

At the same time the concentration and centralization of capital was leading to an increasing size of firm in the advanced capitalist countries and with it important changes in the organization of capitalist enterprise. This has been described by Hymer (1979, ch. 2) for the United States. In the 1870s the typical enterprise in the United States was the single-function firm controlled by an entrepreneur or a small family group. By the early twentieth century this had been replaced by the large corpor-ation carrying out numerous functions and operating several plants. The organization which developed to administer and control these corpor-ations on a continent-wide basis in the US were also well suited to operate plants and subsidiaries in other parts of the world and so the TNC was born. In Europe the so-called Great Depression (1873–96) stimulated the growth of many consumer-good industries as food prices fell, and increasing tariff protection from the 1880s in the USA, Ger-many, France and elsewhere stimulated international production (Wilson 1974).

Many of the earliest TNCs were in the manufacturing sector. In the last quarter of the nineteenth century, firms such as Singer, ITT, General Electric and Westinghouse from the United States, Dunlop and Lever Brothers in the UK and Nestlé and Siemens in Europe estab-lished manufacturing plants overseas. Most of these early manu-facturing investments were in Europe (including Russia) and North America.

The first TNCs to enter the Third World were concentrated largely in the primary sector. Although there were earlier foreign investments in raw material production in the Third World, the emergence of modern TNCs with substantial operations in these areas dates from the turn of the century. These included oil and mineral investments in Mexico, copper mining in Chile, Peru and the Belgian Congo, bauxite in British and Dutch Guyana and oil in the Dutch East Indies.

The expansion of these extractive TNCs was triggered by the rapid growth of demand for certain crucial raw materials which outstripped domestic production capacity in the advanced capitalist economies. New, lower cost sources of supply were eagerly sought by established producers and these were frequently located in the Third World. Thus major TNCs such as Exxon, Royal Dutch Shell, Anaconda, Kennecott and Alcoa were born.

At about the same time, a number of TNCs also began to emerge in agriculture. The United Fruit Company was formed in 1899 and established its 'Banana Empire' in Central America and the Caribbean before World War I. Major US food-processing companies invested in sugar plantations in Cuba and W. R. Grace and Co. began large-scale sugar production in Peru. British TNCs such as Unilever in vegetable oils and Cadbury in cocoa invested in Africa before World War I, while Dunlop owned rubber plantations in Malaya and Brooke Bond set up tea plantations in India and Ceylon. Both in agriculture and in minerals, production had often already been developed by local small-scale producers so that the growth of TNCs constituted a process of monopolization and vertical integration.

At the outbreak of World War I over 60 per cent of all direct foreign investment was located in developing countries (Dunning 1983, table 5.2). Fifty-five per cent of all direct foreign investment was in the primary sector and only 15 per cent in manufacturing (Dunning 1983, 89). Since manufacturing investment was concentrated mainly in the advanced countries (including Russia) and mineral investments mainly in the British Empire and the developing countries, it is clear that the bulk of DFI in the Third World must have been in primary production. This is borne out by data for the United States which indicate that mining accounted for 39 per cent of all DFI in less developed countries in 1914, agriculture for 18 per cent and oil for 13 per cent. Manufacturing on the other hand accounted for only 3 per cent of the total (Figure 1.1).

The inter-war period saw the beginning of operations by manufacturing TNCs in the Third World. The main area for such expansion was Latin America where by 1939 the world's leading TNCs (both US and European) had set up as many as 200 subsidiaries. US firms, such as Ford, General Motors, Goodyear, Firestone, National Cash Register, General Electric, ITT, Singer, Abbott and Parke Davis, and European firms such as Pirelli, Philips, Siemens, Lever, Roche, Nestlé and Olivetti set up subsidiaries in Latin America in this period. In the rest of

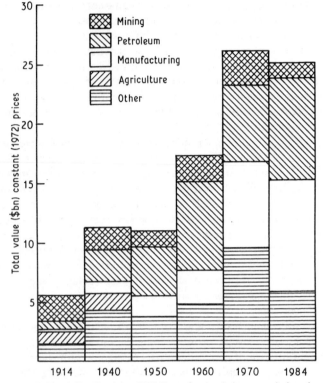

Figure 1.1 Sectoral distribution of US direct foreign investment in less developed countries (%).

Sources: Wilkins (1974), table XIII.2; US Department of Commerce, *Survey of Current Business*, various issues.

the Third World only some 100 manufacturing subsidiaries were formed before the outbreak of World War II, with India as the major destination (Vaupel and Curhan 1973).

However, TNC activity in the Third World continued to be dominated by the primary sector throughout this period. Investments made before World War I were consolidated and expanded while new areas were incorporated as sources of raw materials for TNCs, for example in Africa and the Middle East. These included tea estates and coffee plantations in Kenya, rubber plantations in Liberia, copper mines in Zambia, precious metals in South Africa and oil in the Middle East. As a result, despite a relative decline in the importance of mining after World

War I, the primary sector still accounted for more than half of US investment in the Third World in 1940. Manufacturing on the other hand accounted for less than a tenth of US DFI in these areas at that time (Figure 1.1).

The quarter-century after World War II saw an unprecedented expansion of TNC activity. This was initially led by US capital, but since the 1960s European and Japanese firms have been growing at a faster rate. The growth of TNC activity was facilitated by major advances in technology in the fields of transport and communications. These included the development of jet aircraft, container transport and international telephone and telex links. These developments vastly increased the ease of co-ordinating geographically dispersed operations in different parts of the world. They also reduced the costs of shipping products between these different operations (Vernon 1977, 2).

In the 1950s and 1960s this expansion was reflected in a rapid growth in the number of new subsidiaries established and in the level of direct foreign investment (Buckley and Casson 1976, table 1). In the 1970s, however, changing strategies on the part of TNCs, measures by some Third World governments to unpackage foreign investments, so that the different components – technology, finance, management – were acquired separately, and the growth of non-equity sources of finance, such as the Eurocurrency markets, meant that direct foreign investment declined in significance (Oman 1984). This has been particularly marked in the Third World, where there has been no increase in the real value of DFI since the late 1960s (World Bank 1985, 126). However, this has not meant any diminution in the significance of TNCs for the world economy. Indeed, the sales of the largest 100 TNCs grew faster than the GNP of the capitalist world in the 1970s (UNCTC 1983, 47).

The most rapidly growing sector for TNC activity in the Third World in the post-war period has been manufacturing. Many states followed import substituting policies in the 1950s and 1960s and often a major beneficiary of these policies was the transnational corporation. In the late 1960s and 1970s a number of Third World states adopted more export-oriented industrialization strategies, the manifestation of which was the mushrooming of Export Processing Zones around the world. The attraction of TNCs was again a prime objective of such a strategy. At the same time the importance of the primary sector has declined as a result of nationalization or voluntary divestment. Between 1950 and 1984 the share of US DFI in the Third World which was employed in the manufacturing sector more than doubled from 15 to 37 per cent, while the share of the extractive industries fell from over a half to less than 40 per cent

(Figure 1.1). Data from both host LDCs and other home countries of the TNCs confirm the growing importance of the manufacturing sector.

THE SIGNIFICANCE OF THE TRANSNATIONAL CORPORATION IN THE WORLD ECONOMY

There are two ways of viewing the significance of the TNC in the world economy. The first is quantitative and highlights the size of such companies and their weight in such things as world production, foreign investment, technology creation, finance and trade (see, for example, Lall and Streeten 1977, 11–15). The second is qualitative and looks at the growth of TNCs as a process which is intimately related to, and highlights, key tendencies in the capitalist system.

There is ample evidence of the quantitative significance of the TNC in the world economy today. It has been estimated that some 350 such firms, controlling 25,000 subsidiaries, accounted for 28 per cent of the Gross Domestic Product of the capitalist world in 1980 (UNCTC 1983, 46). In terms of size, the largest TNCs have sales which exceed the total Gross Domestic Product of most Third World countries (see Table 1.1).[2] In many major industries, such as oil refining, aluminium, vehicles and tobacco, a substantial proportion of the capitalist world's production is accounted for by a handful of TNCs.

Not only do the TNCs account for an important share of world production but they also control a major part of all direct foreign investment. According to one recent estimate, 500 TNCs were responsible for 80 per cent of all direct foreign investment (Stopford and Dunning 1983). They are also a major force in world trade. In the early 1980s exports from the home base of 500 TNCs accounted for some $350 billion (Stopford and Dunning 1983, table 4.1), about 28 per cent of total exports from the advanced capitalist countries. If exports by subsidiaries were also included, TNC-linked trade would be even higher. In the case of the United States it has been estimated that as much as 90 per cent of all trade was generated by TNCs (both US and non-US TNCs) in the late 1970s (UNCTC 1978, annex table IV. 9). A similarly high proportion (over 80 per cent) of UK exports was accounted for by local and foreign TNCs in the early 1980s (Business Monitor 1983, table 6.2), and the situation is not very different in other countries.

TNCs are also a major force in the development of new technology. They tend to be concentrated in technology-intensive industries and to spend a higher proportion of their sales on research and development (R & D) than non-TNCs (Hood and Young 1979, 68–9). Not surprisingly then a substantial proportion of all R & D in the advanced capitalist

Table 1.1 World-wide sales of leading TNCs compared to GDP of selected Third World countries, 1984

Company	Nationality	Industry	Sales ($ bn)	GDP ($ bn)	Country
Exxon	USA	Oil	73.6	83.2	South Korea
Royal Dutch/Shell	Neth/UK	Oil	72.6	80.6	Indonesia
General Motors	USA	Motor vehicles	64.4	76.2	Argentina
BP	UK	Oil	44.1	73.5	Nigeria
Mobil	USA	Oil	43.0	50.7	Algeria
Ford	USA	Motor vehicles	40.2	47.5	Venezuela
Texaco	USA	Oil	36.3	47.5	Turkey
IBM	USA	Office equip.	35.2	42.0	Thailand
du Pont	USA	Chemicals and energy	27.6	34.4	Colombia
General Electric	USA	Electrical	21.4	32.8	Philippines
Chevron	USA	Oil	21.4	30.6	Hong Kong
Amoco	USA	Oil	20.7	30.6	Libya
Atlantic Richfield	USA	Oil	18.9	30.1	Egypt
Toyota	Japan	Motor vehicles	18.2	29.3	Malaysia
EN I	Italy	Energy and chemicals	17.9	27.7	Pakistan
Unilever	UK/Neth	Food	16.2	19.8	Chile
Chrysler	USA	Motor vehicles	15.0	18.8	Peru
Elf Aquitaine	France	Oil	14.7	18.2	Singapore
BAT Industries	UK	Tobacco	14.4	15.9	Syria
Hitachi	Japan	Electrical	13.4	13.3	Morocco

Sources: *Times 1000 Leading Companies*; World Bank (1986).

Note: Six Third World countries (China, Brazil, Mexico, India, Iran and Saudi Arabia) had a GDP of over $100 bn in 1984.

countries (the major source of new technology) is accounted for by TNCs. This does not necessarily mean that TNCs are the major originators of inventions and innovations. In fact only about a fifth of a sample of post-war innovations were originally introduced by TNCs (Vernon 1977, 40), but they have played a major role in commercializing new technology.

Within the Third World, although DFI by TNCs makes a very limited contribution to total domestic investment (see UNCTC 1983, annex table II.14 for data on individual countries), and declined relatively in the

Table 1.2 Share of manufacturing industry controlled by foreign firms in selected Third World countries

Country	Year	Foreign share %	Basis of calculation
Latin America:			
Argentina	1972	31	Production
Brazil	1977	44	Sales
Central America	1971	31	Production
Chile	1978	25	Sales
Colombia	1974	43	Production
Ecuador	1971–3	66	Assets of public corporation
Mexico	1970	35	Production
Peru	1974	32	Production
Venezuela	1975	36	Value added
Trinidad and Tobago	1968	40	Employment
Africa:			
Ghana	1974	50	Sales
Kenya	1976	30–35	Employment
Nigeria	1968	70	Assets
Zaïre	1974	30–35	Employment
Asia:			
Hong Kong	1971	11	Employment
India	1975	13	Sales
Iran	1975	10–15	Employment
Malaysia	1978	44	Value added
Philippines	1970	7	Employment
Singapore	1978	83	Output
South Korea	1975	11	Sales
Thailand	1970	9	Employment

Sources: UNCTC (1978), table III, 5.4; Jenkins (1984a), table 2.2; UNCTC (1983), table IV.2; ILO (1981b), table II.3.

1970s as a source of foreign finance (UNCTC 1983, table II.4), a substantial part of non-subsistence production is often accounted for by their subsidiaries. Historically many of the major exports of the LDCs, such as oil, copper, bauxite, bananas and tea, have been produced by TNCs, and although many of these firms have been nationalized in recent years, TNCs continue to dominate the marketing of such products (Clairmonte 1981). In many Third World countries the expanding manufacturing sector, particularly dynamic industries such as chemicals, rubber, machinery and transport equipment, have a substantial TNC presence (see Table 1.2). A substantial portion of manufactured exports are also accounted for by TNCs in many of the newly industrializing countries (Jenkins 1984b).

TNCs have a significance for the analysis of the world economy, over and above that which may be suggested by their quantitative role. They constitute the most advanced form of capitalist production and as such illustrate many of the tendencies of development of the capitalist system as a whole. They are a primary manifestation of the internationalization of capital, the process by which an increasingly integrated capitalist world economy has developed and by which capital has become ever more global in its operation.

First they indicate the continuing concentration and centralization of capital, especially productive capital, which is occurring on an international scale. The output of the world's largest firms (almost all TNCs) has outstripped the growth of world production throughout the 1960s and 1970s (Table 1.3, see also Trajtenberg 1985). Moreover the production of these firms has become increasingly internationalized. Between 1971 and 1980 the share of foreign subsidiaries in the total sales of the world's leading TNCs rose from 30 per cent to 40 per cent and in employment from 39 per cent to 46 per cent (UNCTC 1983, table II.11).

Table 1.3 Growth of the world's largest firms, 1962–82 (% p.a.)

	1962–7	*1967–72*	*1972–7*	*1977–82*
GDP of market economics	8.3	10.7	14.3	9.4
Sales of largest firms	9.3	11.2	15.4	11.2

Sources: Dunning and Pearce (1985), table 6.4; UN *Yearbook of National Account Statistics*, various years.

This internationalization of production has been accompanied by a tremendous increase in the international mobility of capital. One indication of the extent of this increase in the mobility of money capital is that in the run on the pound in August 1947 the maximum amount of daily speculation was less than $100 million, whereas in May 1971 more than $1 billion moved into the Deutschmark in less than an hour (Cooper quoted in Edwards 1985, 182). This is partly a result of the growth of intra-firm trade which gives rise to new opportunities for shifting capital between different countries. It is also a result of the growth of new financial markets (particularly the Eurocurrency market) and the expansion of transnational banking. But these developments were in turn closely related to the expansion of the TNCs. Capital mobility has also been increased by the diversification of TNCs, of which the most obvious recent example has been the move by the major oil TNCs into other fuels and minerals. This is part of a broader development whereby few TNCs are now single line businesses (Stopford and Dunning 1983, ch. 5).

The significant role of TNCs in world trade has already been commented upon. However it has also led to the replacement of market transactions in international trade by non-market relationships between the parent and subsidiaries of the same TNC. In other words the market, held to be the hallmark of the capitalist system, has been increasingly displaced in international economic relations. In aggregate it has been claimed that intra-firm trade accounts for about 30 per cent of all world trade. In the United States it has been estimated that between 40 per cent and 50 per cent of all trade was intra-firm in the late 1970s (UNCTC 1983, table annex IV.9, and Helleiner 1981, 12–13, for two estimates). Data for other countries indicate that between 30 per cent and 60 per cent of exports are on an intra-firm basis (UNCTC 1978, 43). Moreover as the extent of international production by TNCs has grown, so too has the proportion of trade that is intra-firm. In the UK for instance, the proportion of intra-firm exports increased from 26 per cent in 1970 to 31 per cent in 1981 (UNCTC 1978, 43; UNCTC 1983, 160). Similarly data for a sample of German TNCs indicate that the proportion of their exports which were intra-firm increased significantly in the late 1960s and early 1970s (UNCTAD 1977, table 7).

The TNCs are also major agents in the process of standardization of production techniques and consumption patterns on a world scale which is a feature of the internationalization of capital. The use of technology is becoming increasingly international. One indicator of this is the growing proportion of patents which have been issued to foreigners (mainly foreign corporations) in the major advanced capitalist countries in the post-war period (Vernon 1977, table 1). Another is the rapid growth of receipts of royalties and other technology-related payments. Between 1970 and 1981 such payments to the advanced countries increased at an average annual rate of 6 per cent in real terms (Vickery 1984, table 1). Finally the speed with which innovations are diffused internationally has been increasing over time (Vernon and Davidson quoted in Caves 1982, 210) further contributing to international standardization.

Products are also becoming more and more 'international'. One example is the 'world cars' being developed by the major auto TNCs. Another is the international dissemination of that contemporary elixir, Coca Cola. As Raymond Vernon has noted,

> The manufactured products that appear in the stalls and markets of Accra or Dar es Salaam are no longer very different from those in Djakarta or Cartagena or Recife. The plastic pail has replaced the gourd, the earthen pot, and the banana leaf; tin roofs are replacing the local varieties of thatch; electric batteries and electric bulbs are taking over the function of kerosene, wood, vegetable oil and tallow; the portable radio and the aspirin are joining the list of life's universal necessities.   (Vernon 1977, 4)

An indicator of this process has been the rapid growth of transnational advertising agencies which have followed in the wake of their industrial customers (UNCTC 1979a).

Finally, the expansion of the TNCs vividly illustrates the uneven nature of capital accumulation on an international scale. Although this book is concerned with the impact of TNCs in the Third World, it has to be borne in mind that the bulk of TNC operations are concentrated within the advanced capitalist countries. In the early 1980s, slightly more than a quarter of all foreign investment was in the Third World, down from almost a third in 1960 (Stopford and Dunning 1983, table 1.7). Similarly in 1980 just under a quarter of all foreign subsidiaries of TNCs were located in the Third World (UNCTC 1983, table II.8).

What is more, within the Third World, foreign investment is heavily concentrated in a small number of countries. Two countries (Brazil and Mexico) account for over a quarter of the total stock of DFI in LDCs and eight countries make up over half. The share of these eight countries has increased significantly since 1967 (Table 1.4). Most of these countries belong to one of two categories – the so-called newly industrializing countries (NICs) which have a large and rapidly growing industrial sector and the Organization of Petroleum Exporting Countries (OPEC). The NICs which account for 13 per cent of the Third World's population

Table 1.4 Stock of direct foreign investment in less developed countries by major host countries, 1967 and 1983

	1967		1983	
	bn $	%	bn $	%
Brazil	3.7	11.3	24.6	17.5
Mexico	1.8	5.5	13.6	9.7
Singapore	0.2	0.6	7.9	5.6
Indonesia	0.2	0.6	6.8	4.9
Malaysia	0.7	2.1	6.2	4.4
Argentina	1.8	5.5	5.8	4.1
Venezuela	3.5	10.6	4.3	3.1
Hong Kong	0.3	0.9	4.2	3.0
Eight countries	12.2	37.2	73.4	52.4
TOTAL LDCs	32.8	100.0	140.0*	100.0

Sources: UNCTC (1978), table III, 4.7; IMF (1985), table A.2.

* Estimate.

and 31 per cent of its GNP increased their stock of DFI from 25 per cent to 34 per cent in the 1970s, while the least developed countries with a similar share of the Third World's population accounted for only 1.5 per cent of the stock of DFI in 1978 (UNCTC 1983, table II.7). Thus the increasing differentiation of the Third World (see Hoogvelt 1982, ch. 1) between a small group of rapidly growing countries and the rest is reflected in the pattern of TNC accumulation.

CONCLUSION

The above discussion has shown that TNCs are significant, not only in their own right in terms of the size of their operations, but also as the major institutional form adopted by capital in the second half of the twentieth century. It is important therefore to analyse TNCs not simply as institutions but also as a particular manifestation of capitalist development. It is part of the purpose of this book to show that such an approach can provide a much richer understanding of the TNCs than a purely institutionalist approach which takes the TNC itself as the object of study.

NOTES

1 See the glossary for an explanation of certain technical terms.
2 There are, of course, problems with such comparisons. Strictly speaking, value added by TNCs rather than sales should be compared to GDP, which is a value added concept. There is also the question of the meaning of such quantitative comparisons between two quite different institutions, nation states and TNCs (Lall and Streeten 1977, 12). For an attempt to compare value products of TNCs and country GNP, see Buckley and Casson (1976).

FURTHER READING

There are a number of useful sources of empirical data on TNCs. The UNCTC publishes a survey of the activities of TNCs every five years and so far three such surveys have come out (UN 1973; UNCTC 1978; UNCTC 1983). The Harvard Business School has published a number of source books based on their databank (Vaupel and Curhan 1973; Curhan, Davidson and Suri 1977). Statistical profiles of TNCs are also found in Stopford *et al.* (1980), and Stopford and Dunning (1983).

A number of magazines and periodicals provide up-to-date information on the activities of TNCs and related issues discussed in this book. Radical perspectives on TNCs are found in *Transnational Information and Exchange Bulletin* and *Multinational Monitor*. The *CTC Reporter*, published by the UNCTC, is useful, particularly for information on attempts to develop a code of conduct on TNCs within the UN and for references to UN studies. *Multinational Info* is put out by the Institute for Research on Multinationals, a private organization entirely funded by Nestlé. Two journals which focus specifically on labour issues are *International Labour Reports* and *Newsletter of International Labour Studies*. Counter Information Services (CIS) occasionally publish in-depth studies of particular TNCs.

The history of TNCs is discussed from different theoretical perspectives in Hymer (1979, ch. 2) and Dunning (1983). Detailed empirical studies are Wilkins (1970, 1974) on US TNCs, Stopford (1974) on British manufacturing TNCs and Franko (1974) on Continental European manufacturing firms.

A number of campaigning organizations work around TNCs, and related issues. These include Transnational Information Centre, 9 Portland Street, London, W1V 3DG; Women Working Worldwide,

2/4 Oxford Road, Manchester, M1 5QA; Transnational Information Exchange, Paulus Potterstraat 20, 1071 DA, Amsterdam, The Netherlands.

For a recent listing of organizations working on TNCs throughout the world, see *TIE Report* 18/19 (1985, 66–73).

2

Theoretical perspectives on the transnational corporation

Not surprisingly, the intense debate over the impact of TNCs in the Third World has generated a vast literature and throws up a large number of conflicting arguments and positions. In order to bring some order to this literature, a number of writers have attempted to identify different approaches to the TNCs (Lall 1974; Hood and Young 1979, ch. 8). It is obviously useful to distinguish between those writers whose main emphasis is on the positive benefits which TNCs bring to Third World countries and those who adopt a more critical approach, stressing the disadvantages of TNC activities (although in practice there is a continuum with many writers discussing both costs and benefits and differing primarily over the degree to which state intervention is necessary to ensure that the benefits outweigh the costs). Although some writers have been content to adopt a twofold classification along these lines (e.g. Biersteker 1978) this fails to recognize the very real methodological differences between Marxists and non-Marxist writers, which have important implications for their analysis of the TNC. Since Marxists and non-Marxists alike adopt different positions *vis-à-vis* the TNC, it is appropriate to start with a fourfold classification of approaches towards the TNC.

	Pro-TNC	*TNC Critics*
Non-Marxist	Neo-classical (Reuber, Meier, Vernon, Rugman, Balasubramanyam)	Global Reach (Barnet and Muller, Streeten, Lall, Vaitsos, Helleiner, Newfarmer)
Marxist	Neo-fundamentalist (Warren, Emmanuel, Schiffer)	Neo-imperialist (Baran, Sweezy, Magdoff, Girvan, Sunkel, Frank)

The above table identifies four main perspectives on the transnational corporation – the neo-classical, the Global Reach, the neo-fundamentalist and the neo-imperialist – and some of the leading exponents of each approach amongst writers concerned with the impact of TNCs in the Third World. The specific issues debated between these approaches will be discussed in detail in later chapters. The purpose of this chapter is to sketch in broad outline the main features of each perspective.

NEO-CLASSICAL VIEWS

Most advocates of the benefits of foreign investment by TNCs base their arguments on neo-classical economic theory. Although the neo-classical case has developed considerably over the past twenty-five years, a common theme runs through all these writings. It is that the TNCs act as efficient allocators of resources internationally so as to maximize world welfare. The distribution of the benefits from TNC operations are either assumed to accrue to both home and host countries, or is not addressed directly.

Capital flow models

The earliest neo-classical attempts to evaluate the effects of foreign investment regarded DFI as simply a capital flow which increased the stock of capital in the host country. As a result of this capital inflow the total output of the recipient economy would be increased, and under a number of assumptions including that of perfect competition and no negative effects on the stock of locally owned capital, the income of host nationals after deducting profits to foreign capital would also increase.

At a time when shortage of capital was regarded as a major obstacle to development in the Third World, direct foreign investment seemed to offer an attractive way of breaking out of the 'vicious circle of poverty'. Not surprisingly then, mainstream development economists in the 1960s, such as Meier, advocated DFI as a means of supplementing domestic savings and providing valuable additional foreign exchange required for economic growth. Even the less orthodox development theorists of the Economic Commission for Latin America with their critique of comparative advantage, shared this generally favourable attitude towards foreign investment, provided that it was not of the enclave variety (Jenkins 1984a, ch. 1).

In addition to the initial effect of increasing savings and foreign exchange availability, foreign investment is also seen as having a number of further effects. Of these the most important gains are assumed to be increasing technological and managerial know-how and training labour in new skills. Moreover foreign investment not only supplements domestic investment but may also stimulate additional investment in various ways.

Underlying the neo-classical case in favour of direct foreign investment are two crucial assumptions, often supplemented by a third which strengthens even further the case for DFI:

(i) the supplement assumption – foreign resources supplement domestic resources and in their absence there would be no local production;

(ii) the competitive assumption – that markets approximate the perfectly competitive model so that profits are not excessive and that market imperfections where they do arise are largely the result of misconceived government policies;

(iii) the resource generation assumption – that TNCs not only supplement *existing* local resources but they also generate additional local resources or utilize resources previously unutilized.

It is hardly surprising that empirical studies which adopt this theoretical framework conclude that TNC investment in underdeveloped countries generates considerable benefits for the host countries. An extreme example of this type of approach is the studies by May for the Council of the Americas, an organization of US TNCs (May 1970, 1975). The study by Reuber (1973) for the OECD also gives an extremely favourable picture of the impact of DFI in the Third World (see Lall 1974, for a critique of the Reuber study).

The product cycle

During the late 1960s the neo-classical case for DFI shifted its emphasis away from its capital contribution to technology transfer. This was partly a result of the failure of the capital flow model to take into account some of the specific characteristics of TNCs and their operations particularly

(i) the 'package' nature of direct investment which almost invariably incorporated other factors such as technology and management techniques as well as capital;

(ii) the existence of a strong correlation between DFI and concentrated market structures;

(iii) the need to integrate trade theory and the theory of foreign investment.

Drawing on the marketing concept of the life cycle of a new product from its first introduction to maturity, a number of writers at the Harvard Business School developed the product cycle theory. Although primarily concerned with explaining changing patterns of trade and investment, the theory provided some interesting implications for the analysis of the effects of DFI in Third World countries. It predicts that these countries will enjoy a comparative advantage in mature, standardized products. There is therefore a beneficial 'trickle down' as LDCs take over mature products previously manufactured in the advanced capitalist countries. When products are mature and their technology standardized there is considerable competition so that it is possible for host countries to obtain the technology on favourable terms. Thus the competitive assumption is maintained as far as those products of most interest to Third World countries are concerned. Over the life cycle of a product, host countries are able to get increasingly favourable terms as the bargaining power of the TNC declines as technology becomes standardized. This is an important element in the 'obsolescing bargain' view of host government–TNC relations which provides a basis for arguing that TNCs are not all powerful *vis-à-vis* host countries.

In addition to supplying standardized technology to LDCs the product cycle theory emphasizes the importance of TNCs in providing access to overseas markets for Third World exports. Mature products, despite increasing competition, are characterized by substantial barriers to entry especially at the marketing stage. In the absence of multinational links, firms in LDCs would find it very difficult to penetrate these markets especially those of the advanced capitalist countries (Vernon 1973, 105–7).

Internalization

In the last ten years a new neo-classical synthesis for analysing trade and investment by TNCs has emerged. This has been variously termed 'internalization theory' (Buckley and Casson 1976), 'contemporary orthodox approach' (Hood and Young 1979), 'electic theory' (Dunning 1981) and 'transactional approach' (Caves 1982). It has become the approach adopted by most pro-TNC writers in recent years. The major proponents of internalization are quite specific in seeing it as a general theory within which previous contributions can be incorporated (Buckley and Casson 1976; Rugman 1981), regarding it as a synthesis not only of earlier neo-classical contributions but also of some of the critical studies discussed below.

The central argument of this approach is that TNCs exist because of market imperfections. If all markets operated perfectly there would be no incentive for firms to go to the trouble of controlling subsidiaries in different countries and to internalize markets between them, rather than engaging in arm's length transactions with independent firms. Internalization then is a way of bypassing imperfections in external markets.

Imperfections in a number of areas are regarded as being important in explaining the existence of TNCs. Markets for intangible assets such as technology or marketing skills are notoriously imperfect because of their public good nature, imperfect knowledge and uncertainty. This makes it difficult for the seller to appropriate fully the rent from such assets through external market transactions and creates an incentive to internalize. Similarly in vertically integrated industries such as oil or aluminium there are gains from internalization because of the existence of small numbers of oligopolistic firms and large investments which take a long time to mature. Internalization avoids the difficulties of determining market prices and the uncertainties associated with arm's length transactions in such a situation. A further important source of market imperfections internationally is government intervention. The existence of trade barriers, restrictions on capital movements or differences in tax rates between countries provide a further incentive to internalize since intra-firm prices can be set to minimize the effects of such controls.

The analysis of the consequences of the growth of TNCs follows from the view that they are essentially an efficient means of overcoming market failure. They therefore act to increase efficiency in the world economy. As with the product cycle theory, technology or information plays a central role in internalization theory. In analysing the gains to host countries these are not primarily related to the transfer of capital, as in the traditional neo-classical model, but to transfers of technology which would not otherwise take place because of external market imperfections (Casson 1979, 5). More generally it is argued that the activity of TNCs makes both goods and financial markets more efficient than they would otherwise be (Rugman 1981, 36). It has even been suggested that since market imperfections are more pervasive in the Third World than in the advanced capitalist countries, Third World countries are in a position to gain even more through TNC operations which circumvent such imperfections (Agmon and Hirsch 1979).

A crucial assumption of this application of internalization theory to TNC operations is that market imperfections are exogenous, either 'natural' or government induced, and that TNCs do not themselves generate such imperfections. As Rugman (1981, 33) points out:

> The multinational firm is able to circumvent most exogenous market imperfections. Concerns about its alleged market power are valid only when it is able to close a market or generate endogenous imperfections. In practice these events rarely occur.

It is here that the contrast between internalization theory and the Global Reach approach derived from Hymer's work with its emphasis on the creation of market imperfections by TNCs (see below) is most apparent.

Policy implications

Although internalization theory provides a considerably more sophisticated analysis of TNCs than the earlier neo-classical theories of foreign investment, the policy prescriptions of both approaches are extremely similar. Any problems which TNC operations create are generally ascribed to misguided government policies. Thus a major recommendation is the removal of government induced distortions such as high protective tariffs (Reuber 1973, 247–8; Rugman 1981, 138). Such tariffs may give rise to a situation where direct foreign investment reduces income in the host country but the TNCs themselves are not to blame for this.

It follows that since there is, in the absence of misconceived government policies, a net gain to the host country from direct foreign investment (whether through inflows of capital or technology or through more efficient allocation of resources as a result of the elimination of market imperfections) host countries should generally encourage foreign investment, providing a 'favourable climate for investment' (although not to the extent of introducing new distortions by granting large subsidies). In some cases the use of cost-benefit analysis to evaluate major projects is advocated but there should in general be a minimum of red tape. Government efforts to regulate the operations of TNCs are strongly discouraged. 'Regulation is always inefficient. Multinationals are always efficient,' as Rugman puts it (1981, 156–7). Reuber (1973, 248–9) agrees that government attempts to control TNCs probably do more harm than good.

Conclusion

A common thread which runs through the pro-TNC approaches to foreign investment is a primary concern with efficiency in resource allocation. This is of course quite explicit in internalization theory and is the underlying value premise of neo-classical analysis. A second common thread is the belief that direct foreign investment by TNCs is superior to all feasible alternatives. Here one faces the problem of the counterfactual which is at the heart of many of the debates about TNCs, i.e. what would have happened in the absence of direct foreign investment. The assumption of most neo-classical thinking on the subject is that the alternative to DFI is the complete absence of local production. Internalization theory on the other hand emphasizes local licensing as an alternative. Both of these alternatives are generally regarded as inferior to foreign investment.

GLOBAL REACH

A sharply contrasting view of the impact of TNCs is given in the writings of those authors who emphasize the oligopolistic nature of the TNCs. This approach has again been given different labels, for example the 'nationalist approach' (Lall 1974), 'critical approach' (Biersteker 1978) and 'industrial organization approach' (Newfarmer 1985a). A rather more snappy title which captures the essence of this perspective is 'Global Reach', after the title of the best seller on TNCs by Richard Barnet and Ronald Müller (1974).

Central to this approach is the view that foreign investment should be seen as part of the strategy of oligopolistic firms and not simply as a resource flow. Its roots can be traced back to industrial organization theory and the US anti-trust tradition which was first applied to the analysis of DFI by Steve Hymer in the early 1960s. Hymer (1976) identified two major reasons leading firms to control subsidiaries in foreign countries: (i) in order to make use of a specific advantage which the firm enjoys over foreign firms; (ii) in order to remove competition between the firms concerned and to eliminate conflict. While most recent orthodox writings on TNCs have accepted the first point, it is only the Global Reach approach that has continued Hymer's emphasis on foreign investment as a means of restraining competition.

The main focus of attention of this approach is the market power of TNCs. This is seen as deriving from a number of oligopolistic advantages possessed by TNCs particularly access to capital (both internal to the firm and external); control of technology (both product and process technology); marketing through advertising and product differentiation; and privileged access to raw materials. (See Lall and Streeten 1977, 20–9, and Hood and Young 1979, 48–54, for a fuller discussion of these advantages.)

The existence of oligopolistic markets means that firms enjoy considerable discretionary powers rather than being the atomistic firms of neo-classical theory which respond to market conditions. Consequently much of the Global Reach literature focuses on the TNCs as *institutions*, their strategies and tactics. A leading proponent of this approach, Constantine Vaitsos, brings this out clearly in discussing the provision of 'collective inputs' (i.e. a package) as a means of preserving monopoly rents. He concludes, 'Thus a technological monopoly is transformed into an *institutional* one. *Viewed in this light the product cycle theory is seen as a theory of monopoly cycles*' (Vaitsos 1974a, 18; emphasis in the original).

Whereas for neo-classical writers on the TNCs, particularly internalization theorists, market imperfections are exogenous, arising from government intervention or the nature of certain products such as technology, for the Global Reach view the TNCs are themselves major factors creating imperfect markets. Far from TNCs increasing global efficiency through overcoming market failure, they reduce efficiency by making markets less perfect as a result of their oligopolistic strategies.

The Global Reach approach has highlighted a number of consequences of the market power of TNCs for host countries. Each of these hypotheses will be discussed in detail in later chapters, but it is worth listing them briefly here.

Market structure

TNCs have tended to invest in oligopolistic markets in host Third World countries and it has been suggested that they tend to contribute to increased concentration.

Monopoly profits

The market power of TNCs enables them to earn monopoly profits in host countries. These profits, however, do not always appear in the tax returns of the foreign subsidiaries because of various accounting procedures used by TNCs, particularly transfer pricing. There is also the question of how such monopoly rents are distributed between the TNCs and the host countries in which they operate.

Abuse of market power – restrictive business practices

Individually and collectively TNCs act in order to restrict competition in various ways. Individually they impose restrictive clauses on subsidiaries and licensees through technology contracts. These include tying inputs of raw materials, machinery, etc., to the technology supplier or restricting exports in order to divide world markets. Collectively they form cartels or engage in informal collusion through market sharing agreements or the allocation of spheres of influence.

Demand creation

TNCs use their market power to create demand for their products rather than responding to consumer preferences expressed through the market. This leads to 'taste transfer' via the TNC and the expansion of the market for products which are inappropriate for local conditions.

Factor displacements

The package nature of DFI and the monopoly power of the TNCs leads to situations where at least part of the package displaces local inputs (Hirschman 1969). Importing technology which is not available locally and hence supplements local resources could also bring with it imports of capital and management which displace local capital and entrepreneurship. This has led to concern over the denationalization (i.e. the extension of control by foreign subsidiaries) of local industry, which is seen as a reflection of the market power of TNCs rather than their inherently greater efficiency compared to local firms.

Policy implications

A major implication of this view of foreign investment is the need for state control of TNCs. These controls may be imposed either on a national or an international basis. The areas which have been particularly emphasized as requiring regulation are transfer pricing and restrictive business practices. Governments in a number of countries have set up agencies to control foreign investment and technology transfer since the early 1970s, with a view to eliminating practices such as export restrictions and tied inputs, and monitoring TNC behaviour. There have also been steps to develop codes of conduct on TNCs and technology transfer by various international agencies.

The emphasis on TNCs as oligopolists which generate monopoly rents in their activities has also led to the view that the state in the Third World should actively intervene in bargaining with TNCs in order to ensure that a greater share of such rents accrue to the host country. There are two areas in which such an emphasis on bargaining has been of particular significance. First in the extractive industries where host governments have negotiated with TNCs to increase their share of revenue through taxation of profits, royalties, share ownership, etc. Secondly in technology transfer where government agencies have intervened in negotiations often between two private parties in order to reduce the level of royalty payments and hence the outflow of foreign exchange.

A corollary of this emphasis on monopoly rents and the scope for bargaining is that foreign investment projects cannot be analysed along the 'take-it-or-leave-it' lines of conventional cost-benefit analysis. Any such project will itself be subject to bargaining over the distribution of returns with a range of possible outcomes. Thus government policy should not be directed primarily at evaluating whether a proposed foreign investment project has a positive net present value, but rather at getting the best possible terms from the foreign investor.

In so far as the packaged nature of DFI is seen as an important source of monopoly rents for TNCs, there is a case for 'unpackaging' direct investment into its constituent elements. In other words rather than acquiring capital, technology, intermediate inputs, brand names, management skills all from the same TNC supplier, efforts can be made to acquire each component individually. This would permit each to be obtained at the lowest possible cost and for those elements for which domestic substitutes exist to be acquired locally. Such a call for unpackaging has become common in recent discussions of TNCs and technology transfer

A further implication often drawn from this approach is that the state should give preferential treatment to national capital, e.g. in terms of access to local sources of credit. This derives from the view that TNCs tend to displace local firms primarily because of their market power rather than because of greater productive efficiency. The state should therefore attempt to redress the balance in favour of local capital. Indeed it provides a theoretical rationale for forms of bourgeois nationalism as well as greater state intervention in the economy.

Conclusion

The overall framework of this approach contrasts with the pro-TNC writings discussed above in a number of key respects. First, TNCs are seen as important creators of market imperfections rather than as competitive firms or as an efficient response to exogenous imperfections. Secondly, TNCs often substitute rather than complement local factors. In other words the alternative of production under local control is more feasible than pro-TNC authors admit. Thirdly, there is a greater concern with the distributive effects of TNCs both internationally and internally.

NEO-IMPERIALIST VIEWS

The best known Marxist or neo-Marxist approach to TNCs is that represented by the Monthly Review School (especially Baran, Sweezy, O'Connor and Magdoff) and those writers on dependency most influenced by the Monthly Review approach (for example Frank and Girvan). These authors view the TNCs as a major mechanism blocking development in the Third World and an important obstacle to socialist transformation.

The origins of this approach can be traced back to the classical Marxist writings on imperialism in the early twentieth century with their stress on the concentration and centralization of capital and the link between monopolization of industry, capital export and imperialism (Lenin 1917, Bukharin 1917). A central element in the argument was that the monopolization of industry led to a growing mass of profit in the major capitalist countries, while at the same time limiting the possibilities of accumulation at home because of the restrictions imposed on expansion by cartels and trusts. This led capital to seek outlets for this relative surplus of capital overseas (see Olle and Schoeller 1982 for a critique of this view). Furthermore Lenin particularly emphasized the parasitic nature of imperialism stressing that the development of monopoly inhibits technical progress and leads to a tendency to stagnation and decay (Lenin 1917, ch. viii).

This leads to the question of the impact of capital export or more generally imperialism in the countries on the receiving end. Marx himself had stressed the progressive nature of these processes and this view was accepted (although only mentioned in passing) by the major Marxist authors writing on imperialism. However, as Warren (1980, 81–3) has stressed, the implication of this view of a parasitic, decaying monopoly capitalism was that imperialism could no longer play a progressive role in the colonies. It was not surprising therefore that imperialism was recognized as a major obstacle to industrialization of the colonies at the 1928 Congress of the Comintern.

The recent neo-imperialist literature continues Lenin's and Bukharin's emphasis on the rise of monopolies as a cause of TNC expansion, either by reference to the classical theories of imperialism or through the new version of the surplus capital theory proposed by Baran and Sweezy (1966). They argued that a major characteristic of US capitalism was the tendency for the economic surplus, defined as the difference between total output and the socially necessary costs of producing total output, to rise over time. The major cause of this rising surplus was the growth of monopoly and the consequent decline of price competition with the result that increases in productivity did not lead to falling prices as under competitive capitalism, and that the gap between prices and production costs tended to widen. While the surplus tended to rise, the monopolization of the economy limited the opportunities for investment because of the need to maintain monopoly prices (Sweezy and Magdoff 1969, 1). There is therefore a chronic tendency to underconsumption and stagnation under monopoly capitalism.

One of the possible outlets for the surplus identified by Baran and Sweezy was foreign investment. (Others discussed were advertising, government expenditure and militarism.) Thus, although only alleviating temporarily the problem of the rising surplus, because the return flow of profits and dividends to the United States soon exceeded the outflow of new investment, capital export and the overseas expansion of US firms was seen as primarily a consequence of the existence of large monopoly profits and the need to go slow on expanding productive capacity directed at existing markets. Two solutions offered themselves – international expansion or conglomerate expansion (i.e. diversification into new industries in the domestic market) (Sweezy and Magdoff 1969; O'Connor 1970).

It is worth noting in passing that this emphasis on monopoly and the tendency to underemphasize the competitiveness of the oligopolies (cf. Barratt Brown 1974, 217) was also accompanied by the view that the United States enjoyed undisputed hegemony within the international capitalist system. This view characterized by Rowthorn (1975) as 'super-imperialism' plays down the increasing competition between the United States, Western Europe and Japan, both politically and economically, which underlies the alternative 'inter-imperialist rivalry' view of international relations. The downplaying of conflicts between capitals and between advanced capitalist states also tended to go hand in hand with a 'Third Worldist' view which stressed that the struggle against capitalism and imperialism would primarily take place in the underdeveloped countries.

Foreign investment in the Third World is seen as contributing to the 'blocking of development' (Amin) or the 'development of underdevelopment' (A. G. Frank). Three principal mechanisms link foreign capital to underdevelopment. Considerable emphasis is placed on the so-called 'drain of surplus' from the underdeveloped countries in direct opposition to the claim of neo-classical economists that foreign capital supplements foreign exchange earnings and local savings. Thus surplus transfers which add to the problems of surplus absorption in the advanced capitalist countries at the same time deprive the countries of the Third World of the necessary resources for economic progress. The TNCs are viewed as a 'vast suction-pump' for obtaining resources from the periphery. At the same time they are a major part of the balance of payments problems which are so chronic in most Third World countries.

While much of the empirical analysis of the impact of TNCs concentrated on the outflow of capital from the Third World, equal or even greater importance was attached to the impact of foreign investment on the economic and social structures of the underdeveloped countries. As Baran puts it

> The worst of it is, however, that it is very hard to say what has been the greater evil as far as the economic development of underdeveloped countries is concerned: the removal of the economic surplus by foreign capital or its reinvestment by foreign enterprise.   (Baran 1973, 325)

The extension of TNC operations to the underdeveloped countries has also led to the extension of the monopolistic or oligopolistic structures of advanced capitalism to these areas (Dos Santos 1968 on Brazil; Caputto and Pizarro 1970, ch. 11.5 on Chile). Given the association of monopoly with stagnation in the United States, it is unlikely that monopolistic subsidiaries of US firms operating in the periphery will be a major dynamic force. Thus monopolistic firms with high profit rates will tend to repatriate profits, intensifying the drain of surplus and limiting the rate of capital accumulation within the host economies.

In so far as TNCs do reinvest profits locally, they are likely to expand by displacing or acquiring local competitors or moving into new areas of activity (diversification). Thus the twin spectres arise of denationalization (i.e. increasing foreign control over the economy) and the reduction of the spheres available to local capital which is confined to the most competitive and least profitable sectors of the economy. This brings us to a central point of the argument against foreign capital, namely that it reduces the local bourgeoisie in the Third World to the subordinate status of a 'comprador' or 'dependent' bourgeoisie which is consequently incapable of playing its historical role in promoting capitalist development. Baran writing in the 1950s emphasized the strengthening of local merchant capital by foreign capital which was mainly directed towards the export sector, and the consequent blocking of the development of industrial capitalism (Baran 1973, 337). Latin American dependency writers in the 1960s argued that a local industrial bourgeoisie did exist in the region but that its interests were closely tied to those of foreign capital and that it would not provide the basis for a strategy of national development. The crucial decisions on production and accumulation would be made in the light of the global interests of the parent companies of the foreign subsidiaries, and not in the interest of local economic development, a situation which local capital would be unwilling or powerless to alter.

While the drain of surplus, the creation of monopolistic structures and the emergence of a dependent bourgeoisie were the three main ways in which foreign capital contributed to underdevelopment, they were by no means the only consequences of TNC expansion. A common argument is that foreign capital far from supplying basic goods for the mass of the population tends to concentrate on the production of luxuries for a small élite. The extensive activities of the car TNCs are often cited as an example (Frank 1969, 168–9). The tendency for foreign subsidiaries to generate links primarily with the parent company or other affiliates and only to a very limited extent with local suppliers, leads to the development of an economic structure which is not integrated at the local level (Sunkel 1972). Moreover, the TNCs are able to use their political influence in order that public expenditure is allocated to support their investment through the provision of infrastructure.

Political implications

The political conclusion that generally follows from this analysis is the need to break out of the capitalist system in order to transcend underdevelopment. Hostility to TNCs is directed at them as the prime representatives of capitalism in the post-war period. In any case the lack of an authentic national bourgeoisie capable of leading the process, renders national capitalist development in the Third World impossible. Thus only through a socialist revolution can the situation of the periphery be fundamentally altered. Such a socialist transformation will however inevitably have to face the hostility of the TNCs and their home states.

Conclusion

Although many of the neo-imperialist arguments concerning the impact of TNCs in the Third World are similar to those of the Global Reach approach, and the two groups of writers are sometimes considered together (for example by Biersteker 1978), the political conclusions drawn are quite different. This derives from a very different evaluation of the role of the local bourgeoisie in Third World countries and the possibility of state action to control the TNCs.

NEO-FUNDAMENTALIST MARXISTS

In the last decade some Marxists have begun to develop a very different view of the TNCs to that discussed in the last section, arguing that their impact on the Third World is overwhelmingly positive. This is presented as part of a more general picture of the progressive role played by capitalism in developing the forces of production and providing the material basis for a socialist society. These authors trace their roots back to Marx's view (for example in some of his writings on India) that the impact of imperialism in destroying pre-capitalist structures and laying the basis for the development of capitalism was progressive. The clearest exponent of such a position was Bill Warren (1973, 1980; see also Schiffer 1981).

Warren stresses the continued competitive nature of the capitalist system going as far as suggesting that competition internationally has intensified since the loss of Britain's position of world hegemony, despite the rise of oligopolistic market structures within individual countries (Warren 1980, 79–80). Thus he rejects the Leninist view of surplus capital as a cause of capital export and implicitly sees the geographic extension of capitalism as a consequence primarily of the competition of capitals (for a succinct presentation of this view see Cypher 1979).

The main thrust of his thesis is to argue that the impact of imperialism on the Third World is progressive, in the sense that it is developing the productive forces in these areas. As part of this thesis he argues that 'private foreign investment in the LDCs is economically beneficial irrespective of measures of government control' and 'must normally be regarded not as a cause of dependence but rather as a means of fortification and diversification of the host countries. It thereby reduces "dependence" in the long run' (Warren 1980, 176).

The arguments on which he bases this thesis reproduce virtually point by point the claims made by bourgeois advocates of the TNCs discussed above. The three major assumptions of the neo-classical view of foreign investment are all accepted by Warren. First, foreign capital is seen in the main as complementary to local capital rather than displacing indigenous efforts (Warren 1973, 37). Secondly, he points to increasing international competition particularly amongst manufacturing TNCs (Warren 1980, 175), which has increased the bargaining power of Third World states enabling them to reduce the monopoly rents earned by the companies and to obtain technology on more favourable terms. Finally, Warren accepts the neo-classical view that TNCs not only supplement existing local resources but also generate additional local resources or utilize resources previously unutilized (Warren 1980, 173 n. 31).

Not only does Warren share the main assumptions of pro-capitalist TNC advocates, but even on points of detail he reproduces the same arguments. Thus for instance TNCs are seen as playing a major role in opening up advanced country markets for Third World exports (Warren 1973, 26–8), while the 'drain of surplus' view of foreign investment is criticized on exactly the same grounds used by neo-classical economists (Warren 1980, 140–3).

While Warren's position is an extreme one amongst Marxists, other writers who wish to stress that the problem of underdevelopment is a consequence of capitalism and not of TNCs *per se*, and that the foreign or local ownership of capital is not a major factor, come close to his position. Thus Emmanuel in pursuing this line of argument states that 'Whenever we find . . . that in any particular aspect the behaviour of the MNC differs from that of the traditional capitalist undertaking, the specific character of the MNC is generally to its (i.e. development's) advantage' (Emmanuel 1976, 763). Emmanuel stresses primarily the technological contribution of TNCs emphasizing particularly the low cost of imported technology and rejecting arguments of the 'inappropriate technology' variety (Emmanuel 1976, 1982).

Political implications

A major explicit political conclusion of this analysis is the need to distinguish carefully between anti-TNC rhetoric used to serve the interests of an expanding local bourgeoisie in the Third World, and true anti-capitalist struggles. As Warren (1973, 44) concludes 'Unless this distinction is clearly grasped the Left will find itself directly supporting bourgeois regimes which, as in Peru and Egypt, exploit and oppress workers and peasants while employing anti-imperialist rhetoric'. However, the implicit conclusion to which Warren's analysis points is that capitalist development in the Third World should be actively supported since it is removing many of the internal obstacles to growth, and that the TNCs are playing a significant role in this process.

Conclusion

In recent years Marxist views of the TNCs have polarized around two positions which are, in terms of many of their arguments, not very different from those found amongst non-Marxist writers. The neo-imperialist view stresses the qualitative transformations which have taken place within capitalism with the rise of monopoly, and emphasizes the regressive nature of imperialist expansion, particularly the appropriation of surplus value from the peripheral areas. In contrast the neo-fundamentalist view stresses the essentially competitive nature of capitalism despite the concentration and centralization of capital and sees the international expansion of capital as playing a predominantly progressive role in breaking down pre-capitalist structures, and laying the basis for capitalist development.

THE INTERNATIONALIZATION OF CAPITAL

Although most of the current literature on TNCs and the Third World falls more or less neatly into the four categories discussed so far, and this exhausts the typology laid out at the beginning of this chapter, it is my view that none of these approaches offers a completely satisfactory treatment of the TNCs. My reasons for saying this will become clearer in the course of the remaining chapters when different aspects of the operations of TNCs will be discussed in more detail.

Each of the approaches discussed so far is partial in that it emphasizes one level of analysis. The neo-classical, Global Reach and neo-imperialist approaches all focus on the sphere of circulation, that is on relations of exchange and distribution. Obviously this is the case with the neo-classical view of the firm responding to market forces, but it is also true of the Global Reach concern with *market* power and with income distribution both nationally and internationally. Similarly the neo-imperialist approach has also been described elsewhere as exchange-based (Cypher 1979) in view of its emphasis on surplus transfer. On the other hand, the neo-fundamentalist view is a 'productionist' approach (Jenkins 1984b; Hoogvelt 1982, 188–9). Its main concern is with the development of the forces of production and in so far as social relations are considered at all these are derived in a highly mechanistic way from the level of development of the forces of production. None of these approaches is able to successfully integrate the spheres of circulation and production.

Not only are these approaches partial in failing to take account of both the sphere of circulation and the sphere of production, but they also fail to integrate the analysis of TNCs as institutions with a broader analysis of the capitalist system. For both the neo-classical and the neo-fundamentalist approaches with their focus on markets and the forces of production respectively, structural and institutional concerns are largely absent. On the other hand, critics of the TNCs reacting against this neglect 'have gone too far in lodging the laws with which they are concerned in firms as institutions, rather than treating the latter as the forms through which the laws of the market are manifested' (Murray 1972). It is the failure to do this which has led to the position of many Marxist critics of the TNCs who 'having first isolated the MNC as the characteristic evil of the century, they study it concretely as an excrescence of the system' (Emmanuel 1976, 769) which logically should lead them to the conclusion that a reformed capitalism without the TNCs would be perfectly acceptable.

A further unsatisfactory aspect of these approaches is their tendency to reduce a contradictory reality to one or other side of a false dichotomy. TNCs are regarded as either competitive or monopolistic. In the Third World they either contribute to development or increase dependence. TNC–state relations are either harmonious or conflictual and the Third World state is either 'nationalist' or 'comprador'. The dominant tendency in the world economy is either towards greater internationalization or the strengthening of nation states.

All these issues will be taken up in detail in later chapters. The point that needs to be emphasized here is that these polarities around which the debate on TNCs has often revolved can lead to a misunderstanding of the real issues.

Some writers, however, notably Palloix and Murray, have attempted to develop a Marxist framework for analysing TNCs which overcomes these three limitations. Although the term is often used very loosely, I shall refer to this as the 'internationalization of capital approach'. It is far less well represented in the literature on TNCs than any of the other approaches except the neo-fundamentalist position. Part of the purpose of this book, therefore, is to make a contribution to developing and synthesizing this view.

In contrast to other critical writings on the TNCs, the starting point of this approach is not the TNCs *per se* but the self-expansion of capital which can be traced through the circuits of capital discussed by Marx in Volume II of *Capital* (see Fine 1975, ch. 7 for a brief exposition of the circuits of capital). The different aspects of the internationalization of capital are identified with the internationalization of the three circuits of capital. The circuits of commodity capital, money capital and productive capital were for Marx three different aspects of the process of self-expansion of capital. In the context of the internationalization of capital these three circuits have been identified with the growth of world trade, the growth of international capital movements, and the growth of the operations of TNCs and the international circulation of products within such firms, respectively (Palloix 1975). The circuits of capital comprise both the sphere of circulation and the sphere of production.

The growth of TNCs therefore is seen not as a phenomenon in its own right, but as an aspect of a broader process of internationalization of capital which tends to create a more integrated world economy. The driving force which underlies international expansion is capitalist competition (Cypher 1979). It is important to stress that despite concentration and centralization of capital, the TNCs remain subject to the compulsion of competition (although as will be seen in the next chapter competition is understood rather differently in this approach).

This approach stresses the highly uneven nature of development brought about by TNC expansion. Foreign investment has tended to be heavily concentrated in a relatively small number of Third World countries (Weisskopf 1978). Moreover, far from the underdeveloped countries representing a homogeneous block, there is a process of increasing economic differentiation within the Third World with some countries emerging as 'newly industrializing countries' or forming the intermediate 'semi-periphery' (Marcussen and Torp 1982, 28–30; Evans 1979, 291).

Despite the highly uneven nature of its impact, the internationalization of capital is leading to an ever more integrated capitalist world economy. This implies transformations in the relations of production as new areas are incorporated into the circuits of capital. In some cases this involves the extension of fully capitalist relations of production and a corresponding growth of the working class. In other areas it involves modifications to or the reinforcing of existing social relations. The impact of the growth of transnational agribusiness on the relations of production in agriculture provides many examples of such processes as does the incorporation of petty-commodity producers through the use of sub-contracting in manufacturing. Social relations at the periphery are neither frozen into the existing mould by TNC expansion, nor can they be totally neglected. Rather they are being continuously transformed and redefined by the internationalization of capital, but not in any simple or universal way. The creation of a unified capitalist world economy is accompanied by the extension of the competitive process of standardization and differentiation on a world scale. In other words there is a growing tendency for the products and production techniques of TNCs to become similar, while at the same time as part of the competitive struggle capital seeks to differentiate itself attaining super profits through the introduction of new products or new techniques, or taking advantage of different local and national conditions.

A feature of these analyses of the internationalization of capital and dependent development is the role attributed to the Third World state. There is an emphasis on the alliance created between the state, TNCs and local capital which is central to the dynamic expansion of certain Third World economies (Evans 1979; Weisskopf 1978). However, it is also recognized that such an alliance is inherently unstable because of the contradictory position both of the local state and the local bourgeoisie.

Political implications

The analysis of the internationalization of capital focuses attention on two crucial areas of struggle. One is the need to develop international links between workers so that labour is able to combine internationally in order to limit the power of international capital to divide it along national lines (Picciotto and Radice 1971). The second area for struggle is the state itself. In dependent development the state has come to play a central role not only in regulating but also participating directly in the accumulation process. The alliance of foreign capital, local capital and the state is by no means immutable and both internal and international developments put it under stress.

Conclusion

The key features of the internationalization of capital approach are its attempt to locate the TNCs within a broader framework of capitalist development and its integration of the spheres of circulation and production. This enables it to provide a more comprehensive view of the TNC phenomenon which like capitalism itself is recognized as being contradictory in many respects.

FURTHER READING

The typology of theories concerning TNCs and the Third World used in this chapter is not the only possible one by any means. Other attempts to classify different approaches to the TNCs can be found in Lall (1974), Emmanuel (1976), Hood and Young (1979, ch. 8) and Biersteker (1978). The most useful short summary of the neo-classical view of TNCs in relation to the Third World which takes account of the most recent developments is Balasubramanyam (1980). More detailed summaries of all the neo-classical theories discussed can be found in Hood and Young (1979, chs 2 and 5). A useful critique of the neo-classical approach and particularly of Reuber (1973) can be found in Lall (1974). Rugman (1981) is recommended on internalization theory because it goes beyond the tedious discussions found in some of the earlier literature to bring out the normative implications of the approach.

For the Global Reach approach, the book of that name by Barnet and Müller (1974) is very readable and Chapters 6 and 7 are relevant to the discussion in this chapter. For a more academic presentation of this view Lall and Streeten (1977; chs 2 and 3) is particularly recommended. For a criticism of this approach generally and of Lall and Streeten in particular see Lal (1978).

The best critical summary of the neo-imperialist position as exemplified by the works of Baran and Sweezy is Brewer (1980, ch. 6). See also Cohen (1973, ch. IV) for a critical account from a different perspective. Sweezy and Magdoff (1969) provide a short analysis of the TNCs, Sunkel (1972) discusses the impact of TNCs in the Third World, particularly Latin America.

The neo-fundamentalist position is summarized in Emmanuel (1976). It is also found in scattered discussion of the TNC in Warren (1973) and (1980, chs 6 and 7).

Few of the writings of Palloix are available in English and they are in any case extremely dense and difficult to follow. See for example his article in Radice (1975). Cypher (1979) is useful in some respects in contrasting the internationalization of capital with what he terms the Monthly Review School, although he includes Warren in the former. For the contradictory impact of the internationalization of capital on the periphery see Weisskopf (1978) and Cardoso (1972).

3

Transnational corporations, competition and monopoly

INTRODUCTION

It should be apparent from the previous chapter that a major issue which divides the different views of TNCs, both Marxist and non-Marxist, is the extent to which large international firms are essentially competitive in nature or represent substantial concentrations of economic power. A related question is whether direct foreign investment by TNCs serves to increase competition or to monopolize those industries in host countries in which it takes place.

The question of competition is of such importance that it has been seen as the major dividing line between different approaches to foreign investment by some writers. Newfarmer, for instance, distinguishes between the 'workable competition' model and the 'transnational conglomerate power' model of TNC behaviour (Newfarmer 1979, 15–21). Similarly, as was seen in the last chapter, it is an important division between the analysis of the Monthly Review School and other Marxist writers on TNCs and more broadly an issue in the debate over the importance of inter-imperialist rivalry in the post-war period.

It is indeed a vital question for all analyses of the impact of TNCs in the Third World. It raises directly the question of whether TNC profits are simply a 'normal' return on capital, making resources available to the underdeveloped countries at a relatively low cost or, as the critics argue, include significant elements of monopoly rents. It also raises the question of whether TNCs in LDCs merely respond to market forces or in contrast are themselves (as a result of their market power), a major element determining the direction of development in the countries in which they operate. It also poses the question of the dynamic of accumulation within the Third World – is this restricted by monopolistic structures leading to a tendency to stagnation or can the TNCs play a dynamic role in developing the forces of production?

THE DEBATE ON INTERNATIONAL COMPETITION

The main question at issue amongst orthodox economists, is whether the international industries in which TNCs tend to be concentrated are characterized by a trend towards increasing competition or display high and persistent levels of concentration. Is it the case, as Vernon suggests, that there is a cycle in many industries from monopoly to oligopoly to workable competition, i.e. a trend for levels of concentration to fall over time (Vernon 1977, 91) or is Newfarmer correct in arguing on the basis of a number of studies that 'in these industries leading firms have apparently expanded their share of the industry's global production relative to what it was in the 1960s' (Newfarmer 1985b)?

The empirical evidence on trends in international concentration is rather mixed.[1] Vernon (1977, 81) shows a declining trend in concentration between 1950 and 1975 in automobiles, aluminium, petroleum, lead, pulp and paper, slab zinc, copper and styrene monomer. Dunning and Pearce (1985) found that the share of the largest three companies in the sales of the world's twenty largest firms declined in eleven out of seventeen industries between 1962 and 1982. However, in six of these eleven industries declining concentration in the first half of the period was partially reversed in the second part. Studies of specific international industries, such as automobiles, tractors, tyres, electrical equipment and cigarettes also indicate that on certain definitions of concentration, over certain periods since World War II, concentration has increased (Newfarmer, ed. 1985c). What is certainly true, however, is that a small number of firms continue to enjoy large market shares in many of the industries in which TNCs tend to be found (Table 3.1).

A parallel debate in the Marxist literature on the TNCs is between those who characterize the post-war period as one of US hegemony ('super-imperialism') and those who see it as a time of increasing inter-imperialist rivalry (Rowthorn 1975). Although this debate is concerned with the relationships between the major capitalist states, it is premised upon an understanding of the relations between different capitals. It is not surprising, therefore, that those Marxists who stress the monopolistic nature of contemporary capitalism and underemphasize the competitiveness of the TNCs, also tended to hold the view that the United States enjoyed undisputed hegemony within the international capitalist system, while those who stress the competitiveness of capitalism tended to stress inter-imperialist rivalry between the United States, Western Europe and Japan.

Table 3.1 Major TNCs' share of Western world output of selected products

Product	No. of TNCs	% of output	Year
Crude oil	7	25	1979
Refined oil	7	40	1979
Iron ore	7	>50	1976
Copper	7	23	1981
Bauxite	6	45	1982
Alumina	6	50	1982
Aluminium	6	46	1982
Bananas	3	75	1970
Vehicles	8	76	1983
Tractors	10	70	1979
Agricultural machinery	11	73	1980
Tyres	6	>70	1982
Cigarettes	7	59	1974
Tin smelting	4	50	1980
Nickel	4	60–64	1978

Source: UNCTC and own investigation.

THE COMPETITIVE IMPACT OF TNCS IN HOST COUNTRIES

A second area of debate concerns the effects of foreign investment by TNCs on competition in host countries. As in the discussion of international competition, two opposed positions can be identified. Neoclassical writers emphasize the role of TNCs in increasing competition in the markets which they enter, while the Global Reach approach sees them as factors tending to restrict competition. Similarly among Marxists, Warren has stressed that 'the secular trend is towards stiffening competition of manufacturing multinationals in LDCs' (Warren 1980, 175), while a number of dependency writers have pointed to the monopolization of host economies by the TNCs.

A number of studies of individual LDCs have found that investment by TNCs tends to be located primarily in sectors characterized by high levels of concentration. Clearly, the extractive industries such as oil, copper and bauxite, in which TNCs have in the past invested heavily have been characterized by a small number of firms. More significantly perhaps, even within manufacturing industry to which an increasing proportion of DFI in LDCs has been directed, there is a correlation between the presence of TNCs and the level of concentration. (Empirical studies are reviewed in Lall 1980, ch. 2; Dunning 1981, ch. 7; and Newfarmer 1985a.)

TNCs not only tend to cluster in the more concentrated branches of industry but individual subsidiaries also tend to enjoy dominant positions in the markets in which they operate. A number of studies in Latin America (Jenkins 1984a) and other Third World countries, such as Kenya (Langdon 1978) and South Korea (Jo 1976, 54–6), bear this out. The Kenyan study concluded, for instance, that 68 per cent of the sample of foreign subsidiaries analysed were relatively unconstrained by competition.

Unfortunately the existence of a correlation between highly concentrated market structures in LDCs and the presence of TNC subsidiaries says nothing about the causes of such a relationship. In other words it does not necessarily indicate that TNCs are a cause of high levels of concentration. It may equally well be the case that TNCs are found in industries which are in any case concentrated because of the existence of barriers to entry. Moreover it is also possible that although TNCs are found in highly concentrated industries their effect may be to reduce concentration below the levels which would have existed in their absence.

In order to examine in more detail the causal mechanisms involved in this correlation, a distinction is usually made between the first stage or 'at entry' effects of foreign investment and the second stage or 'post entry' effects.

'At entry effects'

The neo-classical view regards it as almost axiomatic that new entry through foreign investment leads to a reduction in concentration and increased competition in host economies (Reuber 1973, 178). Vernon (1977, table 9) presents evidence from Latin America and India to show that the number of foreign subsidiaries producing in each 3-digit industry increased significantly in the 1960s, indicating a sequence from monopoly through oligopoly to workable competition.

The critics question this analysis on a number of points. Firstly, new entry by a TNC often takes place through acquisition of local firms rather than through a 'greenfield' venture. Since the early fifties more than two-fifths of the subsidiaries set up by US manufacturing TNCs in the Third World and more than a quarter of European-owned subsidiaries have involved acquisition of existing firms (UNCTC 1978, tables III.20 and III.22). There is, therefore, no increase in the number of firms in the industry in these cases, particularly since some evidence suggests that most of the acquired local firms could have continued in operation if they had not been taken over (Newfarmer and Mueller 1975). Secondly, TNC entry may take place in new industries rather than increasing the number of firms in an existing industry. This is likely where new sectors are being developed through import-substituting industrialization.

Furthermore, TNCs through their behaviour may well increase barriers to entry in the industries which they enter. In particular, TNCs may raise product differentiation barriers by introducing heavily advertised branded goods, or increase economies of scale or capital requirements by the introduction of large-scale, capital intensive technology (Lall 1980, 66–9). Since the height of entry barriers is held to be a major determinant of the level of concentration in an industry, these characteristics of TNCs are likely to lead to increased levels of concentration in the industries which they enter. Studies in Malaysia and Brazil both indicate that TNCs serve to increase barriers to entry in the industries in which they operate (Lall 1980, ch. 3; Newfarmer and Marsh 1981).

'Post entry effects'

Similarly divergent views exist over the subsequent effects of TNCs on competition. The neo-classical view is that over time competition tends to increase either because the initial TNC entry attracts further foreign investment in the industry, or because technology is diffused to local firms which become increasingly competitive (Vernon 1977, 79). It is also sometimes argued that TNCs may be less prone to collusion than national oligopolists (Reuber 1973, 178).

The critical view stresses the way in which the behaviour of TNCs and the reactions to them tend to reduce competition. The TNCs are able to use the advantages which their size and international spread give them to eliminate local competitors through predatory pricing and the 'deep pocket' of the parent company. As local firms are driven out of the industry, concentration tends to increase. TNC entry may also lead to 'defensive' mergers by local firms in order to remain in the market (Dunning 1981, 198). The TNCs may also restrict competition by restrictive business practices involving collusion on prices, or global market allocation.

A detailed empirical analysis of the Brazilian electrical industry reveals some of the mechanisms which can be used by TNCs to limit competition in a host country (Newfarmer 1979, ch. vii). TNCs in the industry resorted to a number of restrictive practices in order to secure their control over the market. Not surprisingly in view of the existence of an international cartel in the heavy electrical equipment industry, an almost identical cartel operated in Brazil. The companies involved which included General Electric, Westinghouse, Siemens, Brown Boveri, ASEA and Hitachi agreed to rotate sellers designated to win tenders for transformers. This was done on the basis of price lists – firms not designated to win a tender would submit bids 3 per cent, 6 per cent or 9 per cent above the list price in accordance with a predetermined order. If the client failed to allocate the tender to the cartel designated firm, the winner was to raise its price by 5 per cent. Occasionally a member of the cartel would be instructed to win a tender at below-cost prices in order to exclude a non-member firm – in other words to use predatory pricing. As a result of these operations more than seven producers of power and distribution transformers went out of business in Brazil in the 1960s and early 1970s and concentration in the industry increased considerably.

Formal collusion was by no means the only way in which TNCs attempted to limit competition in the Brazilian electrical industry. Newfarmer documents extensive interlocking directorships between major TNCs (i.e. the same person sits on the board of two or more TNC subsidiaries). This tends to encourage co-operation rather than conflict amongst the firms concerned. Philips and Philco which between them controlled two-thirds of the Brazilian market for colour televisions, three-quarters of the market for black-and-white sets and one-third in radios, had such an interlock which must have contributed to the likelihood of limiting competition between the two firms with Philips producing 17-inch and 20-inch colour televisions and one- to four-band radios and Philco producing 22-inch and 26-inch colour televisions, 12-inch portable black-and-white televisions and three- and eight-band radios. Similar patterns of market allocation and mutual forbearance appear to exist in other sectors of the electrical industry.

Consequences

The implications of the neo-classical view (shared by Warren) is clear. TNCs are not an important cause of market imperfections in host countries, indeed they tend to increase competition and improve the functioning of markets. Market imperfections, where they do exist, can be attributed to misconceived government policies, particularly high levels of protection. TNCs do not obtain excessive returns in the form of high profits. In general, profits are kept within limits by competition and where above average profits are obtained this is attributable to some special endowment of the TNC rather than to market power.

In contrast, Global Reach and neo-imperialist interpretations consider that TNCs enjoy considerable market power because they operate in concentrated markets. Moreover, they are factors which tend to reduce competition and increase concentration in the markets in which they operate. As a result, TNCs are able to enjoy persistent monopoly rents reflected in significantly higher than average rates of profit. It is market power rather than greater efficiency that enables them both to earn higher profit rates and displace local competition which leads to the denationalization of the industries which they enter.

THEORIES OF COMPETITION AND MONOPOLY

A major flaw of much of the literature on the competitive or monopolistic nature of the TNCs is the implicit concept of competition which they employ. Most analyses of the TNCs in fact share a common view of competition which has been described as 'the Quantity Theory of Competition' (Weeks 1981, 153). In this view competition finds its highest expression in perfect competition, a situation in which a large number of small firms supply an identical commodity and are 'price takers', that is have no influence over the price at which their commodities are sold, which is determined by market supply and demand. In this framework, monopoly is the exact opposite of perfect competition, a situation in which one firm controls the entire market for a commodity and thus by varying output can control the market price.

There are a number of features of the Quantity Theory of Competition that are worth emphasizing:

- the number of firms and their size distribution is crucial in determining the extent of competition in an industry; the smaller the number of firms, the nearer a market is to being monopolistic and therefore the more likely it is that firms will be able to set monopoly prices through some form of collusion or price leadership;

- it considers competition in the sphere of exchange so that the emphasis is on *market* structure and *market* shares;

- competitive conditions are the starting point of the analysis;

- competition is analysed as a force which tends to bring about a new equilibrium following any economic disturbance;

- competition is viewed as one end of a continuum of market structures.

This view of competition is shared by both neo-classical economists who see capitalism as approximating the perfectly competitive model and, for example, industrial organization theorists who regard various forms of imperfectly competitive markets as being of greater empirical relevance. A similar view also underlies the writings of certain Marxists who argue that with the transition from competitive capitalism to monopoly capitalism, the law of value has ceased to function (Semmler 1982a; Bryan 1985).

A recent revival of interest in classical and Marxist theories of competition has led to a critique of the Quantity Theory of Competition which is of considerable relevance to the discussion of TNCs. A number of features of these alternative approaches to competition distinguish them. In the first place, the classical notion of competition did not refer to perfect competition but to a situation in which the removal of restrictions on the mobility of labour and capital led to a tendency for the rate of profit to be equalized between different industries. Mobility of resources rather than the number of firms in a particular market becomes the crucial determinant of the degree of competition (Semmler 1982b).

Second, competition is not simply an aspect of exchange but affects production, realization, distribution – accumulation as a whole. Thus struggles in production over the labour process, attempts to increase market shares and investment strategies are all aspects of the competitive struggle. It also follows that monopoly cannot simply be reduced to market power and that it is necessary to develop a different concept of monopoly which relates it to the ability to secure and reproduce surplus profit rather than size *per se* (Bryan 1985).

Third, competition is not the starting point in this analysis but a consequence of the self-expansion of capital. As Fine (1975, 35) put it, 'Capital as self-expanding value creates competition which is fought by accumulation.' It is the nature of capitalist commodity production that leads to competition which must, therefore, exist independently of the number of firms in any particular market.

Fourth, competition is not an equilibrating force but a cause of continuous disequilibria in capitalist economies. In the competitive struggle one firm introduces a more productive technique. This leads to a profit rate differential in its favour. Existing fixed capital is devalued, other firms introduce the technique and the value of the commodity falls in line with the reduced socially necessary labour time.

Finally, competition is not analysed as one end of a continuum of market structures, but as a process in which competition and monopoly are not polar opposites but are linked in a dialectical fashion. As Marx argued in *The Poverty of Philosophy*

In practical life we find not only competition, monopoly and the antagonism between them, but also the synthesis of the two, which is not a formula but a movement. Monopoly produces competition, competition produces monopoly. . . . The synthesis is such that monopoly can only maintain itself by continually entering into the struggle of competition.   (Quoted in Weeks 1981, 168)

Competition therefore permeates the capitalist mode of production. It manifests itself in a number of forms: in the competition between capital and labour over the organization of production, in the competition among capitals (both within industries and in the movement of capital among industries) and competition among workers (Burkett 1986; Weeks 1981, ch. VI). Some writers (e.g. Clifton 1977) have argued that far from competition decreasing with the development of capitalism, and the concentration and centralization of capital (as the Quantity Theory of Competition implies and 'monopoly capital' theorists explicitly argue) competition in the classical and Marxist sense increases because the modern corporation involves much greater capital mobility than the small, entrepreneurial firm of early capitalism.

That the earlier discussion of the competitive/monopolistic nature of TNCs is based on the Quantity Theory of Competition is readily apparent. Whether at the international or the national level, the discussion has revolved around questions such as whether the number of firms has increased or what the trend in the concentration ratio has been. Concern over monopoly is directed primarily at the *market power* of TNCs and their consequent ability to charge monopolistic prices and earn monopoly rents. It is only the Marxists who emphasize inter-imperialist rivalry in the post-war period who reject the view that sees monopoly and competition as polar opposites with an increase in one leading to a decrease in the other.

THE MARXIST THEORY OF COMPETITION AND THE INTERNATIONALIZATION OF CAPITAL

It is, however, possible to develop an alternative view of the TNCs based on the classical and Marxist view of competition. If competition is analysed not in terms of the distance from a theoretical model of perfect competition, but in terms of the degree of capital mobility, then as Clifton (1977) has argued,

the competitive firm . . . is the modern corporation, not the atomistic firm of the neoclassical theory of perfect competition. The conditions of free capital mobility which permit maximum flexibility and intensity for an independent unit of capital to directly search out the highest possible rate of return in the market are most closely approximated in the modern corporation.

The TNC permits this maximum flexibility and intensity on an international scale. The growth of the TNC and the developments which in part have made it possible, such as the advances in technology in transport and communications, can therefore be seen as giving rise to a more competitive world economy in which the internationalization of capital has brought ever widening geographical areas within its ambit.

The growth of TNCs should not therefore be seen as a correlate of monopolization of the home economy, but as part of the increasingly competitive nature of the capitalist system. Both the Global Reach approach and the neo-imperialist view have stressed the relationship between monopoly and foreign investment. From the early work of Hymer onwards, the former group has pointed to the tendency for TNCs to come from oligopolistic industries in the United States, while there is a long Marxist tradition which sees a link between the growth of capital exports and the growth of monopoly within national economies. Both these views are open to question. The association of foreign investment with domestic concentration was based on the experience of US TNCs and it is by no means clear that it is universally valid (Ozawa 1979). Even within the United States it appears that it is factors such as firm size, technological intensity and product differentiation rather than market concentration *per se* which primarily distinguish TNCs from non-TNCs.

The Marxist thesis that capital export is associated with monopoly has also been questioned, both in its original Leninist formulation and more recent interpretations such as those of Baran and Sweezy (Olle and Schoeller 1982; Barratt Brown 1974, chs 8–9). The original capital export thesis has been disputed on the grounds that it failed to explain the direction of investment which did not go predominantly to the underdeveloped countries, that in any case the net flow of capital was towards the so-called capital exporting countries, and that the correlation with monopoly was dubious since the major capital exporting country, the UK, was where monopoly was least developed. The first two points can also be made in relation to more recent theories of foreign investment. It has also been argued that foreign investment is not confined to monopolistic firms and that in any case, a broader concept of internationalization of capital is required since foreign expansion can occur in ways other than direct foreign investment.

To emphasize competition as the dynamic element in TNC expansion does not imply that monopolistic positions and monopoly rents are insignificant. As the passage quoted earlier from Marx indicates, monopoly and competition constitute a dialectical unity not opposite poles. It is possible to give a more concrete expression to this view in the context of the internationalization of capital. In contemporary capitalism, competition expresses itself largely as the search for surplus profits by individual firms. Surplus profits may be obtained in a number of ways. TNCs search for ways in which to obtain a rate of profit above the average for the branch in which they operate. This may be done through the introduction of new production processes which reduce their costs below the average for the branch. More commonly, it may be done by introducing new products which enjoy favourable demand conditions initially and a quasi-monopolistic position until other firms bring in similar products. They may enter new geographical markets and again, as the first comer, enjoy a favourable demand situation until other firms follow. Finally, they try to secure cheaper sources of raw materials and thus acquire a cost advantage through differential rent. In the first three of these cases, competitive success in terms of achieving higher than average profit rates sets in motion counteracting pressures as other firms seek to imitate the leader. Success in achieving a quasi-monopolistic position leads to its own destruction.

While TNCs compete to increase their profit rate above the average for the branch or branches in which they operate, they can under certain circumstances attempt to raise the average rate of profit in the branch above the general rate of profit by increasing their share of the total surplus value produced. This can be done by measures designed to limit conflict and competition, such as joint-ventures or cartels. There is of course an inherent contradiction between the attempts of firms to raise profits above the average for the branch which implies competition, and attempts to raise the average which requires collusion. As a result, attempts at cartelization are constantly threatened by the potential of renewed competition. Two tendencies of capitalist development ensure that this potential eventually becomes a reality. The first is uneven development leading to changes in the relative strengths of capitals and a divergence of interests between strong and weak capitals. The second is the tendency to crisis which destabilizes attempts to eliminate competition and intensifies the competitive struggle.

Such an approach to capitalist competition is consistent with the view of recent Marxists who have stressed the importance of inter-imperialist rivalries in the post-war period (Rowthorn 1975; Hymer 1979, esp. chs 7 and 10; Mandel 1975). They have argued (in opposition to the view of US super-imperialism) that the lead of US capital was being narrowed and that some of the alleged manifestations of the strength of US capital in fact represent a weakening of its position. Concentration and centralization of capital in Western Europe and Japan has led to increased international competition. There has been a substantial narrowing of the gap in size between US and non-US capital, as a result of the growing merger movement in these countries and the more rapid growth of their economies. Large US firms which were twice as large as their rivals in the early 1960s were only slightly bigger twenty years later (see Figure 3.1).

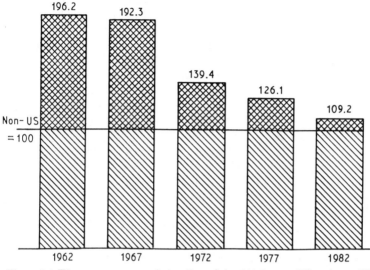

Figure 3.1 The gap narrows: relative size of the 100 largest US and non-US firms, 1962–82.

Source: Dunning and Pearce (1985), table 5.4(a).

Even at the time of greatest concern over the 'American challenge' it has been suggested that the US threat was exaggerated because of a tendency to overemphasize the offensive nature of US foreign investment. In fact, the much faster growth of the EEC and Japan compared to the United States meant that US expansion into these markets was necessary as a means of maintaining corporate growth rates in the face of slowly expanding domestic markets. Moreover, the growth of the EEC economies strengthened European capital posing a threat to the equilibrium of the existing international oligopoly which US capital hoped to maintain, preventing the emergence of a new competitive threat (Rowthorn 1975). Thus US investment in Europe and pressure in Japan to liberalize foreign capital in the late 1960s was a reflection of the undermining of US capital's previously strong position.

The narrowing size differential between large US and non-US capital has undermined one of the pillars of the technological superiority of US capital. In any case, such technological monopolies were inevitably temporary as competing firms imitate the innovator, and require continuous heavy R & D expenditure in order to be reproduced. The loss of technological dominance by US capital has also been accentuated by developments after 1973 when the increase in oil prices put a premium on energy-saving innovation. In a number of such areas, non-US capital enjoyed a technological lead, e.g. Michelin in radial tyres and Bosch and Lucas in fuel injection equipment (Franko 1978, 79).

The decline in US pre-eminence is indicated not only by the relatively slower growth of large US firms, but also by the recent substantial overseas expansion of European and Japanese capital. This is reflected in the declining share of the United States in the total stock of direct investment overseas from 49 per cent in 1960 to 42 per cent in 1980. Over the same period the share of West Germany increased from 1.2 per cent to 7.4 per cent and that of Japan from 0.7 per cent to 7.3 per cent (Stopford and Dunning 1983, table 1.3). A similar pattern emerges from an examination of the setting up or acquisition of new manufacturing subsidiaries abroad. By 1965 large non-US firms were expanding at least as fast as US firms and by 1968 had overtaken them. Moreover, after 1968 the rate of establishing and acquiring new operations abroad by US TNCs began to decline rapidly (Franko 1978, 96). Data on the growth of overseas production by TNCs in recent years confirm that European and Japanese firms have been expanding faster than those from the US (Table 3.2). By the early 1980s US TNCs accounted for a half or less of total overseas production by TNCs (Dunning and Pearce 1985; UNCTC 1983, table II. 32).

One particular manifestation of this 'non-American challenge' in recent years has been the rapid growth of foreign investment in the US economy itself. Between 1967 and 1977 the stock of direct foreign investment in the US increased fourfold. The ratio of the flow of direct foreign investment into the United States to United States investment

Table 3.2 Increase in overseas production by TNCs, by origin

	1974–8	1977–81
USA	50%	68%
Western Europe	89%	91%
Japan	122%	103%

Sources: Stopford et al. (1980), table 14; Stopford and Dunning (1983), table 4.4.

abroad more than trebled from 19 per cent in 1970 to 58 per cent in 1980 (UNCTC 1983, tables II.1 and II.2). Investment by Japanese, Dutch and West German companies in the United States has grown particularly rapidly in recent years (Young and Hood 1980, table 1).

Although Petras and Rhodes (1976) attempted to argue that US hegemony was being reconsolidated in the late 1970s, the evidence of the past decade has tended to confirm the picture drawn by Hymer, Rowthorn and Mandel in the early 1970s. The growth of international competition between TNCs from North America, Western Europe and Japan has been a major feature of this recent period as has the interpenetration of markets. The 1980s are likely to see an expansion of this trend with the growth of overseas production by Japanese firms which have in the past relied primarily on exports of commodities.

THE INTERNATIONAL OIL INDUSTRY

The experience of specific industries suggests that competition and monopoly coexist in the process of capital accumulation and the internationalization of capital. Thus TNCs seek out new ways of making surplus profits such as new products, new technologies and new sources of raw materials. At the same time they try to eliminate competition and conflict through acquisition, joint-ventures, collusion and cartels. But the inherent competitive drive of accumulation tends to eliminate surplus profits through imitation by competitors, while uneven development between different capitals, conflicts of interest between the strong and the weak and periodic crises of capital accumulation, tend to destabilize attempts at collusion. This can be clearly illustrated by a more detailed examination of the international oil industry.

The oil industry is the transnational industry *par excellence* and its leading companies, Exxon, Shell, BP and others, are amongst the first to spring to mind when TNCs are discussed. Four of the world's five largest TNCs are oil companies (see Table 1.1, p. 9). The seven sisters (Exxon, Shell, BP, Gulf, Texaco, Socal and Mobil) are often cited as a classic example of monopolistic control of world markets. The industry is highly internationalized and its history illustrates both the importance of competitive pressures in the world market and the ways in which major TNCs attempt to control and eliminate such pressures.

In the United States, what began as a highly competitive industry with a large number of small firms in the 1850s came to be dominated by Rockefeller's Standard Oil Trust in the last quarter of the nineteenth century. As the United States became the world's largest oil producer, Standard Oil became the leading company dominating both the US and foreign markets. However, new oil discoveries in Russia (developed by the Nobels and the Rothschilds) and the Dutch East Indies (Royal Dutch) in the 1880s led to increasing international competition for Standard. It responded by attempting to control marketing outlets in those countries in which it faced international competition. This proved difficult because of the relative ease with which competitors could establish new outlets and around the turn of the century the strategy switched to one of controlling major sources of supply of crude (Vernon 1973, 27). This gave rise to the typical large vertically integrated international oil company involved in all the stages of production and distribution from the extraction of crude through refining to final sales to the consumer through service stations.

Competition intensified in the early twentieth century with the merger between Royal Dutch and Shell Transport and Trading in 1907 and British discoveries in Iran in 1908 (Anglo-Persian Oil Company, now BP). In 1911 Standard Oil was broken up by a US government anti-trust action into a number of major oil companies, including Standard Oil of New Jersey (now Exxon), Standard Oil of New York (now Mobil) and Socal. As Tanzer (1980, 101) has noted: 'Up until 1928 the history of the international oil industry was a continuous series of fierce struggles for markets and profits, primarily between Standard Oil of New Jersey and Royal/Dutch Shell.'

With the growth of vertically integrated oil companies, existing major oil producers came to see the discovery of new, low-cost sources of crude oil as a major threat to their position. The TNCs, therefore, developed a number of mechanisms to control supply from the late 1920s. A major way in which the seven sisters established this control in the Middle East (the major area of cheap oil potential) was through a series of jointly owned operating companies established in each of the major producing countries (Iraq, Iran, Saudi Arabia and Kuwait). The Iraq Petroleum Company brought together Exxon, Mobil, BP, Shell and CFP; the Arabian-American Oil Company involved Standard Oil of California, Texaco and later Exxon and Mobil; the Kuwait Oil Company comprised BP and Gulf; and after the overthrow of Mossadeq a consortium was formed in Iran which included all of the seven sisters and CFP. These joint ventures were responsible for exploration, development and production of oil, and distributed profits and production to the oil companies in proportion to their ownership shares.

In addition the TNCs used long-term contracts for the supply of oil amongst themselves, subject to highly restrictive terms concerning pricing and marketing. According to the Report of the US Federal Trade Commission on the International Petroleum Cartel

> The operation of these two instruments of control (joint ventures and long term contracts), in effect, brings the seven international oil companies, controlling practically all of the Middle East oil resources, together into a mutual community of interest.
>
> (Quoted in Blair 1976, 43)

Even as late as 1972 the seven sisters continued to account for over 90 per cent of crude oil production in the Middle East.

Although the Middle East was the major source of crude oil, it was by no means the only one, and the TNCs also attempted to control markets to prevent disruption from the uncontrolled producers in the US, Rumania and Venezuela, and to prevent competition for markets amongst themselves. From 1928 the companies entered a number of 'As Is Agreements' designed to maintain existing market shares and a number of national cartels were formed. In addition to fixing quotas, the agreements dealt with price fixing and other conditions of sale (including limitations on non-price competition) and dealing with the problem of outsiders. Independent firms continued to be a problem for the seven sisters and in the late 1930s the majors found themselves unable to stop a price-cutting campaign in the UK (Blair 1976, ch. 3).

In the post-war period formal collusion through cartels gave way to the production-control and price-matching systems which did away with the need for frequent and cumbersome meetings (see Blair 1976, ch. 5 for a discussion of these two mechanisms). This involved the establishment of a predetermined growth rate for production and the use of a basing point system for establishing prices. This system worked reasonably well for the major TNCs until the mid-1960s but then once more intensification of competition from outsiders put the system under strain.

The development of new sources of crude oil with substantial participation of firms other than the seven sisters, particularly in Libya, led to increasing price competition from the early 1960s as the independents attempted to find outlets for their rapidly growing supplies of crude. There was also a growth of independent refiners and retailers in the US and elsewhere. In fact, the share of the seven sisters declined significantly at each stage of production in the international oil industry between 1953 and 1972 (Jacoby 1974, table 9.12). Increasing competition in the industry was reflected in the elimination of surplus profits by the early 1960s. Rates of return in oil which had been more than double those obtained in the mining and manufacturing industries in the

1950s fell to below that in mining and the same rate as in manufacturing in the 1960s (Jacoby 1974, table 10.7).

Looked at from the point of view of conventional indicators of market concentration it would appear that the trend to increased competition and declining market power of the seven sisters continued in the 1970s. Nationalization of their assets in a number of oil producing countries led to a fall in the majors' share of crude oil production from 61 per cent in 1970 to 25 per cent in 1979 and of sales of petroleum products from 50 to 40 per cent over the same period (UNCTC 1983, table V.1). Moreover, oil prices are no longer set by the companies but by OPEC.

However, in terms of their ability to secure and reproduce surplus profits, the power of the oil TNCs has increased. The most clear indication of this is the sharp rise in company profits with the oil price increases of 1973–4 and 1979–80 and the maintenance of higher rates of profit from 1973 onwards than in the 1960s.

It is open to debate whether the oil companies deliberately encouraged OPEC to raise prices from around 1968 in order to increase company profits. However, there is little doubt that they have come out of the changes in the international oil industry very well. They were able to reverse the slide towards intensified competition in a number of ways. First the new Libyan government (of Qadaffi) attempted to raise prices, restricting the output of Libyan producers and subsequently nationalizing or taking a majority holding in the production companies. The fall in Libyan production removed the threat posed by the independents. The majors also succeeded in driving out many of the independent retailers by cutting back oil refinery output and engineering a shortage, the main victims of which were the independents.

This set the scene for the price increases of 1973. Although the oil companies were probably not the primary instigators of these increases, they played an important role in maintaining them through limiting output and allocating markets, which it is doubtful whether the countries themselves would have had the capacity to do. The increased price of crude enabled the companies to increase their rate of return and at the same time shift profits downstream from crude production. Although, as noted above, the seven sisters' share of crude oil output fell sharply in the 1970s, they continue to enjoy access to supplies of crude as a result of long-term contracts with their former subsidiaries (UNIDO 1978, table A.11). They are also involved in providing technical assistance to the nationalized oil companies and the producing countries continue to be heavily dependent on the majors for downstream outlets for their oil.

The rise in profitability in the 1970s has enabled the major oil TNCs to move rapidly into new areas. This has included an extension of their activities in other fuels, such as coal and uranium, which began in the 1960s, so that by the mid-1980s it was expected that oil companies would control 40 per cent of US coal reserves and production. They have also diversified into non-fuel minerals, for example through the acquisition of Anaconda by Atlantic Richfield in 1977 and Kennecott by Sohio in 1981 and Exxon's investment in a Chilean copper mine. In addition, they have pushed downstream into chemical production to such an extent that Shell is now the eighth largest chemical producer in the world. Thus while the *market* power of the oil companies as indicated by their shares in sales of crude oil or petroleum products may have declined, their corporate *monopoly* power in terms of ability to earn surplus profits has increased since the late 1960s. There can be no clearer illustration of the need for a broader concept of monopoly than is provided by orthodox theory.

COMPETITIVE IMPACT IN LDCS

Analysing competition in terms of capital mobility, rather than number of firms, gives new insights into the consequences of TNC entry into host markets. Such entry may take one of two forms. It may involve a greenfield venture or acquiring an existing firm in an already established industry or it may involve a greenfield plant in an entirely new industry thus diversifying the existing productive structure. In the former case, conventional analysis seeks to distinguish between the effects of greenfield ventures and acquisitions as forms of entry because of their different implications for the number of firms and hence the level of competition in the industry. However, this distinction is largely irrelevant when looked at from the point of view of capital mobility.

The more relevant distinction is between entry into existing industry (whether greenfield or acquisition) and entry into an entirely new industry. In both these situations TNCs are likely initially to enjoy high profit rates, but for different reasons. In the former case because TNCs have lower costs then existing local firms they enjoy surplus profits because prices are set initially in relation to the costs of local firms (who represent the average socially necessary labour time for the commodity) (Weeks 1977). In the latter case demand conditions are likely to be extremely favourable in relation to supply so that again high profit rates will be earned.

Neither of these situations permits the TNCs to maintain high profit rates in the long run however. A number of factors tend to modify the situation. Although TNCs may raise barriers to entry which face local capital wishing to enter a particular industry, they are much less capable of raising barriers to entry against other TNCs which have ample capital resources and their own range of differentiated products (Knickerbocker 1976, quoted in Parry 1979; Gorecki 1976, quoted in Connor 1977, 27, on Canada). Thus after entry by a TNC the mobility of capital, as indicated by potential entry by other TNCs, remains high. In some industries there is evidence that rivalry between capitals is so intense that investment by one TNC in a particular country will lead to a 'bandwagon effect' whereby its major competitors follow suit.

This model of TNC behaviour was formalized by Knickerbocker (1973) who dubbed it 'oligopolistic reaction'. It was found that bunching of entry into foreign markets by TNCs in a particular industry was indeed quite common. Moreover, although the direction of causation was not clear, it was also noted that the industries which had the highest rates of profit overseas also showed the strongest level of oligopolistic reaction (Knickerbocker 1973, ch. 7). Thus high profits (and incidentally favourable demand conditions as indicated by market growth) served to intensify competitive rivalry among TNCs.

In some industries, the degree of 'oligopolistic reaction' has been so strong that far from industries in host Third World economies displaying higher levels of concentration than in developed countries, as might be expected from the smaller size of the market (Merhav 1969), they are in some cases more fragmented. This phenomenon, known as the 'miniature replica effect', involving a large number of TNCs crowding in to small markets regardless of the resulting loss of economies of scale, has been particularly marked in the pharmaceutical and motor industries (Evans 1977; Jenkins 1977). It has also been observed in some other consumer good industries such as cosmetics, record players, television sets, electrical appliances and household appliances (Fajnzylber and Martinez Tarrago 1975, 335; Connor 1977, table B1).

Thus far from TNC entry leading to the raising of entry barriers and the development of monopolistic positions, entry barriers facing other TNCs driven by competitive pressures to match a rival's initial move, may be quite low. Nevertheless, this emphasis on the competitive nature of TNCs does not imply a favourable evaluation of their impact in host countries as in the case of the neo-classical analysis. In fact, it shows that in some industries the problems associated with foreign capital derive from too much rather than too little competition. As will be shown below the excessive fragmentation of the motor industry in Third World countries as a result of oligopolistic reaction has given rise to a high-cost, inefficient industrial structure.

A second factor which tends over time to erode the high profits which are earned initially by a TNC entrant into an existing industry is the displacement of local firms. As TNCs come to account for an increasing share of the industry's output, the average socially necessary labour time in the production of the commodity tends to shift towards the level of the TNCs. Thus prices tend to fall in the industry in line with the reduction in values.

A third factor is the modernization of local firms under pressure from TNC competition. This often involves acquiring foreign technology under licence. Thus increased productivity of surviving local firms towards the levels achieved by the TNCs is a further factor putting downward pressure on prices and leading to a reduction in the surplus profits which TNCs earn.

In the case of new industries established through TNC entry where high profits are a consequence of favourable demand conditions, then even more obviously these profits can only be temporary. Once normal conditions of supply and demand are established, it is no longer possible for the commodity to be sold permanently above its value (or price of production). Thus prices tend to fall and surplus profits are again eliminated.

Depending on the extent of the competitive advantage enjoyed by TNCs, and the ability of local capital to modernize, the processes described above will either lead to the complete domination of an industry by foreign capital, as is commonly the case in tobacco, pharmaceuticals, tyres and cars, or to the coexistence of foreign and local capital as is often found in food and beverages, textiles and chemical products. In the latter case, TNCs may continue to enjoy a higher rate of profit than local firms reflecting their lower costs as a result of access to the parent company's technology or economies of scale, but this cannot be too high otherwise it would pay them to expand at the expense of the remaining local firms, or other TNCs would be attracted into the industry with the same effect.

One further point needs to be made concerning this analysis. It should not be read in comparative static terms as a shift from one (pre-TNC entry) equilibrium to another (post-TNC entry) equilibrium situation. The internationalization of capital is a dynamic process of continually recurring disequilibria. The entry of TNCs occurs at different times in different industries. Moreover, the competitive struggle impels firms to look for new areas in which surplus profits can be earned all the time. This involves not only entry into other branches but also the launching of new products and improved production techniques. For TNCs the introduction of new products is a major way in which they seek to create temporary surplus profits because of the monopoly positions to which they can give rise and the temporarily favourable demand conditions which they enjoy.

Despite the emphasis on competition in this analysis, it is very different from the neo-classical approach (and Warren's). TNCs give rise to increased competition because of the greater mobility of capital between industries and countries. But an important part of competition between TNCs is the search for surplus profits which frequently involves the creation of quasi-monopolistic positions and attempts to protect such positions which are under threat from other TNCs.

TNCs may well earn higher profits than local firms on average. Theoretically above average profits for particular firms can be explained in one of three ways. First they may reflect excess demand for a commodity in a particular period. Second they may reflect different levels of productivity and costs within a particular industry. Third they may reflect barriers to the mobility of capital in particular spheres of production (Semmler 1984, 37–8). As far as TNCs are concerned, it is the first two of these factors that provide the explanation for differential profitability, rather than the last, although it is concentration and market power that are commonly emphasized by the Global Reach approach.

TNCS, HOST INDUSTRY STRUCTURE AND PROFITABILITY

In view of the above discussion, two questions need to be examined further. First do TNCs in fact earn higher profits in Third World economies than local firms? Second if so, are differential profit rates explicable in terms of market structure or do they reflect demand and cost conditions? Unfortunately, there are major problems in carrying out such an analysis, and the empirical studies which have attempted to do so are few and far between.

The main problem arises from the existence of transfer prices in the intra-firm trade of TNCs. Thus the declared profits of a subsidiary do not necessarily reflect the true contribution of that subsidiary to the global profitability of the TNC (see chapter 5 below for a full discussion of transfer pricing). There are also other problems associated with any study of profitability, such as the appropriate measure to use, the possibility that monopoly profits may be capitalized leading to an underestimation of profit rates or that the cost of maintaining a monopolistic position may inflate production costs (Semmler 1984, 107). A further methodological problem arises in determining the appropriate technique for comparing local and foreign firms (see chapter 7 below for a discussion of this issue).

Studies in a number of countries have found that foreign subsidiaries have higher profit rates than local firms but the differences, although in the right direction, have not always proved statistically significant. Few studies have concluded that TNC profit rates are on average lower than those of local firms (Jenkins 1986a). In view of the possible underestimation of the profitability of foreign subsidiaries as a result of transfer pricing, the evidence on profitability seems quite consistent with the view that TNCs do have higher profit rates than local firms. Does it then also follow that high TNC profit rates can be principally explained by the tendency for TNCs to operate in concentrated industries and hence to enjoy considerable market power?

Again there is a paucity of detailed empirical studies. Studies of the structure–profitability link carried out in Third World economies have tended in the main to be methodologically unsophisticated (Kirkpatrick et al. 1984, chs 3–4). Although a number of the studies show a simple correlation between profitability and concentration, these do not consider the effects of barriers to entry on profitability. When more sophisticated models are employed then generally concentration ceases to be significant at the 5 per cent level (Jenkins 1986a).

The analysis of the internationalization of capital suggests that TNCs are able to earn higher profits than local firms irrespective of the level of concentration in the industries in which they operate. In fact, given the great mobility of TNC capital and its ability to surmount barriers to entry, then it is reasonable to suppose that TNC profitability is largely independent of local market structures and the barriers to entry that face local firms. Studies of Canada and Spain bear this out, indicating that the profitability of foreign subsidiaries is much less fully explained by conditions in the local market than those of national firms (Caves et al. 1980 and Donsimoni and Leoz-Arguelles 1980, quoted in Caves 1982, 109).

It also implies that intra-industry differentials will exist between the profit rates of local and foreign firms. In the case of Mexico it was found that significant differences in profitability did exist within industries and that foreign subsidiaries earned higher profits in competition with less efficient local firms (Fajnzylber and Martinez Tarrago 1975). While differential profit rates within industries can be interpreted as an indication of market power, where market leaders obtain higher returns, it is also consistent with the view that both large market shares and high profits are a result of the competitive advantage of the TNCs.

There is in fact considerable evidence that TNCs have higher levels of productivity than local firms. In a number of countries it has been found that on average the productivity of labour in foreign subsidiaries is about double that of local firms. Nor can this be attributed entirely to the concentration of TNC subsidiaries in industries which are by their very nature capital-intensive and hence have intrinsically higher labour productivity. Disaggregated data show that TNCs also have higher levels of productivity within industries. In some cases it has also been shown that not only labour productivity, but capital productivity is higher for foreign firms (Jenkins 1986a).

This is not to imply that TNCs are inherently more efficient than local firms. As Lall (1980, 47) has concluded on surveying the evidence,

> We are, therefore, led to adopt an agnostic position about the relative productivities of TNC's and local firms, at least as far as 'efficiency' is concerned. It is likely that TNC's achieve greater output or value-added per worker because they are concentrated in industries which are capital-intensive, they use more modern technology or are able to reap economies of scale.

This is quite consistent with the argument advanced in the previous section that TNCs enjoy a competitive advantage over local firms in the same industry because of their access to more advanced technology or their greater size.

THE LATIN AMERICAN AUTOMOBILE INDUSTRY: INTERNATIONAL COMPETITION AND MARKET FRAGMENTATION

The relevance of the internationalization of capital as an approach to the analysis of the impact of TNCs in host countries can be illustrated with the example of the Latin American motor industry, particularly Argentina and Brazil. The 1950s was a period of increased international competitiveness in the automobile industry as European capital began to challenge the dominance of the US TNCs, particularly General Motors and Ford. This involved a sustained attack by European firms, led by Volkswagen, on the position of US capital in areas where it had previously been unchallenged. One such area was Latin America.

At the same time, from about the mid-1950s onwards, Latin American governments, anxious to further their import substituting industrialization in the field of durable consumer goods and intermediate goods, introduced tariff and foreign investment policies designed to attract foreign capital into these industries. As a result the governments of Brazil and Argentina embarked on the creation of a fully integrated motor manufacturing industry in 1955 and 1959 respectively.

Intense oligopolistic rivalry led to seventeen firms entering the Brazilian motor industry and twenty-two in Argentina. Initially there was considerable excess demand, particularly for cars, since the market had been starved of vehicles for a number of years because of the shortage of foreign exchange. Favourable demand conditions guaranteed high rates of profits for the TNCs in the early years of the industry's development. These market conditions only lasted for about four or five years however (from 1956 to 1961 in Brazil and 1959 to 1963 in Argentina). During the 1960s car prices fell sharply in both countries, by around 40 per cent in relation to other goods. Profit rates also followed the downward trend, particularly in Argentina (Sourrouille 1980, ch. VI).

While the main source of high profits in the Latin American motor industry in the early years of its development were the very favourable demand conditions, even after demand and supply were brought in line, the lower costs of TNC subsidiaries enabled them to earn higher profits than the local firms which produced under licence (Jenkins 1977, ch. 5; Mericle 1984, table 1.1). In the light of the large number of firms which entered the industry, and the fragmented industrial structure that resulted, it is unlikely that market concentration, which was much lower than in the advanced capitalist countries, or barriers to entry could play a major role in ensuring high TNC profits in the industry.

The competitive advantages of the TNCs in the industry led eventually to the disappearance of all the local firms who were either acquired by their licensor, taken over by another TNC or went out of business altogether (Jenkins 1977, ch. 7; Guimaraes 1980, ch. 6). Thus by the end of the 1960s the motor industry in both Argentina and Brazil was entirely controlled by TNC subsidiaries. The displacement of local firms in the mid and late 1960s was accompanied by a continuing fall in the relative prices of vehicles in line with the lower level of costs of the foreign subsidiaries. Once these came to dominate the market however prices no longer fell so rapidly being constrained by the changes in relative productivity.

The experience of the motor industry in Argentina and Brazil also highlights another weakness of the emphasis on market power in explaining TNC profitability. By focusing on the sphere of circulation this approach ignores the crucial role of control over labour in order to ensure profitable production. The profitability of the auto TNCs in Brazil in the 1970s compared to the losses declared by their Argentinian subsidiaries cannot be explained in terms of market structure variables, but has to be seen in the context of the success of capital in its control of labour in Brazil and its failures in Argentina (Jenkins 1986b, ch. 5).

NOTE

1   It should be noted that there are numerous difficulties in measuring international concentration levels. For a discussion of these in the context of the aluminium industry see Litvak and Maule (1984).

FURTHER READING

The orthodox literature on trends in international concentration is reviewed in Newfarmer (1985b) while the Marxist debate on inter-imperialist rivalry is summarized in Rowthorn (1975).

Surveys of the relationship between the presence of TNCs and industry concentration in Third World countries are found in Lall (1980, ch. 2), Dunning (1981, ch. 7) and Newfarmer (1985b).

Clifton (1977), Semmler (1982b) and Bryan (1985) are particularly recommended from the recent spate of Marxist writings on competition theory, although none of them is specifically concerned with TNCs. Olle and Schoeller (1982) provide a critique of monopoly theories of foreign investment and imperialism but is rather hard-going.

There is an enormous literature on the international oil industry; particularly recommended are Blair (1976), Turner (1983), Penrose (1971) and the collection edited by Nore and Turner (1980).

Theoretically and empirically interesting case studies of the impact of TNCs on industry in host countries are Weeks (1977) on Peruvian manufacturing and Evans (1977) on the Brazilian pharmaceutical industry. Kirkpatrick *et al.* (1984, chs 3–4) surveys the literature on the relationship between market structure and firm performance in LDCs. See also Jenkins (1986a) for fuller details of the studies on which many of the statements in the last part of this chapter are based.

See Jenkins (1984a, ch. 3) for a brief introduction to the Latin American automobile industry. For more details see Kronish and Mericle (1984) for a series of essays on the same subject, and Jenkins (1986b).

4

Transnational corporations and technology

INTRODUCTION

Technology plays a central role in most current thinking about TNCs. The product cycle theory of trade and investment hinges on the international diffusion of new technologies and new products and was in many ways developed from earlier 'technological gap' theories of international trade. Internalization theory, with its emphasis on the TNCs as a mechanism for overcoming imperfections in external markets, identifies the market for information as a crucial one in which there are very strong incentives to internalize because of the nature of technology as a 'public good'. The theory predicts that TNCs are particularly likely to be found in R & D intensive industries. From a different standpoint, the Global Reach approach sees the control of technology as one of the most crucial monopolistic advantages of TNCs as they expand internationally.

Marxists writing on TNCs have also stressed the importance of technology. For Emmanuel the introduction of advanced technology by TNCs is a major contribution to development in the Third World (Emmanuel 1982). Here he directly contradicts the more conventional emphasis of the left on 'technological dependence' as a major element in reproducing the subordinate position of Third World countries in the world economy and the identification of the latest stage in the relationship between them and the advanced capitalist countries as 'technological-industrial dependence' (Dos Santos 1970). Even those Marxists who do not share this view of technological dependence still recognize both the role of technological development (the Third Technological Revolution in the words of Mandel 1976) in the growth of TNCs and the importance of the centralized control of technology in the internationalization of capital.

Despite broad agreement on the importance of the technology factor in international trade and investment, the assessment of the technological contribution of TNCs made by various writers differs greatly. The key issues of controversy which will be considered in this chapter are the appropriateness of imported technology; the appropriateness of TNC products; the costs of imported technology; and the implications for local technological development.

These areas of debate have also been central to recent policy concerns relating to technology imports. A number of policy initiatives have been pushed in these areas in recent years. These include the setting up of national agencies in many countries to control and monitor the transfer of technology, attempts to formulate an internationally acceptable code of conduct, the reform of the patent system in a number of Third World countries and pressures to alter the Paris Convention on patents, and the attempts to promote the development of local science and technology involving the creation of a national science and technology plan in a number of countries.

TECHNOLOGY IN ECONOMIC THEORY

Before discussing the role of TNCs in the field of technology it is necessary to clarify certain definitions. Technology has been variously defined as 'organized knowledge for production' (Sachs quoted in Contreras 1976), 'knowledge of how to do all those things associated with economic activity' (Stewart 1979) or 'Knowledge of how to control and exploit natural phenomena for production' (Cooper and Hoffman 1981). Whatever the exact definition chosen, two linked elements constantly reappear – knowledge and production. Technology is distinguished upstream from science and downstream from techniques. The latter are those specific processes usable in production of a given commodity. 'Techniques' constitute a range of processes, 'technology' a range of knowledge (Emmanuel 1982, 10). Techniques can be substituted one for the other while technology tends to improve with the growth of knowledge. Technical progress can therefore be defined as the growth of knowledge about production.

The development of technology

There are a number of distinct approaches to technology in economic theory. The conventional neo-classical treatment of technology identifies it with the array of techniques of production, defined in terms of the different combination of capital and labour required to produce a given output, available at any point in time. It is assumed that a wide range of production techniques exists illustrated by the smooth isoquants of economic textbooks, and that all techniques are available to any firm.

Technological progress can be represented by a shift in the isoquant over time indicating that the same output can be produced with less capital or labour or both. This shift was traditionally regarded as manna from heaven, as something exogenous to the economic system (Kennedy and Thirlwall 1973, 117). Much theoretical discussion revolved around the definition of 'neutral' technical change, but in practice there was little reason for believing that technical progress should be biased in either a capital-saving or a labour-saving direction (Blaug 1971).

More recent developments see technical progress as the result of a deliberate diversion of resources to research and development (R & D) activities. This involves a switch of emphasis to the innovative activities of individual firms. Technology is viewed as an intangible asset resulting from past R & D. The ownership of such assets gives rise to additional profits representing a return on past investment in R & D. This view underlies the 'internalization' approach to TNCs.

Once it is recognized that technical progress is endogenous, then it is possible to emphasize the influence of the historical and economic context in which technology develops. This has been described as the neo-Schumpeterian approach to technology (Fransman 1985). These writers generally adopt a much broader definition of technology than that used in the traditional neo-classical approach including not only factor proportions, but also other variables such as the scale of production, the type and nature of product and material inputs (Stewart 1978, ch. 1). Technological change which emanates largely from the advanced capitalist countries is conditioned by the economic environment of those countries. More specifically technological development has been characterized by increasing capital-intensity, increasing scale of production, increased use of skilled labour and increasingly sophisticated or 'luxury-type' products (Clark 1975; Stewart 1978, ch. 3). Moreover the development of technology over time tends to render previously existing techniques obsolete because they become absolutely inefficient or because the machinery and equipment necessary for their application is no longer available. This implies that the effectively available range of techniques is more limited than neo-classical theorists believe.

Marxist writers have also been particularly concerned with the development of technology. Some interpretations of Marx see him as a technological determinist in the sense that technical change is the independent variable generating social change (see Rosenberg 1982, ch. 2 for a critique of this view). Socialism will be built on the basis of the high level of development of the forces of production brought about by capitalism. In its less deterministic formulation technology is 'if not the "carrier" of social progress, at least in a less mechanist conception its *prerequisite*' (Emmanuel 1982, 105, emphasis in the original).

Other Marxists, however, give much greater emphasis to the non-neutrality of technology under capitalism (Leys 1984). The social relations between capital and labour and the need for capital to secure control of labour within the labour process is seen as the driving force of technical change. This perspective was succinctly put by Marx when he wrote: 'It would be possible to write a whole history of the inventions made since 1830 for the sole purpose of providing capital with weapons against working class revolt' (Marx 1867, 563). Recently a revival of interest in the capitalist labour process has provided new insights into the development of technology. It has been argued that the immanent tendency of the capitalist labour process is for increasing division and subordination of labour and mechanization (Braverman 1974). This has led to the introduction of Taylorist labour processes involving the sub-division of tasks and strict control of operations carried out by labour through time and motion studies, and Fordism, under which operations become machine-paced, for example through the use of conveyor belts in the twentieth century. For Braverman this has led to the degradation of work as a result of the deskilling of the majority of the labour force. There is, therefore, a tendency which derives from the nature of the capitalist labour process itself and not from developments in the sphere of circulation (rising wages, market competition) for increasing mechanization and deskilling of labour with the development of capitalism.

As some Marxists have argued, however, there is a danger in taking this picture too far particularly in so far as it neglects workers' resistance to management strategies (Friedman 1977, esp. chs 4 and 6). The forms of workers' resistance to Taylorism and Fordism have in some cases led to new developments in the labour process involving the recomposition of some tasks, the use of semi-autonomous groups and so-called 'job enrichment'. These new forms which involve only an adaptation of the labour process within mass production have been characterized as neo-Fordism (Palloix 1976).

The commercialization of technology

Once technology is recognized as a commodity which is not universally available to all firms as in the traditional neo-classical model, it leads to consideration of the conditions under which technology is diffused and sold. Although this is usually dealt with under the heading 'transfer of technology' in the literature, it has been argued that the term transfer is in an important sense misleading and that it would be more appropriate to refer to 'commercialization of technology' with its overtones of a business transaction (Vaitsos 1975, 183).

There is widespread agreement that in making technology (or information) available to one individual or firm its availability to another is not diminished (something that is not true of a commodity that is consumed like an apple). It is, therefore, a *public good* and once produced the social marginal cost (i.e. the cost to society of making it available to an additional user) is zero. This presents a problem in terms of neo-classical welfare economics because in order to attain Pareto Optimality (a situation in which no one individual can be made better off without making someone else worse off) commodity prices should be equal to their social marginal cost. This implies that from a welfare point of view technology should be available free of charge to all potential users. However, if this were the case, within a capitalist economy, there would be no incentive for firms to invest in the development of new technology because there would be no return from it.

Of course under capitalism technology is not a free good. In fact there is private appropriation of technology which some Marxists (e.g. Mandel) and even non-Marxists (especially Schumpeter) have argued provides a driving force of capitalist accumulation. Firms invest in new technology precisely because of the surplus profits which can be earned as a result of private appropriation and this is a major form taken by capitalist competition in the age of large oligopolistic firms. There is, however, a problem of 'appropriability' as far as technology is concerned. Because technology is a public good, its ownership and use does not exclude its use by others. In order to ensure the returns to investment in technology it is necessary for the owner of that technology to be able to exclude others from using it in some way. This is of course the purpose of various forms of legal protection of intellectual property such as patents, copyright and trade-marks. The patent system, for instance, grants a legal monopoly for a number of years through which a producer may earn a return on the technology which he developed, in return for publication of the information through registration. Appropriability may also be achieved through industrial secrecy for unpatented know-how.

From the welfare maximization point of view the private appropriation of technology is objectionable because by charging for a commodity whose social marginal cost is zero, demand for that commodity is reduced below its optimum level. Proposals to overcome this problem whether through the state taking over the production of all technology, making it available to all potential users free of charge (Arrow 1962), or through the owners of technology practising price discrimination

(Casson 1979), only serve to underline the problem of eliminating imperfections in the international market for technology in the real world.

A second specific characteristic of technology is what Arrow has called the 'information paradox'. In order to make rational choices a purchaser must have information about the commodities which he is proposing to buy. When, however, that commodity is information this presents a difficulty since the buyer needs information about information (Vaitsos 1975). This is problematic because the two are often the same thing so that buyer uncertainty is almost inevitable in the technology market. It is, in fact, a concomitant of the need to exclude other users in order to ensure appropriability.

There are different ways of interpreting the peculiarities of technology. For some writers it is merely a technical economic problem which can be resolved by some form of state intervention. It is thus seen as inherent in specific characteristics of a particular commodity. But, as is often the case, behind this apparently technical problem lie particular social relations. First, and most obviously, the social relations of the capitalist mode of production which imply the private appropriation of surplus value. But it also reflects the way in which the labour process has developed under capitalism. Although specialization and appropriation of knowledge is not unique to the capitalist mode of production (Cooper and Hoffman 1981), the growing division of labour under capitalism and the increasing complexities of technology lead to increased scope for such appropriation, as knowledge is separated from the direct producer.

Some of the more perceptive writers on the problem of 'appropriability' have noted that this has implications for the nature of technical change (Magee 1977). Generally speaking capital intensive techniques are associated with more complex production processes, while labour intensive techniques tend to be relatively simple. It is more difficult to ensure appropriability in the latter case because of the ease with which imitators can steal the ideas. Thus TNCs are reluctant to engage in R & D expenditure on technologies whose appropriability is likely to be low and may even delay the introduction of such techniques where it poses a threat to existing high appropriability techniques.

A comprehensive analysis of technological change under capitalism must therefore relate it to both the competition between labour and capital and the competition between capitals. The dynamic of the capitalist labour process makes mechanization the dominant form of technical change under capitalism. On the other hand it is the competition of capitals and the drive to secure surplus profits which determine which of the potential mechanized techniques are introduced in practice

(Shaikh 1980, 75). Under the specific conditions of modern capitalism, this creates a situation in which firms devote R & D to developing more complex and capital-intensive techniques and seek quasi-monopolistic positions through the introduction of new products.

APPROPRIATE TECHNOLOGY

The debate

A major issue in the debate over TNCs is whether the techniques of production which they use in Third World countries are appropriate or not. In general, pro-TNC writers view these techniques as appropriate or where they are inappropriate attribute this to government induced distortions in host countries. On the other hand, critics of the TNCs emphasize the inherently inappropriate nature of TNC technology.

Despite a common concern with 'appropriateness' there are considerable differences in the definition of what is appropriate. For non-Marxist writers appropriateness is defined in terms of the material aspects of the techniques concerned. This may be defined either narrowly in terms of factor proportions by neo-classicals, or more broadly to include additional variables such as the scale of production and the type of products produced, by the critics. For the neo-fundamentalists such as Emmanuel, the most appropriate technology is generally the most advanced technology. Neo-imperialist writers go further than this, posing the question 'Appropriate for whom?' and concluding that only a socialist technology is appropriate for Third World countries (Amin 1977).

Whether a technique will be appropriate or not in any of the above senses depends on the range of techniques available, in other words the existing technology, the selection of particular techniques by TNCs and the adaptation of techniques. The neo-classical view is that a wide range of techniques of production exists, as illustrated by significant substitution possibilities between capital and labour (Little 1982). Under perfect market conditions firms will choose the optimal combination of capital and labour given the relative cost of the factors of production. Where excessively capital-intensive techniques are chosen this is usually attributed to government intervention. In particular, policies which cheapen the cost of capital (e.g. negative real interest rates, duty free imports of machinery) or increase the cost of labour (e.g. labour legislation, social security payments) are regarded as major factors which limit the incentive to use more labour-intensive techniques (Vernon quoted in Biersteker 1978, 37). A second factor that is also laid at the door of host governments is the lack of competition in certain LDC markets resulting from excessively high levels of tariff protection. This it is argued removes the pressure for adapting technology to local conditions which exists in more competitive industries (Wells 1973). The implication is that more 'appropriate' policies by LDC governments would lead to more 'appropriate' technology being transferred by TNCs.

The Global Reach approach emphasizes that the nature of technological change in the advanced capitalist countries means that the range of available techniques is narrower than neo-classical theory would imply. Indeed some industries are particularly prone to technical rigidities which limit the scope for substituting labour for capital (Forsyth *et al.* 1980). Nevertheless over and above this it is argued that even when there is scope for choice, TNCs' techniques are biased away from those most appropriate for the Third World.

Three interrelated reasons are held to account for the failure of TNCs to adopt more appropriate techniques. The first is succinctly put by Lall:

> One of the main sources of the TNCs special 'advantage' which enables them to grow is precisely the possession of advanced technology . . . which can be applied with little adaptation in different areas. It is not to be expected, therefore, that they will undertake *major expensive alterations* to suit the relatively small markets of LDCs or to take advantage of differences in labour costs which form a small proportion of total cost. (Lall 1980, 48)

In terms of the earlier discussion the return to the investor on existing technology which is available at zero marginal cost is greater than the return which could be obtained by making further investments in the development or adaptation of more labour intensive technology.

Secondly the market power of TNCs enables them to pass on the higher costs of inappropriate techniques to consumers in Third World countries (Newfarmer 1985a, 43–4). Thirdly once the specific product form is determined then there may be very little choice of technique so that TNCs wishing to market their international products may be heavily constrained from choosing more appropriate techniques (Stewart 1979, 85).

What both the neo-classical and Global Reach approaches have in common is a belief in the optimality of the competitive capitalist economy. The sub-optimality of techniques used in Third World countries arises largely out of market imperfections which are either exogenous to the TNCs, resulting from government policies, or endogenous caused by the monopoly power of the TNCs themselves.

An alternative view which emphasizes the sub-optimality of competitive markets in terms of technology choice is provided by Emmanuel (1982, 76–7). He stresses that it is in the nature of capitalism to waste labour and save capital, because a machine will only replace labour when its cost (per unit of time) is less than the wages of the labour which it replaces. However, since the capitalist only pays the worker for the equivalent of a part of the working day (the remaining part being surplus value appropriated by the capitalist), a machine which is as expensive as the worker which it replaces is always produced by less labour than it displaces. In this way capitalism puts a brake on the use of machines. The technique that maximizes profit for the capitalist is not therefore optimal from the point of view of society as a whole. If then TNCs, as is often alleged, choose capital-intensive techniques in Third World countries, this is all to the good.

Neo-imperialist writers see the inadequacy of techniques as first and foremost a political problem. The adoption of capital-intensive techniques is a reflection of a coincidence of interest between the local ruling class in LDCs and the TNCs. From the point of view of local ruling classes there is little to be gained from developing local technological capabilities, or promoting more appropriate products or techniques (Cooper 1973). Their primary interests lie in participating in the monopoly rents generated by foreign technology either as part-owners in joint-ventures or through kickbacks to government officials. Thus whatever the theoretical 'pros and cons' of more appropriate technology, moves in this direction are severely circumscribed by class interests.

Some neo-imperialist writers go further. The technology of TNCs is inappropriate in a more fundamental sense, in that it is *capitalist* technology (Amin 1977, ch. 10). This takes very seriously the view that technology is not neutral. 'Borrowing a technology from the capitalist world is never "innocent" because this technology supports class relations of production' (Amin 1977, 176–7), and further

> this technology is excessively costly, not only because of its capital-intensive nature, but because of the wasteful consumption patterns it brings with it, the excessive exploitation of natural resources that it implies etc. In other words, this technology presupposes imperialism, i.e. the excessive exploitation of labour in the periphery.
>
> (Amin 1977, 173)

Critique

The notion of what is 'appropriate' in Third World countries is clearly not neutral. For neo-classical writers appropriateness is defined in terms of the correspondence between the imported technology and the factor endowments of the host country. The notion of factor endowments is itself profoundly ideological since it reduces 'capital' to an endowment on a par with land or natural resources. It also implies that lack of employment opportunities in the Third World is a technological problem which can be resolved by more appropriate technology and has nothing to do with capitalist relations of production. Although the Global Reach approach takes a rather broader view of technology, at a deeper level there is a parallel notion of what is appropriate to local conditions in the Third World.

On the other hand Marxist discussions of appropriate technology have tended to be excessively mechanistic in their analysis of the relationship between technology and social change. While it may be true that socialist relations of production require a certain level of development of the forces of production, it does not necessarily follow that the most advanced technology is the most appropriate in that it will hasten the development of socialism as Emmanuel seems to imply. Nor does capitalist technology inevitably generate capitalist relations of production independently of the local class struggle as Amin suggests (see Muller 1984, on this point).

This is not to suggest that the nature of technology imported by TNCs into Third World countries is not a matter of considerable importance. However, to criticize TNCs either for failing to fulfil neo-classical criteria of optimality or for transferring capitalist technology to capitalist Third World countries is not a very useful way to address the problem. In fact to pose the analysis of technology imports in terms of appropriate technology is singularly inappropriate.

There is also a very narrow focus to this discussion. As was pointed out above, the development of the labour process in the advanced capitalist countries has involved increasing mechanization and the growth of Taylorism, Fordism and most recently in certain areas neo-Fordism. However, there is very little consideration of the nature of the labour processes introduced by TNCs in Third World countries. It is such questions of the transformation of the labour process as a result of the internationalization of capital and the implications for class struggle in the Third World that need to be addressed.

The internationalization of capital

As was pointed out above, a major element in both the neo-classical and the Global Reach explanations of why TNCs use relatively capital-intensive production technologies in the Third World countries is a lack of competition. In the neo-classical case this is attributed to government policies, particularly tariff protection which creates a permissive environment, while in the Global Reach view it results from the inherently monopolistic nature of TNCs. The internationalization of capital on the other hand stresses the competitive nature of TNC expansion and by extension technology transfer. Firms do not 'choose' techniques but are *forced* by the competition of capitals to introduce the techniques with the lowest cost of production (Shaikh 1979).

If then firms use relatively capital-intensive techniques and do not adapt them in a more labour-intensive direction in response to lower wages in Third World countries, why are these the lowest cost techniques? Part of the answer is of course that TNCs do adapt to some extent, particularly in making greater use of labour in peripheral activities such as packaging and transport (Lall 1980, 48), and that they do tend to be more labour-intensive than their parent companies (ILO 1984, 9; Lipsey *et al.* 1982). Furthermore failure to adapt the central production processes is not a result of monopolistic considerations. First the development of technology may well result in more mechanized techniques being capital-saving (in terms of investment cost per unit of output) as well as labour-saving. A recent ILO Report suggests that the choice of capital-intensive techniques is in fact competitive in terms of costs (ILO 1984). Secondly the advantages in terms of labour costs may be less than differences in wages suggest because of lower levels of productivity. There is indeed some evidence indicating that this is the case in a number of Third World industries although productivity differences are less than the wage differential (Moxon 1979; Pack 1981). If machinery and equipment is available to the TNC at roughly the same price anywhere (contrary to the neo-classical view that the price of the factor capital should be high in Third World countries), then there may be no saving in cost through the use of less mechanized techniques.

Thirdly the tendency for more mechanized techniques to be associated with deskilling may make them relatively attractive in countries in which skilled labour is in short supply (Helleiner 1975, 168). Indeed there is evidence of TNCs in Nigeria wishing to use more automated processes in order to economize on skilled labour (ILO 1984, 23).

This is not to suggest that TNCs will use the very latest technology in their Third World subsidiaries. Clearly there will be a time-lag between the introduction of new technology at home and in an LDC and lower wages may lead to the use of older vintages of equipment. One study of a sample of US firms estimates an average time-lag of ten years between the introduction of a new technology in the United States and its first introduction in the Third World (Mansfield and Romeo 1980).

It has also been suggested that an important aspect of internationalization of capital is the opportunity which it gives for using second-hand machinery in subsidiaries in the Third World. Rapid technological change and rising wages in the advanced capitalist countries may lead to the obsolescence of equipment well before the end of its physical life. However, this equipment can continue to generate profits for the TNC through its use in subsidiaries in the Third World, where different conditions prevail (Salama 1978). Empirical studies confirm that the use of second-hand machinery by TNCs in the Third World is by no means uncommon (Strassman 1968; Langdon 1981, 103; ILO 1984, 23).

Far more important than differences in wages in making highly mechanized techniques higher-cost in Third World countries is the large scale of production for which much modern equipment is designed. If this equipment were introduced in unmodified form in the restricted markets of the Third World, then there would be substantial excess capacity and far higher depreciation per unit of output and higher unit costs than in the advanced capitalist countries. Not surprisingly TNCs in Third World countries have responded to this problem by scaling down plants. In fact a number of studies have concluded that such adaptation to the small size of the local market is much more common than adaptations to make greater use of labour (White 1978, 43; Morley and Smith 1977).

This factor together with the increased importance of quality help to explain why, when TNCs locate production in Third World countries for export to world markets, they tend to use the most modern techniques and avoid the use of second-hand machinery (Baer 1976, 127). This is clearly seen in the recent developments in the car industry in Mexico and Brazil where new factories, particularly engine plants, have been set up to manufacture for export which produce on as large a scale as those in the US or Western Europe and use the latest technology (Jenkins 1986b).

So far, however, the discussion is missing a crucial aspect. The import of technology in Third World countries involves not simply technical characteristics, but also the introduction of a labour process. When considered from the point of view of the labour process it can be seen that TNC operations in the Third World, far from being 'inappropriate' and unadapted are in fact extremely well adjusted to local conditions (from the point of view of capital of course).

The emphasis of labour process analysis on the need for capital to control labour in order to extract surplus value is crucial to an understanding of this point. The labour process develops in response to this need, but it does not develop in a vacuum. It is conditioned for instance by conditions in the labour market, the extent and forms of trade union organization and state intervention in capital–labour relations (Schmitz 1985, ch. 11). Thus the form of labour process introduced by TNCs in a particular Third World country needs to be adjusted to these external factors which condition capital–labour relations within the labour process. An excellent example of this is provided by the use of a Fordist labour process involving high wages, a high level of labour discipline and labour rotation (frequent firings and hirings) in the Brazilian car industry (Humphrey 1982, ch. 4). This 'was made possible by State control over unions and rank-and-file militants, and functioned within the official industrial-relations system which reinforced it' (Humphrey 1982, 105). The significance of local conditions in determining the type of labour process and managerial strategy is illustrated by contrasting the situation in Brazil with that found in the Mexican motor industry (Jenkins 1986b).

It is also worth noting that TNCs are quite willing to vary the labour process used in their countries of origin when these are introduced in the Third World. Thus firms which have responded to workers resistance at home by introducing semi-autonomous groups and other neo-Fordist practices, are able to continue employing Fordist techniques in Latin America (Hirata 1981). This sometimes involves the use of women workers in areas which are usually the preserve of male workers in the advanced capitalist countries as in the case of engine assembly at the GM plant in northern Mexico (Jenkins 1986b).

Another area in which the labour processes introduced by TNCs in Third World countries are particularly well adapted to local conditions (in terms of exploiting labour) are in those labour-intensive products and production processes which have been transferred to export processing zones in the Third World and which are characterized by typically Taylorist forms of labour process (Lipietz 1982).

Neo-classical writers of course would also argue that the labour-intensive nature of production in export zones make it particularly appropriate but this is not the point that is being made here. One element in the relocation of these plants to Third World countries was the adverse effects of labour shortages and unrest in the US and the growing unwillingness of US workers to take on the precise, monotonous assembly work involved (Lim 1980, 112). Therefore, issues of labour control are significant in these industries. This is clear both from the preference of capital for employment of women in export processing zones because of their supposed docility and patience, and from the opposition to trade union organization in such factories. The precise forms of labour process and management strategy in these factories are carefully attuned to take advantage of local conditions, reinforcing those cultural and social traits which contribute to increased productivity (Lim 1980, 125–8).

APPROPRIATE PRODUCTS?

Parallel to and linked with the debate over appropriate technology is that on appropriate products. In its simplest form the argument of both Global Reach and neo-imperialist writers is that TNCs produce luxury products which are only accessible to local élites while neglecting the 'basic needs' of the mass of the population (Griffin 1978, ch. 7). Consequently they are regarded as having a vested interest in the preservation of income inequalities which are the only means of guaranteeing a market for their products (Frank 1969, 168–9).

The response to this criticism from pro-TNC writers, both neoclassical and Marxist, is that the problem lies in the structure of income distribution in the Third World countries and that all that the TNCs are doing is to respond to the demand for these goods which would otherwise have to be imported (Balasubramanyam 1980, 50; Emmanuel 1982, 99). There is an element of truth in this argument, although it should be noted that local production may well give TNCs greater influence over consumption patterns because of the vested interests created locally.

However, it also accepts the basic premise that TNCs do produce largely for a small élite in the Third World, and in doing so underestimates the pervasiveness of the impact of TNCs. In fact the internationalization of capital tends to standardize the consumption patterns of a large proportion of the world's population (cf. Vernon 1977, 4). It is not the production of cars or colour televisions for a small élite that constitutes the major impact of TNCs on Third World consumption, but the introduction of Coca Cola, American style cigarettes and powdered baby-milk which reach low-income consumers. This is borne out by the few studies which have attempted to estimate the impact of a more equitable distribution of income on the demand for goods produced by TNCs which conclude that TNC growth would not be substantially reduced by redistribution (Morley and Smith 1973 on Brazil; Lustig 1979 on Mexico).

A more sophisticated argument has been developed by some Global Reach writers to support the view that the products of the TNCs are inappropriate for Third World countries. This is almost exactly parallel to the argument that TNC production technology is inappropriate. It is argued that new products introduced in the advanced capitalist countries tend to increasingly emphasize high-income (or 'luxury') characteristics as opposed to low-income (or 'essential') characteristics (Helleiner 1975; James and Stewart 1981). This is analogous to the tendency for production technology to become increasingly capital-intensive over time.

The introduction of new products in Third World countries may cause a deterioration in the welfare of low-income consumers if it involves the replacement of an existing product whose characteristics are more oriented toward 'essentials' than 'luxuries' or if demand is diverted from an existing 'low-income' product leading to an increase in the price of the latter because of the loss of scale economies. Against this it might be argued that generally new products serve to widen choice or represent an improvement in terms of both 'luxury' and 'essential' characteristics. Indeed what little empirical evidence exists suggests that consumer choice is indeed generally widened by the introduction of new products in Third World countries (James and Stewart 1981).

A problem with this approach parallels the limitation of the Global Reach interpretation of technological change. It is that changes are seen as mainly a response to market conditions, in the case of production technology to rising wages and in the case of new products to increased incomes (cf. Stewart 1978, 7–9). However, as was emphasized above, the drive to mechanization is independent of factor prices. Similarly the drive to introduce new products is independent of rising incomes. It is the competitive search for super-normal profits through the establishment of quasi-monopolistic positions that leads firms to introduce new products, not changing incomes and tastes. Thus it is by no means necessarily the case that new products will generally involve more luxury characteristics.

A further argument is used to reinforce the Global Reach case that TNCs produce inappropriate products in Third World countries. So far individual tastes have been taken as given but it is strongly argued by both Global Reach and neo-imperialist writers that TNCs play a major role through advertising and product differentiation in creating consumer preferences. Indeed for many writers their control of market-place ideology is a fundamental source of TNC power. As Barnet and Müller (1974, 172) write: 'The role which the Ministry of Propaganda plays in shaping values, tastes and attitudes in what the US Government likes to call "closed societies" global corporations are playing in many parts of the "free world".' Neo-classical writers on the other hand continue to stress consumer sovereignty and the information content of advertising by TNCs (Balasubramanyam 1980, 52).

There is little doubt that the internationalization of productive capital in the form of the TNCs has been closely followed by the growth of transnational advertising agencies and increasing advertising expenditure in Third World countries. Overseas billings by US advertising agencies increased from less than a third in the mid-1950s to almost a half by the mid-1970s (UNCTC 1979a). In the Third World more than two-thirds of all advertising agency revenue is controlled by foreign agencies (Chudnovsky 1979a, table 4). As a result the proportion of GNP devoted to advertising in many Third World countries is comparable to that found in the advanced capitalist countries despite the substantial gap in per capita income (UNCTC 1979a, table I.4).

An institutionalist approach to the TNCs sees heavy advertising by firms playing a dual role, creating demand for the firm's (differentiated) product and erecting barriers to entry by new competitors. Taking the host economy as a whole then the promotional activities of TNCs tend to distort consumption in favour of heavily advertised TNC products and to increase the market power of TNCs and the scope for making monopoly profits.

There is some evidence from Third World countries to support the view that advertising is a significant barrier to entry, particularly in consumer good industries, and that high levels of advertising are associated with above average profits (Newfarmer 1985a, 37–9). On the other hand the evidence that TNCs distort consumption patterns is often largely anecdotal and it is not clear how far advertising by TNCs affects overall patterns of consumption and how far much competitive advertising is self-cancelling. While advertising may bring about shifts between different brands or different product forms, the evidence that advertising can shift consumption between products may be viewed more sceptically.

This is not to deny that the consumption norms of the advanced capitalist countries have been increasingly diffused to the Third World in recent years. There is ample evidence of this. The proportion of registered trademarks in the Third World which are owned by foreigners rose from just over a quarter in 1964 to almost a half ten years later (Chudnovsky 1979a, table 1). It also appears that the lag between the time when a product is first sold in the advanced capitalist countries and its introduction in the Third World is on average getting shorter. This cannot, however, be attributed exclusively or perhaps even primarily to the advertising practices of the TNCs.

The problem with this approach is that it fails to break with the individualistic assumption of neo-classical theory, merely modifying it by introducing TNC advertising which distorts and moulds individual preferences. It fails to recognize that consumption like production is fundamentally a social activity. Wants are socially constructed and TNC advertising is only one of many factors involved. The internationalization of capital, of which the growth of TNC activities is only one aspect, is integrating the LDCs more closely into the capitalist world economy. This is promoting Western style consumption patterns in a number of ways, e.g. through the 'demonstration effect' of films, television programmes and tourists, as well as through the direct sales efforts of the TNCs. Indeed without the back-up of these other forces it is unlikely that TNC advertising would be nearly so effective.

It is illusory to suppose that measures to control certain TNC practices such as advertising can significantly alter the situation described in this section. Integration into the capitalist world economy leaves a country exposed to so many other forces which tend to structure consumption in favour of the patterns which prevail in the advanced capitalist countries. Even the socialist block countries have not been entirely immune from such forces as the demand for jeans in the Soviet Union illustrates.

THE COST OF TECHNOLOGY

In addition to questioning the appropriateness of TNC technology and products in the Third World, critics have also pointed to the excessive cost of imported technology to the importing countries. Empirical studies of the costs of technology usually distinguish between direct costs (payments made for technology) and indirect costs in the form of certain restrictions which are imposed on the buyer (Stewart 1978, ch. 5). The OECD has estimated that the total direct cost of technology to Third World countries in the early 1980s came to around $3 billion.

There are, however, a number of problems in identifying the direct cost of technology to Third World countries with explicit technology related payments. First where technology transactions are between a TNC and a subsidiary the division between dividends on the one hand and technology payments on the other may be determined by considerations such as tax rates or foreign exchange regulations rather than reflecting returns on different kinds of assets. Secondly imported machinery may include an element corresponding to a charge for technology. If this represented only 10 per cent of the value of machinery imports to LDCs the cost of technology would be doubled (Stewart 1978, 124). It is, however, impossible to determine the extent to which machinery incorporates a return on technology. Thirdly transfer pricing of imported parts may be used to repatriate and hence hide part of the cost of technology. Thus the overt payments for technology identified may only be the tip of the iceberg as far as direct costs are concerned (Stewart 1979) or may overstate the true cost of technology because dividends are often disguised as royalties (Casson 1979, 19–20).

In addition to the direct costs of technology transfer, certain indirect costs have been found to exist which limit the benefits to the recipient of the technology obtained. Indeed much of the discussion of international codes of conduct and the creation of national systems of control of technology transfer has been concerned with the restrictive business practices of TNCs which are imposed through licensing agreements. By now there is ample evidence of the extensive use of a number of restrictions in technology contracts. They include the tying of purchases of imported inputs and capital equipment, restrictions on exports, control over production patterns, 'grant back' of any improvement made by the licensee to the technology supplier and restrictions on sub-licensing to third parties.

A requirement that the technology importer obtains its inputs and its machinery from the technology supplier or a firm named by the supplier is extremely common. In the Latin American countries for instance such a clause was found in the majority of contracts studied. Elsewhere such a stipulation is found less frequently but still crops up (see Table 4.1). Moreover it is by no means always necessary to include such a clause since for many products there is a technological tie-in which makes it inevitable that inputs will come from the technology supplier. Restrictions of one kind or another on exports by a licensee are even more common than tying of inputs. These restrictions may involve a total prohibition on exports, permission to export only to specific countries, a ban on exports to certain countries or a clause requiring prior approval of the technology supplier before any exports can be made.

The indirect costs which such restrictions can impose on the technology importer are clear. Tying of inputs secures a captive market for the technology supplier enabling him to overprice imported parts and machinery. Restrictions on exports enables the technology supplier to segment international markets maintaining those from which the buyer is excluded for his own direct sales or in order to license another local producer there. Thus the growth potential of the licensee may be constrained. From the point of view of the importing country both measures have an adverse effect on the balance of payments.

Documenting the costs of technology imports does not of course indicate whether or not such costs are excessive. Some writers claim 'that competition assures that prices charged by multinationals for their . . . technology by and large do not contain significant elements of monopoly' (Grubel 1977, 296). On the other hand Helleiner (1975, 162) has pointed out that 'Oligopolistically organized multinational firms are the principal owners and sellers of industrial technology, on markets in which many of the purchasers are extremely badly informed and thus

Table 4.1 Restrictive clauses in contractual agreements for the transfer of technology (%)

	Tied inputs	Export restrictions
Argentina	n/a	74
Bolivia	83	83
Brazil	24	21
Chile	14	93
Colombia	77	79
Ecuador	67	75
Mexico	n/a	97
Peru	62	99
India	5	43
Pakistan	44	44
Philippines	26	32
Turkey	30	39
Ethiopia	86	71
Kenya	n/a	60

Sources: UNCTAD (1972), tables IV.2 and IV.4; Fung and Cassiolato (1976), table 4.30; INTI (1974); Radhu (1973), table VI; Erdilek (1982), 76, 194; Langdon (1981), table 5.7.

Note: Data for different countries are based on different sized samples for different time periods and are not therefore strictly comparable.

possessed of a minimum of bargaining strength'. Once more the debate turns on whether the markets in which TNCs operate are competitive or not.

The Global Reach approach considers that both for the theoretical reasons put forward above and for institutional reasons, technology markets are highly imperfect. Although TNCs are not a prime source of original inventions, their financial and marketing capabilities make them most able to develop and commercialize new techniques and products (Vernon 1977, 40). R & D in the advanced capitalist countries tends to be concentrated in a relatively small number of large firms (Freeman 1974, table 23), most of which tend to be TNCs. In the United States for instance it has been estimated that TNCs account for over 80 per cent of R & D expenditure in high technology industries (Lall and Streeten 1977, 14).

The peculiar nature of technology as a commodity and the specific institutional features of international technology markets means that the price of technology cannot be determined in the conventional way through the intersection of supply and demand curves. When technology is sold by a TNC to an independent local firm its price is established through bargaining between the parties to the transaction. The final price must fall within a range determined by the minimum price which the supplier is prepared to accept and the maximum price which the buyer is prepared to pay. Within this range, the price is determined by relative bargaining strength.

The Global Reach view is that there exists a wide range within which bargaining takes place. The minimum price is determined by the cost of imparting information and the monetary loss which the seller incurs, for example through the loss of export markets or the dilution of monopoly power. This is generally thought to be fairly low. The maximum price on the other hand depends on the value of technology to the buyer which will be determined by the value placed on the technology (i.e. the expected effect on future profits) and cost of alternatives including both known alternative sources of the technology and of developing the technology oneself (Stewart 1978, 125–9). In Third World countries with limited technological capacity, this is likely to be high. Furthermore, technological dependence and lack of information in Third World countries also weakens their bargaining power so that the final price is likely to be near the top of the range. As a result the monopoly rents to be earned from technology sales are very unequally divided between TNC suppliers and host countries.

Neo-classical approaches suggest that the extent of monopoly rents are considerably exaggerated by TNC critics. Their empirical evidence is illusory since such profits constitute a return on past investment in R & D which do not appear in the accounts of foreign firms, leading to understatement of the capital base (Balasubramanyam 1980, 32–3). Moreover there are substantial real costs involved in transferring already developed technology to the purchaser. Theoretically the scope for monopoly rents is much lower than the critics suggest, either because the maximum price is lower or the minimum price is higher than the above analysis suggests. Thus, for example, the product cycle theory implies that as products mature and the technology becomes more standardized (and hence LDCs acquire a comparative advantage in them), increasing competition in the technology market reduces the cost of alternative sources and hence the upper limit of the range. At the same time increasing sophistication on the part of technology buyers tends to add to their bargaining power and thus to drive the price towards the lower end of the range (Vernon 1977, 151).

The appropriability and internalization theories of TNCs not surprisingly emphasize that the risk of diffusion of technology when foreign firms are licensed may be considerable. This leads TNCs to prefer to transfer technology to subsidiaries rather than licensees and to charge a substantial premium when technology is licensed in order to cover this risk. This implies a substantial increase in the minimum price which the seller is prepared to accept and a narrowing of the range within which bargaining takes place (Cooper and Hoffman 1981, 21). It is also argued that, over time, the public good character of technology erodes the advantages of the TNCs as skills are acquired by local firms and individuals thus strengthening the bargaining position of the host country (Agmon and Hirsch 1979).

Some Marxists adopt a not dissimilar position. Thus Emmanuel stresses the low cost of technology which, he argues, more than offsets any excessive profits which may be earned by the seller of technology. Costs he believes are low because of the substantial subsidy which the state in the advanced capitalist countries in effect gives to research and development. This makes technology 'the most under-valued commodity on the international market' (Emmanuel 1976, 765). He also echoes internalization theory in arguing that because of the problem of appropriability, the social benefits of technology are greater than the private returns (Emmanuel 1982, 68–9). This leads him to the conclusion that there are substantial advantages in relying on imported technology rather than trying to develop it locally.

These points can be illustrated diagrammatically as follows (see Figure 4.1). Case 1 represents the situation described by Vaitsos and others. Case 2 represents the neo-classical situation. In Case 1 the minimum price is low but the maximum price is very high giving rise to a wide bargaining range. Unequal bargaining power means that the price is established near the top of the range so that of the total benefit of technology transfer the greater part (B) accrues to the TNC in the form of monopoly rents and only a small share (C) to the technology importer. On the other hand in Case 2 the maximum price is lower because of competition between different suppliers in the technology market, while the minimum price is higher because of the problem of appropriability and the firm's fear that technology will be diffused to rivals. The bargaining range is thus much narrower – (B + C) – and the price settles near the bottom of the range, so that monopoly rents are fairly small (B) and the gain to the importing country (C) relatively large, particularly when this is regarded as a saving compared to the alternative represented by the maximum price, rather than emphasizing the loss of potential benefits represented by monopoly rents.

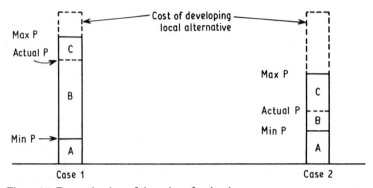

Figure 4.1 Determination of the price of technology.

The analysis so far has dealt only with direct costs but similar arguments exist in the case of the indirect costs of technology. Internalization theorists have developed a defence of restrictive business practices by TNCs arguing that they play a positive role in facilitating the flow of technology to the Third World and that if they were controlled such flows would be curtailed (Casson 1979; Teece 1981). What these arguments boil down to is that licensing agreements secure some of the advantages of internalization. Since internalization is seen as an efficient response to market imperfections, restrictive clauses in licensing agreements are seen in a similar light.

The Global Reach view is that such restrictions are an abuse of the market power of the TNC. Far from facilitating the flow of technology to Third World countries, restrictive clauses act to limit the diffusion of technology in order to maintain the monopoly profits of the TNCs (Vaitsos 1974a, 42). The indirect costs of technology are on this view excessive in relation to what would be required in order to secure foreign technology.

A related issue is the extent to which the existence of patent protection is a necessary condition for technology transfer, or whether as some critics suggest it serves mainly to strengthen the monopoly position of the TNCs. The conventional rationale for the patent system is as an incentive to invention and innovation (overcoming the appropriability problem) and as an incentive to disclosure and hence diffusion which might otherwise be inhibited by secrecy. In the context of the Third World it is further argued that TNCs will be reluctant to invest or to license local firms in the absence of adequate patent protection. TNC critics of the operation of the international patent system (the Paris Convention) in the Third World point to the fact that the bulk of patents are owned by foreigners; that many are not exploited through local production but used to protect the market for the patent holder's exports; and that TNCs are able to use their ownership of patents to restrict competition (O'Brien 1974; Vaitsos 1973).

Internationalization of capital and the cost of technology

As was seen above, one of the crucial differences between critics of the TNCs and those who emphasize the benefits to be derived from the transfer of technology is over the extent to which international technology markets are competitive or monopolistic. However, as was argued in the last chapter, the concepts of monopoly and competition used in most of the literature on TNCs is inadequate in a number of respects. In practice innovation under capitalism is the product of the dialectic between competition and monopoly as firms introduce new products and new processes in order to secure surplus profits.

In general the introduction of new technology into a Third World country will lead to surplus profits either as a result of a reduction in costs or the introduction of a new product for which demand conditions will be particularly favourable, as argued in chapter 3. Where this is done by a TNC through a local subsidiary then this is exactly the same case as was considered in chapter 3. This is in fact by far the most important form of technology transfer. This is illustrated particularly clearly by the data for the proportion of US recipients of royalties and management fees which are intra-firm – 81 per cent in the case of Latin America and 88 per cent for other Third World countries (Chudnovsky 1981b, table 13; see also Madeuf and Michalet 1978, table 3). Although technology transfer to independent firms is more important for non-US TNCs it is clear that a significant proportion of all technology transfer does not involve arm's length transactions. In this case, the direct cost of technology is largely arbitrary since the prices charged are transfer prices not market prices.

The analytically more interesting case is where technology is sold by a TNC to an independent local firm. Again the introduction of new technology will lead to surplus profits being made. The question then is how this surplus profit is divided between buyer and seller. In the absence of state intervention, there are two constraints which severely limit the ability of the local firm to participate in the surplus profits which arise. First, the degree to which capital is mobile within the host economy limits the ability of one local firm to earn surplus profits. In other words competition between capitals locally for the licence will prevent the licensee from earning profits significantly above the average for the economy as a whole. Secondly, even if local capital is not highly mobile and competition for licences is limited, the firm which owns the technology has the option of exploiting it through direct investment. Since, as was seen in chapter 3, there are few barriers to entry to TNCs in foreign markets, the international mobility of capital also constrains the ability of the licensee to obtain surplus profits.

The conclusions drawn here are similar to those reached by the Global Reach approach by a different route. The emphasis here is on the competitive nature of capitalism rather than on market power in explaining the distribution of the surplus profits from the introduction of new technology. It also brings out much more clearly that the issue which is often discussed as though it were a question of distribution between TNCs and LDCs is in fact a question of distribution between capitals.

This approach also suggests a number of ways in which the host government could reduce the share of TNCs in the surplus profits generated by introducing new technology locally. Measures to limit competition locally for licences could ensure that part of the surplus profit accrues to local capital. Similarly, limits on the free entry of TNCs to particular industries could also increase the bargaining power of local firms in negotiating with technology suppliers. Equally clearly however, the primary beneficiaries of such measures would be local capitalists who were able to obtain foreign licences and not necessarily the country concerned.

The contractual restrictions which are often imposed by TNCs when they sell technology to third parties can be understood in the light of the firms' need to secure and reproduce surplus profits. Tied inputs ensure a captive market for the technology supplier enabling him to appropriate part of his profit through transfer pricing and guaranteeing a market for the output of the parent company or its subsidiaries. Restrictions on exports enable the technology supplier to prevent the buyer from threatening his position in third markets. Provisions which prevent the licensee from sub-licensing third parties can also be seen as a means of limiting the diffusion of technology in order to secure the reproduction of surplus profits. Similarly any improvements made to the technology by the buyer have to be made available to the seller free of charge, again guaranteeing that the licensee will not be able to obtain a technological lead over the supplier.

Patents are an element, but only one element, in the reproduction of surplus profits. They are in fact heavily concentrated in a few sectors such as chemicals, particularly pharmaceuticals, while in most industries other factors such as economies of scale in R & D, the complexity of non-patented know-how or product differentiation are far more significant as sources of TNC power (Lall 1981, ch. 6). The experience of countries such as Mexico, India and Colombia which substantially modified their patent laws in the 1970s, and Turkey which abolished patent protection on pharmaceuticals in the early 1960s, suggests that reform of the patent system alone is not sufficient to affect the power of TNCs. However, these countries have also not experienced the adverse effects on foreign investment and technology flows which advocates of the patent system predicted (UNCTAD 1981; Kirim 1984).

The view that TNCs do obtain substantial surplus profits from technology sales to local firms in Third World countries is supported by the experience of those countries where the state has intervened to control technology transfer. In a number of cases, technology payments have been reduced and restrictive business practices eliminated since the early 1970s without the inflow of technology being adversely affected (UNCTAD 1980; see also chapter 8 below for a more detailed discussion of the Andean Pact countries).

FOREIGN TECHNOLOGY AND LOCAL TECHNOLOGICAL DEVELOPMENT

In addition to the short-run costs and benefits of technology imports discussed in the last section there may be longer-term effects on local technological development in Third World countries. These include both the technological efforts of TNCs themselves in host countries and their effect on technological development by local firms.

TNCs tend to concentrate the bulk of their R & D in their country of origin. In the case of US TNCs only some 10 per cent of all R & D is carried out overseas and although this proportion has been increasing in recent years, overseas R & D is concentrated mainly on development rather than basic research (Caves 1982, 199). It is also concentrated mainly in other advanced capitalist countries with very little being undertaken by subsidiaries in the Third World. This is confirmed by studies of R & D by foreign subsidiaries in Third World countries which invariably show little or no R & D being undertaken (see below, chapter 7).

Different perspectives on the TNC tend to interpret the lack of R & D by TNC subsidiaries in Third World countries in different ways. TNC managers and academic defenders of the TNCs explain this tendency to concentrate R & D in the home country in terms of comparative advantage. It is claimed that there are significant economies of scale in R & D and problems of co-ordinating decentralized units. Therefore it is more economic to have a centralized R & D unit rather than several dispersed ones. It is also argued that R & D requires constant contact with production and markets so that processes and products can be modified and developed. This implies that the centralized activities should be located in the country where major production facilities and markets are found which is usually the home country. Finally it is pointed out that R & D requires skilled manpower which is usually unavailable in Third World countries (Germidis 1977; Vernon 1977, 43–5). Similar arguments are put forward by neo-fundamentalist Marxists such as Emmanuel (1982).

Plausible though these arguments may seem, they provide an inadequate explanation of the extreme reluctance to decentralize R & D activities. If relative cost considerations are dominant it is to be expected that government subsidies for R & D will have an important impact on its level, but this does not appear to have been the case for US subsidiaries in Canada (Rugman 1981, ch. 6). It is also by no means the case that all LDCs are characterized by an absence of skilled manpower. Indeed in view of considerable graduate unemployment and much lower wages in a number of LDCs, there might even be a case for arguing that from the point of view of costs, TNCs could achieve savings by relocating certain research activities to countries such as Argentina, Brazil or India.

An alternative view emerges from the neo-imperialist approach to TNCs. Since technology is central to the continued dependence of the Third World it is held that it would be against the interests of TNCs to locate R & D activities in the LDCs because this could increase the bargaining power of the host country, increase their ability to imitate technology and promote the building-up of a national scientific and technological system (Nadal 1977, 239). This line of argument is not entirely convincing since it fails to explain why the setting up of an R & D facility owned by the TNC in a host country should have any of these effects. It is also questionable because it assumes a high degree of collusion by TNCs in preventing the establishment of R & D overseas.

The Global Reach approach provides a more coherent interpretation of the reluctance of TNCs to decentralize R & D. It is seen not as part of a conspiracy to limit technological development in the Third World, but rather as a consequence of the 'appropriation problem'. Since technology is an important source of the market power of TNCs, parent companies seek to control R & D activity tightly to avoid leakages to their competitors. Since it is more difficult to control geographically dispersed facilities this can be best achieved through centralization of R & D in the home country (Newfarmer 1985a).

This is a view shared by the internationalization of capital approach, although it should be stressed that the 'appropriation problem' is not merely a technical issue of market failure. Behind it lie the broader issues of the increasingly social nature of the productive forces and the conflict with the private ownership of the means of production. Nor should R & D location be seen purely in terms of institutional considerations internal to the TNCs. These modify the influence of external factors such as relative costs of skilled labour and state controls on R & D, but do not render them totally irrelevant as the growth of overseas R & D by TNCs in recent years indicates.

Another qualification that needs to be made is that by exclusively focusing on formal R & D activities the extent of technological activity in Third World countries, both by TNCs and local firms, may have been considerably underestimated. There is now considerable evidence of incremental locally generated technological knowledge in existing plants involving adaptations or improvements. This is often based on imported technology and is therefore complementary to technology transfer. However, the fact that it is based on imported technology also tends to limit the extent of technical changes involved, which are mainly directed to minor adaptations and increasing the capacity of existing plant rather than to major innovations (Katz 1984; Teitel 1984).

The neo-imperialist view of the Third World depending on foreign technology which serves mainly to reinforce the domination of the centre is too static to take account of the technological developments that are taking place in some Third World countries (Soete 1981). On the other hand it is by no means the case that unrestricted inflows of foreign technology will have the most beneficial impact on local technological development. The Global Reach approach emphasizes the need for selective imports of foreign technology along the lines pioneered by Japan (Stewart 1978, 133–5).

The development of a local technical capacity in certain LDCs, to the extent to which it does occur, raises once more the question of who benefits? Much of the discussion of technology transfer, as was mentioned above, is couched in terms of relations between TNCs and LDCs. However, just as technology in the advanced capitalist countries is privately appropriated by the TNCs, so technical improvements in LDCs are appropriated by capital, often by the TNCs themselves (particularly bearing in mind the 'grant back' provision found in many licensing agreements). Even where learning by local firms is not captured by TNCs in this way, the benefits of increased technical capacity (e.g. the ability to negotiate more favourable terms with technology suppliers) accrue to the firm and not necessarily to the society at large.

TECHNOLOGY IN THE INTERNATIONAL
PHARMACEUTICAL INDUSTRY

The international pharmaceutical industry provides a very good example of many of the aspects of technology generation and commercialization discussed above. It is an industry which spends heavily both on research and development and on sales promotion, and it is highly internationalized.

Technological development

Product innovation in order to obtain surplus profits through the establishment of quasi-monopolistic positions, usually protected by patents, is the main form of capitalist competition in the industry. The returns on the introduction of a successful new product can be extremely large. However the competitive struggle also means that the introduction of a successful new product, patent protection notwithstanding, leads to other firms attempting to replicate the new product through the introduction of what are known as 'me-too drugs' (similar products produced through molecular manipulation). Consequently, a significant part of R & D in the industry is spent on trying to develop such drugs.

Since patent protection is only partially effective in providing a firm with a monopolistic position, and is in any case granted for only a limited period of time, a second major feature of competition in the industry is sales promotion. Drugs are given brand names by their manufacturers who seek through heavy promotion, mainly by sales representatives (detailmen) visiting doctors, to maintain or establish a preferential market position. The result is a proliferation of different names for pharmaceutical products.

Process innovation has played a much less important role in the pharmaceutical industry. This in part reflects the relatively small share of production costs in the total value of output in the industry. Given also that quality control is absolutely vital in a product such as pharmaceuticals, assuring quality rather than minimizing costs may often prove to be the major consideration in process innovation.

'Technology transfer'

Although some form of pharmaceutical industry exists in all but the smallest and least developed Third World economies, in most countries the extent of technology transfer is limited to the repackaging of formulated drugs or the processing of bulk drugs into dosage forms. The key processes, namely the manufacture of intermediate chemicals and R & D have been transferred to only a handful of Third World countries (Gereffi 1983, table 6.5). The main feature of technology transfer to the Third World in this industry therefore is the introduction of a stream of new products which result from R & D in the advanced capitalist countries. Discussion of appropriateness in this industry has therefore been focused on appropriate products and marketing rather than production technology.

The consequences of capitalist competition in the pharmaceutical industry include excessive product differentiation, misleading advertising and the sale of drugs in the Third World which are positively harmful and have been banned in the advanced capitalist countries. It is also sometimes argued that the kinds of drugs produced by TNCs in the Third World are inappropriate in that they do not correspond to the major diseases prevalent in Third World countries and that the research priorities of the TNCs are oriented towards the maladies of the developed world. In so far as this is true, it clearly reflects the fact that R & D priorities are determined by considerations of exchange value and not use value, that is by commercial not social criteria, rather than any inherent bias on the part of pharmaceutical TNCs.

The most fundamental way in which the products of the pharmaceutical TNCs are inappropriate in the Third World is in their emphasis on curative rather than preventative medicine. It has been estimated that 80 per cent or more of the significant diseases in the Third World fall into two main groups: nutritional deficiencies and communicable diseases such as intestinal infections, acute chest infections and other specific communicable diseases such as malaria, bilharzia, tuberculosis and leprosy (Segall 1975, 5). Most of these diseases are preventable by technically fairly simple means which are generally much cheaper than curative services, such as improved agricultural and nutritional practices, improved sanitation and water supplies, control of mosquitoes and immunization.

However the adoption of Western medical practices cannot be explained primarily by the promotional practices of the TNCs as some critics suggest (e.g. Gereffi 1985, 277). While these may be a contributory factor, as was argued above, the forces tending to lead to the adoption of the consumption norms of the advanced capitalist countries in the Third World, are much more extensive than the operations of a handful of TNCs. As Illich (1973) has pointed out, exactly the same tendency to adopt the models of the advanced capitalist countries exists in education as in health, despite the lack of any group of TNCs with a vested interest in education comparable to the pharmaceutical TNCs in health.

The cost of technology

There are substantial costs associated with technology imports in the pharmaceutical industry. Royalty rates are amongst the highest in any industry and rates of 5 per cent or more on sales are common. Over-pricing of intermediate imports is also common in the industry and this constitutes a hidden form of payment for technology. In addition there are substantial indirect costs of importing pharmaceutical technology in the form of restrictive clauses on exports and tie-in clauses for imports (see Table 4.2).

Table 4.2 Restrictive clauses in contractual agreements for the transfer of technology in the pharmaceutical industry

	Tied inputs	*Export restrictions*
Bolivia	80	80
Colombia	>95	81
Peru	61	100
India	n/a	29
Philippines	n/a	52

Sources: UNCTAD (1972), table IV.5; Vaitsos (1975), 197; Germidis and Brochet (1975), table 11.

Compared to the costs of developing new drugs however, these costs are modest. It has been estimated that in the early 1970s each successful new drug cost an average of $10 million to develop, and costs have continued to rise since then. This is more than the total amount paid in royalties on all drugs in a large Third World producer such as Argentina in a single year. Even if the hidden costs of imported technology in the industry could be calculated, it seems unlikely that the sums involved could approach the amounts which would be required to develop the technology locally. This is reinforced by the heavy level of state support for R & D in countries such as the United States and Britain where it is twice or three times the level of privately funded research (UNCTAD 1975, 35).

This is not to deny that substantial surplus profits are made by the pharmaceutical TNCs. Indeed the nature of the technology transferred suggests that a substantial part of the cost of technology is in fact surplus profit earned from quasi-monopolistic positions created by the introduction of new products. Thus when all the different channels through which profits can be remitted are taken into account, very high profit rates have been found in the operations of pharmaceutical TNCs in Third World countries (see for example Vaitsos 1974a, ch. IV). Further indirect evidence of the existence of surplus profits comes from the success of a number of countries in reducing the cost of pharmaceutical technology without adversely affecting the availability of drugs (Gereffi 1983). Similarly despite vehement protests from the TNCs that adequate patent protection is essential to secure the development and transfer of new technology, a number of countries have relaxed or abolished patent protection for pharmaceuticals without adverse effects (Chudnovsky 1983; Kirim 1984).

Local research and development

Pharmaceutical TNCs have shown a distinct reluctance to decentralize their R & D activities. In the case of US TNCs, 93 per cent of all R & D expenditure was in the United States in the early 1970s and most of the remaining 7 per cent in Western Europe (US Senate, Committee of Finance, 1973, 582). This tendency to concentrate pharmaceutical research in the country of origin cannot be explained either in terms of large economies of scale in R & D or the lack of an 'appropriate research environment' overseas.

Since the new products that result from R & D are a major source of surplus profits in the pharmaceutical industry, control over the flow of innovation acquires a crucial importance. Because patent protection is never completely effective, it is in the interest of firms to ensure close control over the output of its research laboratories. Thus the need for control is an important factor inhibiting the location of R & D facilities in Brazil or Argentina, thousands of miles away from head office (Evans 1979, 179–84).

Other factors may enter into locational decisions to tip the balance in a different direction. In recent years, increasingly strict control over pharmaceutical products, particularly in the USA, has led to some decentralization of R & D activity. In other words TNCs have to balance the risks of loss of control over new technology against the gains from operating in a less restrictive environment in terms of state regulation. Nevertheless the limited extent of this relocation confirms the importance of centralized control over technology for continued capital accumulation.

FURTHER READING

There are a number of studies of 'technology transfer' to Third World countries from different perspectives. Helleiner (1975) and Stewart (1979) are two comprehensive surveys by critics of the TNCs. For an alternative neo-classical viewpoint see Balasubramanyam (1980) especially chapters 3 and 4. Emmanuel (1982) challenges most of the conventional wisdom in this field from a neo-fundamentalist point of view and is definitely worth reading. For a marked contrast see Amin (1977, ch. 10) for a statement of the neo-imperialist position. Both these last two are rather thin on empirical support for their arguments.

The best general discussion of appropriate technology is Stewart (1978) especially chapter 3 although it is not specifically focused on TNCs. Surveys of some of the empirical evidence can be found in Lall (1980, ch. 2), White (1978), Moxon (1979) and ILO (1984). There are few studies of the labour process in the Third World. An exception is Schmitz (1985) but this again does not look specifically at TNCs.

Two short articles by leading critics of the TNCs focus on their role in meeting basic needs (Griffin 1978, ch. 7; Streeten 1981). The discussion of 'appropriate products' is covered in Helleiner (1975) and extended in James and Stewart (1981) which also provides empirical examples. Barnet and Müller (1974, 142–7 and 172–84) discuss the impact of TNCs on consumption in the Third World. Transnational advertising and the role of trade-marks are dealt with in UNCTC (1979a) and Chudnovsky (1979a).

For a theoretical discussion of the cost of technology, see Vaitsos (1975) and Stewart (1978, ch. 5). The former also gives some empirical evidence on the costs of technology in Latin America, while UNCTAD (1972) gives global estimates and illustrative examples. These include evidence on the extent of restrictive business practices in Third World countries. Teece (1981) argues that these practices do not involve a cost for Third World countries. His thesis is strongly challenged by Yamin and Nixson (1984). Contrasting views on the impact of patents can be found in Vaitsos (1972) and Lall (1981, ch. 6).

There has been a spate of recent literature on local technological development. Fransman (1985) provides a recent review. For an excellent discussion of why TNCs in a particular industry (in this case pharmaceuticals) tend to centralize R & D in their home country see Evans (1979, ch. 4).

There are a large number of studies on the international pharmaceutical industry. Particularly recommended as general overviews of the industry are Gereffi (1983, 1985) and UNCTC (1979b).

5

Capital flows, accumulation and the balance of payments

INTRODUCTION

Although the focus of discussions of the impact of TNCs has in recent years switched to the question of technology, the effects of such firms on capital flows, local accumulation and the balance of payments is still a subject of controversy and debate. Advocates of foreign investment claim that they provide much needed finance and foreign exchange while critics stress the limited inflow of capital, the displacement of local firms and the adverse balance of payments consequences associated with TNC operations.

Unlike some of the other issues discussed in this book there are close parallels between the arguments of Marxists and non-Marxists in this debate, so that it is unnecessary to distinguish between neo-classicals and neo-fundamentalists or between the Global Reach and the neo-imperialist approaches. This chapter also shows how the internationalization of capital perspective differs from the more common approaches found in the literature.

Although the analysis of capital flows, effects on local accumulation and the balance of payments are clearly interrelated, for ease of exposition each will be examined separately. Finally, the issue of transfer pricing will be discussed, both because of its implication for the analysis of the balance of payments impacts of TNCs, and because it provides a clear illustration of the different approaches outlined above.

CAPITAL FLOWS

From the early formal model of MacDougall, neo-classical analyses of foreign investment have regarded a significant inflow of capital as almost tautological. Critics however have been quick to point out that much direct foreign investment takes place with a minimal inflow of capital from abroad. As Table 5.1 indicates, a very small proportion of the funds

Table 5.1 Sources of funds of majority-owned foreign affiliates of US companies in LDCs, 1966–72 (%)

	Latin America	Other developing countries (including international and unallocated)
Internal funds		
Reinvested profits	13	22
Depreciation	42	28
Total	55	50
External funds		
US sources	7	14
Non-US sources	36	31
Total	42	45
Other	3	5

Source: Hood and Young (1979), table 1.17.

employed by US TNCs in less developed countries come from the United States. About a third of all funds comes from foreign borrowing, mainly involving capital raised locally in the host country, while half or more of the total is made up of reinvested profits and depreciation allowances of the subsidiaries. It is this extensive use of local funds and re-invested earnings which explains the apparent paradox whereby inflows of new direct foreign investment account for a very small share of gross fixed capital formation (less than 5 per cent in Latin America and Asia) while TNCs control a large share of production in many Third World countries.

An important motive for using local funds as far as the TNCs are concerned is the availability of cheap credit. This has been particularly true in certain Latin American countries where the existence of high inflation rates combined with controls on interest rate levels has often led to negative rates of interest in real terms (see Lall and Streeten 1977, 118, on Colombia). In addition TNCs with subsidiaries in countries subject to inflation and frequent exchange rate adjustments have tended to borrow locally as a hedge against devaluation. Unfortunately the data in Table 5.1 do not resolve the debate between advocates and critics of foreign investment. As was indicated above, at least a half of the total funds employed by US subsidiaries come from reinvested profits and accumulated depreciation provisions. Pro-TNC writers argue that because the assets that generate these funds are themselves foreign then the funds should also be regarded as deriving from abroad (May 1975, 10). For the critics however these funds represent locally produced profits which are appropriated by the TNC and therefore constitute a local source of funds. At this level however the debate is purely semantic. The significant questions are the implications of foreign investment for local accumulation and the balance of payments.

A first step towards answering these questions is to consider the net capital flows associated with foreign investment. As Table 5.2 indicates there is clear evidence that the outflow of capital in the form of profits, dividends, etc. from the Third World as a whole is considerably greater than the inflow of new foreign direct investment. It is this net outflow of capital which TNC critics have in mind when they point to the 'drain of surplus' from the underdeveloped countries. The TNCs are conceived of as a gigantic 'suction pump' extracting capital from the Third World.

Table 5.2 Current inflow of direct foreign investment and outflow on accumulated past direct investment, of developing countries, 1970–80 (millions of dollars)

	Inflow	Outflow	Net flow
1970	1,834.0	5,693.0	−3,859.0
1971	2,863.5	6,659.8	−3,796.3
1972	2,585.1	5,510.0	−2,924.9
1973	3,978.1	8,107.7	−4,129.6
1974	508.7	10,856.2	−10,347.5
1975	7,764.5	7,526.5	+238.0
1976	2,830.9	8,700.5	−5,869.6
1977	6,313.9	10,821.7	−4,507.8
1978	7,446.9	11,979.1	−4,532.2
1979	8,819.2	10,540.1	−1,720.9
1980	7,654.3	15,833.1	−8,178.8

Source: UNCTC (1983), tables II.2 and II.4.

The neo-classical response to this criticism is to deny that such comparisons of inflows and outflows of capital are in any way meaningful. Essentially they are two completely different things and there is no reason why they should be compared. Outflows of profits and dividends are a return on the accumulated stock of foreign investment made in the past, while inflows of foreign investment are new additions to that stock.

Despite this neo-classical response there is a substantive issue here. If the initial capital inflow associated with foreign investment is short-lived, giving rise to a net outflow within a few years, then the contribution of TNCs in terms of foreign exchange must be sought elsewhere. However, critical accounts of the 'drain of surplus' are unsatisfactory in that they remain at the level of appearances, being content to show the existence of a net outflow of capital without providing an adequate theoretical explanation. This gives rise to an apparent paradox wherein TNCs are seen as exploiting less developed countries by making excessively high profits, while at the same time they repatriate rather than reinvest profits despite such high profit rates. More generally it is possible to ask what is the theoretical status of the 'drain of surplus' – is it a cause of underdevelopment as many TNC critics imply, or a consequence? Given the importance attributed to the outflow of capital in explaining underdevelopment, the critics are surprisingly vague when it comes to accounting for this phenomenon. Some document the outflow with no explanation of its causes (Frank 1972, ch. 8). Others refer in passing to political instability (Barnet and Müller 1974, 153), while still others refer to the life cycle of capital flows for the individual firm (Sunkel 1972, 221–2). None of these seems to provide an adequate theoretical account. The life cycle hypothesis does not explain why, for instance, US investment should lead to a drain of surplus from Latin America but not from Europe. Between 1960 and 1972 repatriated dividend income by US subsidiaries in Latin America exceeded net inflows by over $9000 million, while in Western Europe the inflows of US capital exceeded repatriated dividend income by over $5000 million (Newfarmer and Mueller 1975, tables 1–4). Moreover political stability is not unknown in the Third World and political instability is not exclusively a Third World phenomenon.

One way of approaching this question is through an analysis of the financial strategies of the TNCs. A distinction has been made in the managerial literature on TNCs between two types of subsidiary – those oriented towards reinvestment and those oriented towards remittances (Brooke and Remmers 1973, 177). The former operate in countries where there are substantial opportunities for investment and local earnings are insufficient to cover investment requirements, while the latter exist in cases where, although the initial investment may have been highly profitable, possibilities of new investment are limited. As a result the profits generated are in excess of the funds needed for reinvestment, so that a significant proportion of profits are exported. Chudnovsky (1981a) has applied this distinction to US subsidiaries, suggesting that those in Europe were oriented towards reinvestment, while those in Latin America were oriented towards remittances.

Such a difference is not the result of any bias in favour of Europe on the part of US TNCs, but must be explained in terms of objective conditions in the two regions. Chudnovsky emphasizes the difference in competitive conditions between Europe and Latin America. The integration of the European economy and intense oligopolistic rivalry gave rise to major opportunities for new investment and increasing capital requirements in order to finance the introduction of new product lines. In contrast the small size of Latin American markets, with high tariff barriers and considerable institutional barriers to new entries, meant much less competitive pressures on US subsidiaries which often had excess capacity and therefore little incentive to invest further.

The analysis in chapter 3 of the effects of TNC entry on host countries permits us to go beyond a purely market oriented (circulationist) explanation of the low level of reinvestment in Latin America. The internationalization of capital approach relates high rates of profit remittances to the relations of production which characterize Third World economies, and in particular the coexistence of capitalist and pre-capitalist relations of production (Weeks 1977). Central to this argument is that wage goods are produced under pre-capitalist relations of production. In the advanced capitalist countries, where capitalist relations of production have become generalized, the major way in which the rate of surplus value (s/v) is increased is through increases in the productivity of those industries producing wage goods which enter into the value of labour power (v). This is what Marx described as increasing relative surplus value and it implies that for a given standard of living, fewer hours of socially necessary labour time are required to produce the goods consumed by workers, thus increasing the part of the working day which is available for producing surplus value.

Where pre-capitalist relations are dominant in the production of wage goods (particularly foodstuffs but also possibly some artisan-produced manufactures) the drive for increased productivity characteristic of capitalism is absent and so the tendency for relative surplus value to increase is weak. If productivity in wage-good production is stagnant the rate of surplus value can only be varied by what Marx describes as increasing absolute surplus value through lengthening of the working day or increasing the intensity of labour (speed ups, etc.). However there are physical limits which prevent absolute surplus value being increased beyond a certain level.

As was argued in chapter 3, foreign capital when it enters a particular branch of production in a less developed country is able to earn surplus profits because its costs are lower than those of existing firms or (in the case of a newly established branch) demand is in excess of supply. However, over time, capitalist competition tends to eliminate such surplus profits bringing the rate of profit down to the average for the economy as a whole. If the branch concerned does not enter into the cost of reproduction of labour power, variable capital remains unchanged and the rate of surplus value for the economy as a whole is unaltered. Thus opportunities for temporary high profits exist in the short run but, over a longer time period, profitability in a particular branch is low and there is little incentive to rapid capital accumulation.

As already indicated, a crucial assumption of this analysis is that wage goods are produced under pre-capitalist relations of production and as such are not subject to the same dynamic of increasing labour productivity which characterizes the capitalist mode of production. This is clearly an empirical question whose validity must be determined in individual countries. In a number of Latin American countries it does not appear to hold. In Brazil, for instance, it has been shown that industrial goods, and even consumer durables produced under capitalist relations of production, constitute a substantial part of worker consumption and that these branches have been characterized by rapid increases in labour productivity (Serra 1979). Moreover, with the rapid penetration of capitalism in agriculture and the growth of transnational agribusiness, the picture of foodstuffs being supplied by pre-capitalist producers is becoming less true.

Finally, the argument is couched in terms of a constant rate of surplus value (s/v). This, however, is consistent with an increase in the rate of profit $\left(\frac{s}{[c + v]}\right)$, if the value of constant capital (c) is reduced. Thus, for the argument that the *rate* of profit is unaffected by the inflow of foreign capital in the long run to hold, it must be assumed that the branches concerned not only do not enter into the value of labour power (v) but also that they do not produce inputs or machinery which constitute constant capital. The argument would therefore only seem to apply at a particular stage of economic development, where local industrial production is largely of consumer goods and when the bulk of workers' consumption is of food which is supplied by a predominantly pre-capitalist agricultural sector.

One significant implication of this analysis is that, as capitalist relations of production are extended, the process of industrialization diversifies into intermediate and capital goods, and workers' consumption increasingly incorporates industrial goods, it becomes possible to increase relative surplus value and to cheapen constant capital so that the scope for profitable capital accumulation broadens.

This is precisely the process that has occurred, particularly in the more advanced countries of the Third World in recent years. In Latin America, for instance, intermediate and capital goods production accounts for an increasing proportion of industrial output (UNIDO 1983, table III.1) and capitalist development in agriculture has proceeded rapidly since World War II (Burbach and Flynn 1980, ch. 4).

The result has been a growing tendency for TNCs to reinvest their profits in the region in recent years. Table 5.3 shows a steady increase in reinvestment by US subsidiaries since the mid-sixties in successive four-year periods both for all sectors and for manufacturing taken separately. This is not the result of any subjective change of heart on the part of US capital in its attitude towards Latin America. It reflects the changing objective conditions for profitable accumulation in the region. While this may partly result from changes in market conditions and government policies, and the relatively rapid growth of the region in the 1970s, it is also a reflection of a longer term trend which can only be explained in the light of changes at the level of the relations of production.

Table 5.3 Reinvestment by US subsidiaries in Latin America, 1966–81

	Income, fees and royalties	Reinvested earnings of incorporated affiliates	Reinvestment ratio (2) ÷ (1)
	(1)	(2)	(3)
All sectors			
1966–9	6,662	1,203	0.18
1970–3	7,997	2,462	0.31
1974–7	15,166	5,635	0.37
1978–81	26,440	11,705	0.44 (0.45*)
Manufacturing			
1966–9	1,705	729	0.43
1970–3	2,761	1,345	0.49
1974–7	4,734	2,562	0.54
1978–81	7,772	3,903	0.50 (0.61*)

Source: US Department of Commerce, *Survey of Current Business*, August 1979 and August 1983.

* Data for the period 1978–81 are based on the 1977 Benchmark Survey of US Direct Foreign Investment and is not directly comparable with the earlier data which are based on the 1966 Benchmark Survey. Comparisons of the 1977 data calculated on both bases suggest that the calculated reinvestment ratio is significantly lower when the 1977 basis is used, particularly for manufacturing. The figure in brackets represents an adjustment to make the reinvestment ratio comparable with that of earlier years.

LOCAL ACCUMULATION

The impact of TNCs on local capital accumulation must be looked at both in terms of their direct effects on savings and investment and their indirect effects through backward and forward linkages. A crucial issue is whether foreign investment is a supplement to or substitute for domestic savings and investment. This is an area in which the same information is interpreted in radically different ways according to the theoretical perspective employed. Thus, for instance, the extensive use of local funds by foreign subsidiaries observed in Table 5.1 is interpreted by the critics as evidence of the preferential access which TNCs obtain to local credit at the expense of national firms (Newfarmer and Mueller 1975, 16) while pro-TNC writers interpret the same figures as evidence of the great capacity of TNCs for mobilizing local resources which would not otherwise be available (Vernon 1973, 169; Warren 1980, 173 n. 31).

Clearly, reference only to the level of local borrowing cannot resolve this issue. Other evidence however does suggest that subsidiaries gain preferential access to conventional sources of funds rather than tapping entirely new local sources. As one manager put it, 'We are able to borrow from American banks at slightly lower than normal banking rates because of the association with our parent company. . . . We are treated rather as a son of a rich father' (Robbins and Stobaugh 1974). In the not uncommon situation in which credit is in short supply and has to be rationed then the preferential access, which part of a large international operation is bound to enjoy, will push less credit-worthy local firms down the queue.

An alternative approach to the fundamental question of whether foreign investment supplements or displaces local investment is through econometric analysis. Most of the work of this kind that has been done has focused on capital inflows as a whole rather than direct foreign investment *per se*. A number of studies using both cross-sectional and time series data indicated a negative correlation between capital inflows and domestic savings, supporting Griffin's original contention that foreign capital tended to displace local efforts (Griffin 1970; see also Newfarmer 1985a, appendix A, for a brief review of this debate). However, in view of the complexity of the relationships involved, too much weight cannot be placed on such results.

Another indicator of the possibility that TNCs displace rather than supplement local investment, is the prevalence of acquisitions of domestic firms (see chapter 3). Of course, the existence of acquisitions is not *per se* an indication that foreign capital displaces local capital – this depends on what the local capitalist does with the purchase price of his enterprise. If this were reinvested productively then there would still be a net increase in accumulation equivalent to the new inflow of foreign capital. Unfortunately, evidence on what happens in such situations is rather limited. What little there is suggests that a significant portion of the capital displaced in this way is not reinvested locally in productive activity but may rather go abroad (often illegally) or into property (see Jenkins 1984a, for a discussion of this in Latin America).

The indirect effects of TNCs on accumulation are potentially at least as important as the direct effects. These include backward linkages when new supplier industries are created to provide inputs for the foreign subsidiary and forward linkages when firms are set up which use the TNCs' product as an input. One of the main criticisms directed at TNCs in the Third World is that they operate as enclaves (particularly in extractive industries and in export-oriented assembly activities), creating few linkages and integrating their activities globally within the company rather than nationally within the host country.

Extractive industries

The classic examples of TNC enclaves in the Third World have been the oil and mineral companies which relied largely on inputs imported from the parent company to which the subsidiary repatriated the bulk of its profits. Moreover the raw materials were usually exported in unprocessed form for refining in the advanced capitalist countries. A number of empirical studies have measured the extent of backward linkages from such enclaves using the concept of *retained value* (Mikesell 1970; Murray 1972; Thoburn 1977; Pearson and Cownie 1974). The general definition of retained value (RV) used is as follows:

$$RV = W + L + P + T$$

where W – local wages and salaries
     L – local inputs
     P – profits accruing to local shareholders
     T – local taxes.

A more restrictive definition of RV is sometimes used:

$$RV = (W - W_M) + (L - L_M) + P + (T - T_M)$$

where W_M – expenditure of wages and salaries on imports
     L_M – import content of local inputs
     T_M – government expenditure on imports.

Retained value can be expressed as a percentage of the total value of exports. Where this percentage is very low then the industry is regarded as an enclave. This was the situation which existed in the early years of operation of many oil and mineral TNCs in the Third World. The wage bill was a small proportion of total costs, inputs were supplied by the parent, profits were repatriated and tax rates were low. This situation is illustrated by the case of Chilean copper in the late 1920s when the estimated retained value was as little as 17 per cent (Mamalakis 1970).

Nevertheless, as pro-TNC writers are quick to point out, there has been a tendency for retained value to increase over time, so that the traditional picture of a total enclave is no longer valid. In Chile, for instance, retained value in the copper industry reached almost 70 per cent in the 1950s (Mamalakis 1970). In Zambia retained value in copper rose from 50 per cent in 1956–7 to 70 per cent in 1967 (Thoburn 1977, 238). In these countries and elsewhere, the major cause of the increase in retained value has been the rising government tax share. In recent years, estimates of retained value in mineral and petroleum industries in various countries have been in the region of 60 to 70 per cent (Mikesell 1970).

In addition to creating few backward linkages, apart from those which arise through government revenue, TNCs in the primary sector often export the raw materials which they produce in a relatively unprocessed form (Helleiner 1979, table 4). Thus they carry out processing activities, which tend to be characterized by high value added, in their home countries, and fail to create forward linkages in Third World countries.

Although these facts are widely accepted the interpretation put on them differs. For neo-classical writers the location of production is determined primarily by comparative advantage and limited local linkages are seen as a reflection of the disadvantages of producing inputs and undertaking processing in the less developed countries. Moreover, the 'obsolescing bargain' between TNCs and host governments has led over time to a shift in relative bargaining power towards host governments which has enabled them to obtain better terms from the companies, reflected in higher retained value and more local processing (Vernon 1973, 53–65; Bergsten, Horst and Moran 1978, 130–40).

TNC critics on the other hand emphasize the way in which the specific institutional form of the TNC militates against the creation of domestic linkages. Girvan (1976a, 32–3) cites a number of reasons why mineral producing subsidiaries tend to prefer to import inputs rather than purchase them locally:

(i) The parent company often produces the input itself.
(ii) Purchase of materials and capital equipment for all subsidiaries will

probably be centralized in order to obtain economies in purchasing and standardization of processes used, so that it is natural to use well-established metropolitan suppliers.

(iii) The real cost of transport may be low when inputs can be imported in the company's own empty ships after unloading the exported raw materials.

(iv) Although foreign exchange may be in short supply for the host economy, it is not scarce for the TNC.

In brief, these are all ways in which the global integration of the TNC militate against its integration into the national economy.

Similar arguments have been advanced to explain the reluctance of TNCs to process minerals locally in the less developed countries prior to export. TNCs often found it more economical to expand processing capacity in plants in their home countries which were originally built to utilize local raw materials, rather than investing in entirely new production facilities overseas. This has a further advantage of enabling the companies to draw on raw materials from different foreign sources without being tied to any single source. Furthermore it is held that TNCs are anxious to minimize their exposure in areas which are regarded as being of high risk politically, a point often made by the TNCs themselves, despite the fact that cases of expropriation without compensation have been quite rare in the past (Williams 1975). Although higher tariffs on imports of processed products than on raw materials also act to discourage processing in the Third World, this is not regarded as a full explanation, which must be sought in the internal functioning of the TNC (Girvan 1976a, 34).

In trying to counter the neo-classical view which sees the international division of labour in which less developed countries specialize in the production of raw materials, while the advanced capitalist countries undertake processing and supply capital goods and inputs, as a natural state of affairs dictated by comparative advantage, Girvan and others have leaned too far in the opposite direction, neglecting the material basis of this division of labour and seeing it primarily as a result of the way in which TNCs are organized. The internationalization of capital approach emphasizes that TNCs are an institutional form taken by competing capitals, and that the location of productive activity must be derived from the laws of motion of the capitalist system (which may indeed be modified by the organization of TNCs) and cannot be derived from a study of the firms as institutions. It is only within such a framework that one can understand the tendency for production to be concentrated in the advanced capitalist countries in the past and the trend to increased geographical relocation in recent years.

The centripetal tendencies of capital accumulation are well known. In the absence of counteracting tendencies capital accumulation tends to be geographically self-reinforcing. Murray (1972) has termed these agglomeration tendencies which arise both from economies internal to the firm and external economies. As a result of these agglomeration tendencies capital tends to be attracted to existing poles of capital accumulation. This analysis implies that the lack of a local infrastructure or inadequate supplies of skilled manpower (making it necessary to employ high-cost expatriate labour) are important material bases for the lack of local processing or backward linkages. These agglomeration tendencies may of course be reinforced by differential freight and tariff rates between processed and unprocessed raw materials.

Such an emphasis on the material basis of TNC locational decisions is better able to explain the trend towards increasing local processing in less developed countries in recent years, than an approach which stresses the nature of TNC organization. (See Helleiner 1979, table 4, and Radetzki 1977, table 1, for evidence of this trend.) Important factors leading to such relocation have been increasing environmental costs in the advanced capitalist countries, the availability of low-cost energy supplies, particularly hydroelectric power and natural gas, in the Third World, more developed local infrastructure and the growth of a more skilled local labour force.

The different implications of the two approaches are clear. TNC critics (such as Girvan) who stress the institutional form of the TNC imply that if mines were controlled by national capital then there would be greater use made of local inputs and more processing would take place locally. Those (such as Murray) who stress the underlying material conditions imply that local capital would not behave very differently from the TNCs if it controlled the industry. The same fundamental factors would lead the firms to import machinery and inputs and export raw materials for processing abroad. This, of course, is not to deny that the host government may intervene to modify these decisions but this applies independently of ownership considerations.

(A) The international bauxite/aluminium industry

The international bauxite/aluminium industry provides a good illustration of the interplay of factors which determines the location of production and accumulation in a TNC dominated industry. Five or six companies have dominated the capitalist world's production of aluminium throughout the twentieth century. Since World War II the six leaders have been Alcoa, Alcan, Reynolds, Kaiser, Pechiney and Alusuisse. These companies have been characterized by a high degree of vertical integration. They account for more than half the capitalist world's production at each of the three stages of production (bauxite, alumina and primary aluminium) as well as playing a dominant role at the first fabrication stage which often absorbs over 90 per cent of the company's aluminium ingot production.

Although there has been some decline in the share of the six major companies in world production in the last two decades, this has been much less marked than in other natural resource industries, such as oil or copper where nationalization by Third World states has made substantial inroads into the main TNC's share (Table 5.4). The maintenance of control by a small group of TNCs in this industry has undoubtedly been aided by the high degree of vertical integration in the industry.

Table 5.4 Share of world bauxite, alumina and aluminium capacity controlled by big six TNCs

	Bauxite		*Alumina*		*Aluminium*	
	World	*Capitalist world*	*World*	*Capitalist world*	*World*	*Capitalist world*
1962	n/a	n/a	60.7	78.7	54.8	72.7
1968	51.8	59.8	59.9	76.4	50.3	62.7
1975	53.5	62.8	52.0	63.3	42.4	53.4
1982	46.3	53.8	50.4	61.2	44.5	56.3

Sources: Thym (1981), table 4.1; UNCTC (1983), table V.6.

The expansion of the aluminium industry into the Third World began during World War I with the depletion of bauxite reserves in the advanced capitalist countries. In 1916 Alcan acquired control of British Guiana's bauxite deposits and subsequently those of Dutch Guiana (Surinam). During and after World War II there was further expansion in the Third World by other TNCs with bauxite production beginning in Jamaica, Haiti, Ghana and Guinea. In this way a characteristic division of labour emerged in which the greater part of bauxite production was concentrated in the Third World (approximately 60 per cent in the period 1955–65), while over 95 per cent of primary aluminium production was in the developed countries (UNCTC 1981a, tables 3 and 10). Some alumina production took place in Third World countries by 1960, mainly in Jamaica where Alcan built an alumina plant in 1950, but Third World production was less than 15 per cent of world output at this time. Since bauxite accounts for only about 10 per cent of the total cost of

primary aluminium and alumina for less than 30 per cent the significance of this international division of labour for the distribution of the
gains from the industry is very clear.

Not only were forward linkages into alumina and aluminium production limited in the period up to 1960 but so too was backward
integration with the TNCs relying heavily on imported inputs for their
Third World operations. This is illustrated by the low proportion of the
export value of the bauxite producing countries that was retained locally
in this period. In the case of Jamaica this came to less than 40 per cent in
the late 1950s and early 1960s (Girvan 1971, table 3.1). In Guyana it was
about 35 per cent in the 1960s and in Surinam 38 per cent in the late
sixties (Girvan 1976a, 117). In Guinea in the 1960s the figure was as low
as 25 per cent (Murray 1972) and in Haiti only 28 per cent (Girvan
1976a, 127).

Why did the aluminium TNCs create so few linkages in the countries
from which they extracted bauxite? The lack of forward integration into
alumina production can be explained by the possibility of obtaining both
internal and external economies of scale through expanding existing
plants in the advanced countries. A study of Jamaica concluded that
these considerations rather than differences in fixed costs, strategic
reasons, taxation or fear of nationalism led the US TNCs to locate
alumina production in the United States rather than in Jamaica (Murray
1972, quoting Huggins 1965).

The major cost factor operating against forward integration into
aluminium smelting is the importance of energy costs. Aluminium production utilizes twice the energy required for copper smelting and five
times that used in steel production. Energy on average constitutes
between a fifth and a quarter of the total cost of aluminium. The major
source of energy has been hydroelectric power and countries with ample
sources such as Canada, Norway and Iceland have become major producers of aluminium. The lack of local energy sources has been a major
factor preventing the development of aluminium smelting in an important bauxite producing country such as Jamaica.

Changing cost conditions since the 1960s have led to increasing
production of alumina and aluminium outside the traditional centres in
North America and Western Europe. In the case of alumina there has
been a trend for new investment to be located near bauxite mines,
particularly with the growth of Australia and perhaps in the future Brazil
as a major producer. Increased pressure from host governments has also
led to some bauxite producing countries beginning to produce alumina.

A more striking development has been the growing relocation of aluminium smelting to energy-rich Third World countries. The share of

LDCs in world production of aluminium rose from a mere 2 per cent in 1960 to 5 per cent in 1970 and 10 per cent in 1980 (Thym 1981, table 5.5b). It is expected to double again to at least 22 per cent by 1990, and to 44 per cent by the end of the century (OECD 1983, table 9). Energy costs in a number of Third World countries are anywhere from a half to one-seventh of the average levels found in the United States and Western Europe and there is massive unutilized hydro-power potential in Asia, Africa and Latin America (OECD 1983, ch. III and table 8). This has made aluminium production costs significantly lower in the Middle East, West Africa and Brazil than in the USA (Woods 1979, table 7.2).

Pollution costs have also increased the capital costs of mining and processing facilities by as much as 25 per cent, although government subsidies in the advanced capitalist countries may have limited the importance of this factor as an incentive to relocation to Third World countries with less stringent controls.

The low level of retained value in the bauxite industry in Third World countries is primarily a result of the low level of taxation. In the case of Jamaica, for instance, imported intermediate inputs were only 11 per cent of the value of output, and the bulk of payments to labour were local (Girvan 1971, ch. 3). It was therefore the high share of after-tax profit that was the main determinant of the low local share in the industry. Similarly in Guinea the major factor in the low level of retained value was the low proportion going to the state (Murray 1972), while in Guyana the government only received 3.4 per cent of the total value of exports in taxes between 1963–8 (Girvan 1976a, 164). In the 1970s increased taxation, particularly in the Caribbean, has tended to increase local retained value. In Jamaica, for instance, retained value had reached over 60 per cent by the mid-1970s compared to around 40 per cent a decade earlier (Girvan 1976b, tables 13 and 14).

The case of bauxite illustrates the importance of agglomeration tendencies in determining the location of capital accumulation. It also shows the way in which changing cost conditions can bring about industrial relocation and that the TNCs far from blocking such changes can, through the great internal mobility of capital within their organizational structures, bring this about and perhaps even accelerate it. Finally, it brings out the importance of the state in determining the extent to which value is retained within the local economy.

Import-substituting industries

The issue of backward linkages is also relevant in the case of foreign investment in import-substituting industries. It is possible that such investment is engaged in putting the finishing touches to basically imported consumer goods or involved in final assembly of imported inputs with a very limited impact on the host economy. Although such situations have undoubtedly existed in certain industries, in particular countries at specific times, it cannot be generalized as the typical situation in foreign investment for the local market. Reuber (1973) indicates that 70 per cent of the total cash outlays made by his sample of foreign firms were spent locally and that on average each project gave rise to thirty suppliers (backward linkages).

Although manufacturing subsidiaries do usually purchase local inputs, it is often held that they tend to import a higher proportion of their total inputs (or have a higher ratio of imports to sales) than their locally owned counterparts. There are two main *a priori* reasons for expecting this to be the case, particularly where such imports are provided by the parent company (or another affiliate). First, any price over and above the marginal cost of producing the input represents additional profit to the global system, and where there are economies of scale this price may be less than average production costs. Secondly, continuing to import inputs provides opportunities for transfer pricing which would be lost with local sourcing (see below for a fuller discussion of transfer pricing). Both these factors imply that a TNC will prefer to continue importing unless the price of a local substitute is well below the import price, whereas a local firm (other things such as quality and delivery dates being equal) will prefer a local product on a straight cost comparison.

Clearly, such considerations are important where differences in production costs between developed and less developed countries are small. Where such differences are large, with substantially lower production costs in the developed countries, local firms and TNC subsidiaries have a common interest in opposing domestic vertical integration (cf. Hirschman 1968).

Studies in a number of less developed countries have shown that on average TNCs tend to import more in relation to sales or total purchases than do locally owned firms (see below, chapter 7, for a fuller discussion). As one recent survey concludes, 'the balance of evidence suggests TNCs do have a greater import propensity, though in some cases the differences may be minimal' (Newfarmer 1985a). Other factors such as the particular industry, the level of industrial development in the country concerned or host country policies are however likely to be more important factors in explaining the overall dependence on imports (Lall and Streeten 1977, 145). As in the case of the extractive industries, therefore, foreign ownership modifies the parameters set by material conditions for the accumulation of capital, rather than providing a complete explanation of import dependence.

Manufactured exports

One area of manufacturing investment in which the view that TNCs operate as enclaves is much more accurate, is that of manufactured export production which has come about as a result of the relocation of particular labour-intensive processes to the Third World. Not surprisingly, since these are often set up in free trade zones to assemble or undertake a specific portion of the manufacturing process, they tend to be highly dependent on imports and create few local linkages. One study of a sample of foreign firms found that local cash outlays of firms producing for export were only 34 per cent of the value of sales compared to 70 per cent for firms which produced for the domestic market (Reuber 1973). Dependence on imported inputs is particularly significant in those industries such as electronics where international production is directly controlled by TNCs. In these cases virtually the only local linkages come from wages. In the Mexican border industry, for instance, local materials account for only 0.3 per cent of all bought inputs in the electrical/electronic industry (ECLA 1976, table 20). Moreover, unlike the situation in oil and minerals, government tax revenues are also minimal since production is based on freedom from controls and generous tax exemptions.

As in the case of the extractive industries however the lack of linkages from such manufactured exports must be explained in terms of the dynamic of capital accumulation and the locational tendencies which derive therefrom. In particular it reflects the importance of reducing labour costs in particular production processes in certain industries which act as a counteracting tendency to the normal centripetal forces of capital accumulation. However, such counteracting tendencies are only relevant within certain rather restricted areas of production, so that the greater part of the production process is retained within the advanced capitalist economies. The inevitable result therefore is the high import dependence and limited local linkage creation of such export production. (See chapter 6 for a further discussion of such export-oriented manufacturing investments.)

BALANCE OF PAYMENTS

The preceding analysis of capital flows and local linkages have obvious implications for the analysis of the balance of payments impact of TNCs and it is to this issue that we now turn. TNC critics often point to the negative impact which foreign firms have on the balance of payments of the countries in which they operate. The main focus of the debate is manufacturing investment, since it is unlikely that extractive industries which export virtually their entire output would lead to a net outflow of foreign exchange. A first approximation of the balance of payments impact of foreign investment is the *direct balance of payments effect*. Following Lall and Streeten (1977, ch. 7) this can be defined as

$$B_d = (X + I) - (C_k + C_r + R + D) \qquad (i)$$

where X – value of exports
  I – inflows of equity capital and loans from abroad
  C_k – value of capital goods imported
  C_r – value of raw materials and intermediate goods imported
  R – royalties and technical fees paid abroad
  D – dividends and interest accruing abroad.

Put another way, the direct balance of payments effect is made up of the net capital flow $(I - R - D)$ and the trade balance $(X - C_k - C_r)$ associated with foreign firms. It has already been indicated that the net capital flow tends to be negative, and that TNCs have a significant dependence on imports of capital goods and intermediate inputs. Unless these negative items are offset by substantial exports the direct balance of payments effects of foreign capital will be negative.

In fact, despite the growth of manufactured exports from certain Third World countries in recent years, manufacturing TNCs continue to direct the bulk of their activities towards the domestic market. Data on the principal market of foreign subsidiaries show that only 6 per cent of US, UK and Continental European subsidiaries export more than half their output (Trajtenberg 1976, 13). In aggregate more than 90 per cent of the sales of the US TNCs in less developed countries are made to the local market (Helleiner 1976, table 9). As a result, it is not unusual for manufacturing subsidiaries in the Third World to have substantial negative trade balances. In Mexico in the early 1980s, for example, imports by TNCs were running at more than three times the level of their exports and the resulting trade deficit was greater than the deficit for the economy as a whole (Minian 1983, table 5).

The direct balance of payments effects of foreign investment in manufacturing are likely to be negative. This is borne out by studies of samples of foreign firms. Lall and Streeten (1977, table 7.1) found that 122 out of 133 foreign controlled firms in their sample had such negative effects and that for two-thirds of the firms these negative effects were more than 20 per cent of the value of sales. Similarly Reuber (1973, 162) reports a negative effect on the trade balance of the host country on average for the firms in his sample.

Such analysis of the direct balance of payments effects is criticized by pro-TNC writers for failing to include the major contribution which manufacturing TNCs make to the balance of payments of Third World countries, namely its import substitution effect (May 1975). These writers argue that equation (i) should be rewritten as equation (ii)

$$B_d = (S + X + I) - (C_k + C_r + R + D) \tag{ii}$$

where S – domestic sales valued at international prices.

More generally the criticism is that by focusing on actual flows associated with TNCs, the analysis of direct balance of payments effects does not consider what would have happened if direct foreign investment had not taken place. Two extreme assumptions about the alternative position (counterfactuals) are often made. The first assumes that in the absence of direct foreign investment the goods produced by the TNC would have been imported. The second assumes that DFI is primarily defensive and that local production without foreign capital is feasible.

A number of empirical studies have illustrated the crucial nature of the assumptions made. In Latin America, for instance, the positive impact of foreign investment on the balance of payments, if imports are replaced, becomes negative if it is assumed that local production is feasible (Vernon 1973, table 5.2). Similar results have been obtained for a sample of foreign firms in Nigeria (Biersteker 1978, ch. 5). It is by no means inevitable, however, that even if the alternative is assumed to be importing the same products, that the balance of payments effects will be positive when both sales and inputs are valued at international prices. A number of examples have been found of car assembly plants in Third World countries which make a negative contribution to the host country's balance of payments (Little, Scitovsky and Scott 1976, appendix to ch. 4). However, the balance of payments effects will generally be even less favourable if production by a local firm is considered to be feasible.

It is in the nature of things difficult to know what the alternative situation would have been in the absence of foreign investment. The most detailed attempt to answer this question on a case-by-case basis estimated that 30 per cent of the sample of foreign firms considered could be replaced completely by local firms using local technology or easily available imported technology, and that a further 50 per cent could be partially replaced. Only 20 per cent of the firms were considered impossible to replace by a local alternative because of either the complexity or restricted availability of the relevant technology (Lall and Streeten 1977, 179–80). Obviously, such an evaluation is highly subjective, but it represents an advance on the more extreme assumptions that all foreign subsidiaries are either irreplaceable or totally replaceable. The full balance of payments effects of foreign investment are thus likely to be somewhere in between the two extremes on which the debate is often focused.

This type of analysis of the balance of payments impact of TNCs is subject to a number of further limitations in addition to the difficulty of determining the appropriate counterfactual assumptions. It is assumed that TNC investment is marginal to the economy, it ignores externalities and it assumes that levels of demand are unaffected by the activities of TNCs. It also assumes that other aspects of the behaviour of firms are unaffected by ownership.

However, the most telling criticism of these approaches is that they really focus on the wrong issue. The effects of the internationalization of capital cannot be considered in terms of marginal contributions to the balance of payments of host countries because 'the fact represented in the balance of payments accounts – the fact that a transaction has taken place between one supposed economic unit, one nation, and another – is simply wrong' (Harris 1977, 125). In other words, the significance of the internationalization of capital is that it creates a world economy in which capitals rather than nation states are the basic units. The growth of TNCs has made the traditional analysis in terms of market transactions between national firms and consumers, which has been the primary concern of international economics in the past, less relevant, giving rise to a new 'transnational economics' (Murray 1981a, 1–2; Madeuf and Michalet 1978). On this view the internationalization of capital raises the question of the relevance of the national economy as a unit of analysis, and the feasibility of national economic management. This question will be discussed in more detail in chapter 8. In the present context, however, it leads to the question of the extent to which international trade is nowadays intra-firm trade and the related issue of the transfer pricing practices of TNCs.

TRANSFER PRICING

Strictly speaking, transfer prices are administered prices charged on transactions between different parts of the same corporate organization. They are contrasted with the 'arm's length' prices which are set in external markets for transactions between independent parties. The

term transfer pricing can be used broadly to apply not only to transactions in goods, but also services (royalties and fees) and financial
charges (interest) between related parties when these are determined
administratively. While transfer pricing can be used by multi-plant
national firms when transactions between different factories are valued,
it acquires particular significance in the context of TNCs because their
operations are spread across a number of national jurisdictions and are
carried out in different currencies. The existence of transfer pricing is
of particular concern because of the possibility that TNCs may *manipulate* such prices in order to disguise profits or shift funds internationally.

Numerous writers have focused on transfer price manipulation as a
major problem posed by TNCs for host governments in the Third
World. It is argued that there is considerable scope for such manipulation because of the growth of intra-firm trade, and that transfer prices
deviate substantially from arm's length prices. Such practices are seen as
a result of the global strategies of the TNCs and are held to be systematically biased against less developed countries. This view has been
opposed by those pro-TNC writers who have considered the issue. They
argue that the scope for transfer pricing has generally been exaggerated;
that TNCs' transfer prices do not usually deviate greatly from arm's
length prices; that where transfer prices are manipulated this tends to be
the result of government policy; and that there is no reason to suppose
that transfer prices should operate against the interests of less developed
countries in particular.

The scope for transfer price manipulation

One indicator of the extent of transfer pricing internationally is the
degree to which trade in goods and services takes place within firms. The
best estimates of this are for the United States. A fifth of all US exports
and a third of imports involve trade between US TNCs and their majority
owned foreign affiliates (Helleiner 1981, tables 1 and 3). That this tends
to underestimate the full extent of intra-firm trade is illustrated by the fact
that imports from related parties (defined as firms in which at least 5 per
cent of the voting stock is owned by the other party to the transaction)
accounted for almost a half of all US imports (ibid., table 5). The
proportion of royalty payments which are intra-firm is even higher, over
80 per cent of all US royalty receipts (Chudnovsky 1981b, table 1). The
situation in other countries seems broadly similar. In Britain intra-firm
trade accounts for about 30 per cent of all manufactured exports
(Business Monitor 1983, table 6.2), while in West Germany 43 per cent

of the exports of twenty-seven major TNCs went to foreign affiliates (UNCTAD 1977, table 7).

While the extent of intra-firm trade is now generally recognized, some writers have argued that this substantially overestimates the real scope which TNCs have for *manipulating* transfer prices (Chudson 1981). As much as 60 per cent of intra-firm exports by US TNCs consists of finished goods for resale abroad by sales subsidiaries, and a further portion is made up of standardized products. In both these cases it is argued transfer price manipulation is easy to detect and unlikely to be practised. However, studies of the pricing practices of TNCs show that non-market-based prices are extensively used by TNCs in their intra-corporate trade (Benviganti 1985; Lecraw 1985). Moreover, substantial price differentials are often observed for finished goods in different markets and transfer price manipulation has been discovered in such standardized products as bananas (Ellis 1981) and aluminium (Roumeli-otis 1981).

Levels of transfer pricing

The level of overpricing or underpricing of intra-firm transactions is normally defined in terms of the deviation from the corresponding arm's length price. The formula usually used is $\dfrac{Pa - Pw}{Pw} \times 100$

where P_a – actual price paid
P_w – arm's length or world price.

The pioneering study of transfer pricing in a Third World country was carried out in Colombia in the late 1960s (Vaitsos 1974a). It found that TNCs overpriced the intermediate inputs which they sold to their Colombian subsidiaries by an average of 155 per cent in the pharmaceuticals industry, 54 per cent in the electrical industry, 44 per cent in rubber and 25 per cent in chemicals. For individual products levels of transfer pricing of as much as 3000 per cent were recorded. Subsequently, similar studies in other Latin American countries and elsewhere in the periphery (e.g. India, Iran and Greece) have provided further evidence of substantial deviations from arm's length prices (including both the overpricing of imports and the underpricing of exports from host countries) (UNCTAD 1977, 37–43).

Some commentators have attempted to play down the spectacular evidence of overpricing which the Colombian study uncovered, arguing that they reflected very specific circumstances and have led to a quite unjustified exaggeration of the importance of transfer pricing. These circumstances include a ceiling on permitted profit remittances from Colombia; government price controls on goods which took the declared cost of imported inputs into account in setting prices; and a heavy bias in the sample towards the pharmaceutical industry which was held to be untypical because production costs are a low proportion of total costs (Vernon 1977, 154–5). However, the accumulating evidence that transfer price manipulation is common in countries other than Colombia and industries other than pharmaceuticals tends to undermine such arguments.

Causes of transfer price manipulation

The critical literature on TNCs provides a number of reasons why the transfer prices used by TNCs might deviate from arm's length prices (Vaitsos 1974, ch. VI; Lall 1980, ch. 5). The most important are the following:

(i) To reduce the overall tax burden of the TNC on its global operations. Generally speaking if the tax rate is higher in the host less developed country than elsewhere, there is an incentive to use transfer pricing in order to declare profits in a lower tax country.[1] This is particularly attractive when transactions can be routed through countries which act as tax havens.

(ii) To avoid limits on profit remittances. If a subsidiary wishes to remit profits above the permitted ceiling it may choose to do so through the use of transfer prices.

(iii) To take advantage of a more favourable exchange rate where, under a multiple exchange rate regime, differential rates apply to profit remittances and imports.

(iv) Where the subsidiary is a joint-venture with local capital, declared profits have to be shared proportionately to share ownership. Profits transferred through the use of transfer prices, however, can accrue exclusively to the parent company. If, however, the local firm is an active partner, this may place a constraint on the ability of the TNC to manipulate transfer prices in this way.

(v) Foreign investment is a sensitive issue in many countries. High profit rates can easily lead to accusations of 'imperialist exploitation' being directed at the TNCs concerned. It may therefore be politically expedient to under-report profits in the host country and make up the difference through the use of transfer pricing.

(vi) Many Third World countries provide tariff protection to local production and determine price ceilings on the basis of information on costs provided by the firms themselves. In such a situation it may pay a TNC to inflate its import costs in order to obtain higher prices or more protection.

(vii) 'Relative expenditures requirement' arises even if tax rates are the same in the two countries if the total costs of the firm in the home country (including managerial expenses, R & D and financial and management costs, as well as direct operating costs) exceed the revenue from sales in the domestic market plus exports to non-affiliates abroad. In this case it pays the firm to transfer untaxed income from its affiliates to cover these costs.

(viii) To obtain greater flexibility since transfer prices can be used to generate a continuous flow of funds as imports and/or exports are made, whereas profit remittances must usually await the end of the financial year. Particularly in countries characterized by high rates of inflation and periodic devaluation there is an advantage in shifting profits sooner rather than later. This flexibility can also be used to maximize exchange gains and minimize exchange losses when exchange rates change.

The factors listed above all provide TNCs with an incentive to remit profits through manipulating transfer prices. There is some empirical evidence that firms prefer to use non-market-based prices in cases where there are large differences in tax rates between home and host country, where there are restrictions on profit remittances, where price controls are in force and where a particular country is perceived as risky, and that the gap between intra-firm and inter-firm prices widens as these factors become more important. However, as the share of local ownership increases, market-based prices become more common and the gap between intra- and inter-firm prices narrows, suggesting that TNCs enjoy less scope for manipulating transfer prices in joint-ventures (Lecraw 1985).

This approach has much in common with the managerial literature on TNCs, in that it takes as its starting point the individual firm and considers the implications of different transfer pricing strategies for the firm. While focusing on the benefits of transfer pricing for the individual TNC it tends to ignore the costs, such as the difficulties of motivating local management when declared profits are not an accurate indication of real profitability, and the difficulties of managerial control which may arise from too frequent manipulation of transfer prices.

A theoretical critique of the transfer pricing argument is provided by internalization theory (Rugman 1981, 83–6). This sees transfer prices as an efficient response to the exogenous market imperfections which are at the heart of the internalization explanation of TNCs. Criticism of the transfer pricing practices of TNCs are based on two errors. First, in practice, arm's length prices often do not exist because it is the absence of external markets which gives rise to TNCs. Secondly, since transfer prices are created by TNCs in response to market imperfections, the reasons for transfer pricing must be sought in the causes of market imperfections rather than in the strategies of TNCs. More specifically it is government policy which often creates these market imperfections. Therefore, the first best solution to the problems posed by transfer pricing is to harmonize different national tax rates, eliminate exchange controls, etc., in order to remove the incentive to internalization and transfer pricing, rather than introduce further government controls as the critics of transfer pricing argue. This, however, seems virtually to amount to saying that if an international state system existed, the problem of transfer pricing would lose its significance, as it has within national boundaries.

There is, however, another view of the problem of intra-firm trade and transfer pricing which parallels the criticisms made earlier of focusing primarily on the institutional form of the TNC. Rather than relating intra-firm trade and transfer prices to the growth of TNCs, the internationalization of capital approach locates it within the development of the capitalist mode of production and in particular the socialization of production and the changing role of the market in allocating resources. Murray (1981b, 152–6) has argued that the development of capitalism has been accompanied by a growth of 'awkward' sectors where the market mechanism is unable to function as an adequate allocator of resources. This is related to the increasing importance of fixed costs which has led to a widening of the gap between average and marginal costs, and the tendency for more and more commodities to become the output of joint production. These factors provide the material basis of the growing displacement of the market by administrative decisions over large areas of economic activity of which the growth of intra-firm trade is a manifestation.

Such an approach provides a number of important insights into the issue of transfer pricing. First, it indicates that internalization theorists are quite correct in arguing that arm's length prices often do not exist and are difficult to determine. For instance, a number of US government studies have found it impossible to establish comparable arm's length prices in a majority of cases which they examined (IRS 1984, graph 2). Thus approaches to transfer pricing which depend on restoring the market either by account (i.e. by valuing intra-firm transactions at arm's length prices) or in reality (i.e. through anti-trust action to break up

TNCs) ignore the underlying forces which have given rise to transfer pricing. Similarly, since the intervention of the state in the economy is a consequence of certain tendencies in the development of capitalism and not an exogenous cause of market imperfections, the policy proposals derived from internalization theory are equally invalid. It suggests that, since administered prices prevail over a large and growing area of economic activity, the relevant relationships are not market relationships but power relationships between the state and the TNCs or class relations.

Transfer pricing and the Third World

While the above analysis suggests that transfer pricing is not necessarily manipulated exclusively to the detriment of the interests of Third World countries (as indeed the overpricing of Librium and Valium by Hoffman la Roche in Britain indicates), there are *a priori* reasons to suppose that they will be particularly adversely affected (Plasschaert 1985). The prevalence of foreign exchange controls, limits on profit repatriation, price controls, weak currencies and the political sensitivity of foreign investment in many less developed countries all provide incentives to transfer price manipulation. (It is not clear that differential tax rates are a major factor, since they are not systematically higher in the Third World than elsewhere.) Moreover, the capacity to control transfer pricing, whether by the state or by local capital in joint-ventures with TNCs, is likely to be less than in the advanced capitalist countries.

In these circumstances transfer price manipulation by TNCs operating in the Third World has three major implications. First, the declared profits of their subsidiaries may substantially underestimate the true contribution of these countries to the global profitability of the TNCs. In the Colombian pharmaceutical industry, for instance, the declared profits of foreign firms made up only 3.4 per cent of their effective profitability, the remainder being accounted for by royalties (14 per cent) and overpricing of imported inputs (82.6 per cent) (Vaitsos 1974a, 62). Secondly, such practices represent a substantial cost to the balance of payments of the host country. The additional cost of imports in the Colombian pharmaceutical industry as a result of overpricing was estimated at $20 million a year. Finally, there is a substantial loss of government tax revenue where transfer pricing is used to underreport profits. In the Colombian case the loss of government revenue as a result of transfer price manipulation in the pharmaceutical industry alone would have amounted to $10 million a year.

CONCLUSION

This chapter has shown that much of the debate over the impact of TNCs on capital flows, accumulation and the balance of payments has either been theoretically inadequate or empirically inconclusive. The criticism that TNCs 'drain surplus' from the Third World has not usually been adequately explained in terms of the nature of capital accumulation in these areas. Similarly, the limited, or possibly even negative, effects on local capital accumulation have either been denied or entirely attributed to the machinations of the TNCs. The balance of payments implications of foreign investment (either positive or negative) have tended to be exaggerated by both sides of the debate, while the real issue is the way in which the internationalization of production via the TNCs has transcended the limits of the nation state, limiting the significance of national economic categories. This has indeed been brought out in the discussion of transfer pricing. However, TNC critics have failed to locate the growing importance of intra-firm trade and transfer prices in relation to the process of capitalist development. As a result, some of their proposals for controlling TNCs have been misconceived.

NOTE

1   The manipulation of prices would also have to take account of the effect of transfer pricing on payments of import duties and/or export taxes or credits.

FURTHER READING

For general discussions of most of the issues covered in this chapter, see Barnet and Müller (1974, 152–62), and Lall and Streeten (1977, 47–64), both critical of TNCs; for a more favourable picture, see Vernon (1973, 151–7, 168–79); for a Marxist approach, see Murray (1972).

Capital flows and the balance of payments impacts of TNCs are discussed in Lall and Streeten (1977, chs 7–9). There is also a useful discussion of contrasting perspectives and methodological issues with a Nigerian case study in Biersteker (1978, 3–7, 28–31, 49–51 and 85–102).

The impact of TNCs on local accumulation is the subject of an extensive literature. For a review of this literature, see Newfarmer (1985a, appendix A). The extent of linkages by TNCs is analysed in Girvan (1976a, ch. 1) (for mineral export industries), Murray (1972) and Lall

(1980, ch. 2) (for manufacturing). Factors affecting the processing of raw materials in the Third World are also discussed by Radetzki (1977).

For analysis of the impact of the bauxite/aluminium TNCs in the Third World, see Girvan (1976a) on the Caribbean and Graham (1982) on Africa, particularly Ghana. For a general survey of the international structure of the industry, see UNCTC (1981a).

There is now an extensive literature on transfer pricing by TNCs. These include the seminal work of Vaitsos (1974a), especially 42–118. Other useful references are Lall (1980, ch. 5), Murray (1981a) especially Introduction, chs 1 and 10, and Rugman and Eden (1985), especially chs 12 and 13.

6

Transnational corporations and labour

The growing internationalization of capital in the post-war period has led to an increasing number of workers being employed by TNCs. In 1980 world-wide employment by such firms, including the parent companies, was estimated at around 40 million of which some 4 million were in the Third World (ILO 1981a, 21, 111). Direct employment by TNCs in less developed countries grew rapidly in the 1960s and 1970s averaging over 6 per cent per annum between 1960 and 1977 (calculated from ILO 1981a, table II.1), although growth probably slowed down in the late 1970s and early 1980s.

These figures are put in some kind of perspective when it is realized that they represent only 0.5 per cent of the total labour force of the Third World even when China is excluded (ILO 1981a, 21). Nevertheless the growth of TNC activities raises a number of questions which relate specifically to employment and labour which will be considered in this chapter. In particular we shall look at the consequences of direct foreign investment for jobs, wages and working conditions in host Third World countries; the implications of the transnational organization of capital for the bargaining power of workers and the strategies open to workers to deal with TNCs.

THE IMPLICATIONS OF TNCS FOR THIRD WORLD LABOUR

The debate

For neo-classicals 'by virtue of their very existence in host nations, MNEs [multinational enterprises] clearly make some contribution to increasing the level of employment' (Hood and Young 1979, 202). Indeed by relaxing the full employment assumption for the case of less developed countries, it can be shown, using a conventional capital flow model, that foreign investment reduces the level of unemployment and underemployment and tends to bid up wages (Meier 1972, 418; Reuber 1973, 175).

The assumption that foreign investment is a supplement to domestic saving implies that the whole of the employment by TNCs in the Third World involves the creation of additional jobs. Moreover, it is frequently maintained that this underestimates the total employment impact of the TNCs because it does not include the secondary employment effects generated through forward and backward linkages. When these are taken into account the contribution of TNCs to employment exceeds the number which they directly employ (Reuber 1973, 167–8). Moreover, TNCs also provide training to their workers which constitutes a significant external benefit to the host country which obtains a more skilled labour force (Reuber 1973, 197–207).

Global Reach critics argue that job creation by TNCs is minimal compared to the employment problem of the Third World. They also claim that the figures for direct employment by TNCs, far from underestimating their effect on unemployment as the neo-classicals claim, tend to exaggerate their true impact, for a number of reasons. First, the prevalence of TNC entry through acquisitions of local firms means that often no new employment is created as a result of foreign investment. In the case of Mexico when employment growth as a result of acquisitions were discounted, the contribution of TNCs to increased employment was cut by half (Bernal Sahgun 1976, 156–61).

Secondly, it is claimed that TNCs make a limited contribution to employment because they use capital-intensive production techniques imported from their countries of origin, with minimal adaptation to make greater use of local labour. Thirdly, it is also pointed out that they tend to prefer to import intermediate inputs rather than buy locally so that the secondary employment effects through local linkages are also limited. Finally, in a dynamic context, the fact that a significant proportion of profits are repatriated rather than being used for further local accumulation also limits the long-run employment contribution of TNCs (Vaitsos 1974b, 1976).

Although it is recognized that occasionally TNCs provide some training for their workers in host countries, the significance of this contribution is regarded as minimal for two reasons. First, any skills acquired by workers are specific to the company in which they are employed and therefore there is little or no spillover to the economy as a whole. Secondly, any training that is provided needs to be put against the displacement of skills that occurs as a result of the 'package' nature of technology inputs which limits the development of general skills in areas such as detail engineering, product design, feasibility studies, etc. (Vaitsos 1974b, 341-3).

Whilst it is recognized that TNCs tend to pay higher wages than local firms, it is also pointed out that this is more than offset by the higher productivity of TNC subsidiaries (Vaitsos 1976; Fajnzylber 1976). Consequently the share of wages in the value added by TNCs tends to be lower than for national firms, despite the higher absolute level of wages. This is seen as contributing to income concentration in the host country.

The view that TNCs create limited employment opportunities in Third World countries is shared by neo-imperialist writers. They go further, however, in drawing out the implications of foreign investment for the local class structure. Workers employed by TNCs are seen as sharing in the monopoly rents generated by the TNCs, either as a result of their bargaining power (Quijano 1974) or their power to influence government (Arrighi 1970). Capital-intensive production means that labour costs are a relatively low proportion of total costs, making firms more ready to concede wage increases.

This provides the material basis for the development of a 'labour aristocracy' in Third World countries (Arrighi 1970). These workers, as well as receiving higher wages, enjoy better working conditions, receive more fringe benefits and have greater security of employment. They form a privileged minority who are politically and ideologically divided from the mass of the working class and the peasantry, with an interest in preserving the status quo. The argument that TNC workers constitute a labour aristocracy is generally developed in the context either of extractive industries or of manufacturing for the domestic market. Paradoxically when neo-imperialist writers turn their attention to manufacturing production for the world market, their emphasis is on the low wages, long hours of work and poor working conditions that constitute super-exploitation of labour in the Third World (see below).

Critique

The debate over the employment impact of TNCs is largely inconclusive because, like so many of the other controversies concerning TNCs, it depends on the assumptions made concerning the substitutability or complementarity of foreign investment and domestic accumulation. Empirical estimates of the employment effects of TNCs are therefore often couched in very cautious terms (see, for example, ILO 1981a). The quantitative results obtained depend on the assumptions made about the alternative situation, particularly as far as indirect employment effects are concerned. They therefore do not provide any way of determining the employment impact of TNCs.

The evidence on training, although scanty, tends to support the view that TNCs do not contribute a great deal in terms of human capital formation. The development of the labour process has led to deskilling of large sections of the labour force, so that there is little training required for most production workers. Assembly line workers can be trained in as little as two days (ILO 1981b, 5–6) and training of manual workers generally is 'often brief and mainly on the job' (ILO 1981b, 126). Moreover, for training to be socially beneficial then it must be diffused to other sectors of the economy. However, there is evidence that labour turnover is highest and therefore implicitly diffusion is greatest amongst the least skilled categories (Reuber 1973) while it is relatively low amongst skilled workers (Enderwick 1985, 60).

Although there is considerable agreement between defenders and critics of TNCs that they tend to pay higher wages than local firms (Biersteker 1978, table 3.6), the argument of some critics that this leads to the creation of a labour aristocracy is open to a number of objections. In this general form, it fails to distinguish between different types of foreign investment and different levels of capitalist development found in the Third World. The labour aristocracy thesis was first advanced by Arrighi (1970) in the context of foreign investment in tropical Africa in the 1960s. The region's level of capitalist development was extremely low and TNC investment was particularly heavily concentrated in the extractive sector. As Arrighi himself emphasized TNCs paid high wages in order to obtain a stable labour force, at a time when proletarianization of labour (i.e. the severance of its ties with an extended family in the rural areas) was limited. In other words, the creation of a 'labour aristocracy' was a specific managerial strategy which corresponded to a certain stage of capitalist development in the region. This is supported by the finding that in Latin America the gap between the wage rates paid by TNCs and local firms tends to be inversely related to the level of development (Taira and Standing 1973).

Consequently the labour arisocracy thesis cannot be generalized to the operations of TNCs at all times, in all sectors. Indeed, it is by no means the only strategy which can be pursued in the case of extractive industries in Africa as the use of labour reserves in southern Africa illustrates. A number of writers have questioned its validity even in tropical Africa and Saul, a proponent of this view in the 1960s, has backpedalled considerably in the face of criticism (see the various contributions in Sandbrook and Cohen 1975). At a more advanced stage of capitalist development, when TNC investment is directed more towards the manufacturing sector, as for example in the larger Latin American countries, the view that TNC workers constitute a labour aristocracy is even more debatable.

The internationalization of capital

It is necessary to go beyond static comparisons of TNCs and local firms or TNCs and imports in order to analyse the broader systemic effects of the internationalization of capital on labour in the Third World. As was argued in chapter 5, there is a tendency for the subsidiaries of TNCs in Third World countries to be oriented towards repatriation rather than reinvestment. At the same time, as was seen in chapter 4, the trend to increasing mechanization derives from the nature of the capitalist labour process itself, and there is a tendency for TNCs to introduce ever more capital-intensive technology. Moreover in seeking to compete with TNCs, local firms also tend to mechanize (see chapter 7).

Consequently the balance between labour displacement as a result of technological change and investment, and labour absorption as a result of increased output is likely to lead to very limited employment creation in the industrial sector as a whole. In Latin America this has been particularly marked since the mid-1950s which has seen a new pattern of capital accumulation characterized by expansion of industrial output based on increased labour productivity rather than expanded employment (Salama 1976, 130–8).

This helps explain the apparent paradox that in some countries, sectors dominated by local capital have generated little additional employment. Not only has the internationalization of consumption patterns tended to favour the growth of output of TNC dominated sectors, but there has also been a rapid modernization of those traditional, low productivity industries, frequently associated with the import of foreign technology (Fajnzylber and Martinez Tarrago 1975, 470–511, on Mexico; Luiz Possas 1979, 92–3, on Brazil).

There is considerable evidence that, on average, TNCs tend to pay higher wages than local firms, although how far this is a result of foreign ownership and how far it derives from differences in the size of firm or composition of the labour force is not entirely clear (Enderwick 1985, ch. 4).

Interpretation of relatively high wages in TNC subsidiaries requires some analysis of their labour control strategies in host countries. Contrary to the assumptions of those who see high wages as a consequence of TNCs' need for a stable and skilled labour force, TNCs have in some cases been found to follow a deliberate strategy of 'labour rotation' with regular firing and hiring of labour. This has been particularly noted in Brazil (Arruda *et al.* 1975; Humphrey 1982, ch. 3), but the evidence of significant labour turnover, particularly amongst unskilled production workers, in TNC subsidiaries generally, suggests that this is not uncommon. The combination of relatively high wages and high labour turnover make possible high levels of labour intensity with the ever present threat of significant loss of income as a result of dismissal.

This has important implications for the view that workers in TNC subsidiaries constitute a labour aristocracy. Often, the relatively high wages of TNC employees, far from being an indicator of a relatively privileged position, are associated with insecurity of employment, and intense exploitation. Although difficult to measure, there is considerable anecdotal evidence of the high (and often increasing) intensity of work in such plants. Humphrey, for instance, quotes a Brazilian car worker:

> They use time and motion to force the pace. At the moment it's getting worse. Very often you can't even go to the toilet. It's got worse. For example, there are people who have to work while they have their coffee. (1982, 82)

Clearly from these examples it cannot be assumed that because the average level of wages in TNC subsidiaries is higher than the average in local firms, that TNC workers constitute a privileged minority.

The evidence of considerable labour turnover also undermines the view that TNC workers constitute a distinct section of the working class. Evidence from Latin America indicates considerable mobility between jobs in large-scale foreign subsidiaries and in small and medium sized, mainly locally owned firms (Nun 1979, 53–4). Thus workers in TNCs are not a permanent group of privileged persons, and there is arguably a tendency for a homogenization rather than a differentiation of the working class.

The concept of 'labour aristocracy' involves more than simply a situation of economic privilege enjoyed by a group of workers. It also implies a different ideological orientation and political practice on the part of such a group. The evidence to support such a view is not that strong. Indeed there are numerous examples of Third World situations in which workers in foreign subsidiaries have played a vanguard role in terms of working-class struggle. These include the Venezuelan oil workers in the 1930s (Lucena 1979), the Iranian oil workers in the late 1970s (Turner 1980), the Argentinian car workers in Cordoba in the late 1960s (Evans *et al.* 1985) and the Brazilian metal workers of São Bernardo do Campo since the late 1970s (Humphrey 1979).

In Iran, Argentina and Brazil these apparently privileged workers played a crucial role in the opposition to authoritarian regimes pursuing rapid capitalist development in close association with foreign capital. In the case of Chile it has been found that miners, many of whom were employed by the US-owned copper companies, were an important force in politicizing the Chilean countryside (Petras and Zeitlin 1968). Clearly being well-paid employees of TNCs does not disqualify workers from playing an important role in the wider class struggle.

In so far as there are differences in orientation and ideology within the working class of Third World countries, these owe more to differences in skill levels, ethnic origins or cultural factors than to a division between TNC workers and others.

TNCS AND 'WORLD-WIDE SOURCING'

One of the areas which has given rise to most heated debate is the role of TNCs in relocating industrial production to Third World countries and the associated growth of 'export processing zones' (EPZs) around the world. By 1980 there were 53 such zones located in 30 less developed countries, with a further 25 planned or already under development (Samuelson 1982). The speed of proliferation of these zones is indicated by the fact that they first began to appear in the mid-1960s, by 1971 they were in operation in 9 Third World countries and by 1975 in 25 countries (Frobel, Heinrichs and Kreye 1980, 304, 316). The main geographical areas in which they have been concentrated have been East and South Asia and the Caribbean basin (see Figure 6.1). They have been enthusiastically promoted by international agencies such as the United Nations Industrial Development Organization (UNIDO).

Evaluations of this development in the world economy differ sharply. One view is that TNCs are in an ideal position to perfect an international division of labour based on comparative advantage.

> MNEs [multinational enterprises] can seek out the lowest cost site for even individual components and cross-haul them to various assembly points. Such a high degree of specialization and exchange would have warmed the heart of Adam Smith, and it is possible mainly because it is done within a single enterprise.
>
> (Krause, quoted in Franko 1976, 2)

Such a view sees an important role for export processing zones in developing exports of manufactures from the Third World since they removed the artificial impediments which government policies such as tariffs, minimum wages, etc., placed in the way of a truly global division of labour.

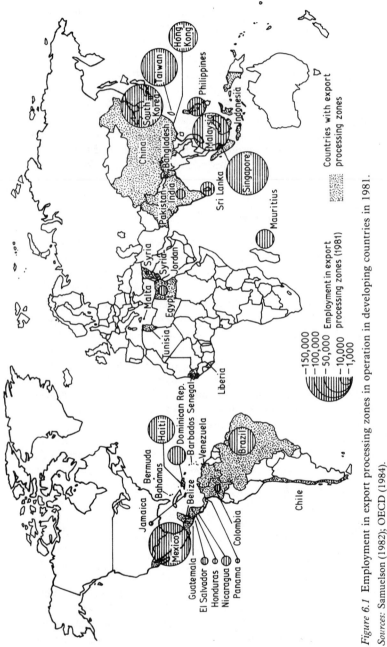

Figure 6.1 Employment in export processing zones in operation in developing countries in 1981.

Sources: Samuelson (1982); OECD (1984).

Notes: The map includes all countries with export processing zones in 1981. Employment is indicated where figures are available. With exception of Singapore (1974), Hong Kong (1975), Republic of Korea, Colombia, El Salvador, Haiti, Jamaica, Nicaragua, Panama, Jordan and Syria (1978), all figures are for 1981. Includes only employment in foreign-owned firms in Hong Kong.

It also saw an important role for TNCs in developing such exports because of their ability to grant access to developed country markets (Vernon 1973, 107).

A much more sceptical view is offered by Global Reach critics who stress a number of limitations of this type of industrialization model (Vaitsos 1976; Helleiner 1976). They point to the limited extent to which TNCs have been involved in production for export in the Third World and the continued predominance of manufacturing for local markets. They argue that in terms of the need for jobs in the Third World as a whole the employment created by such exports is minimal, and moreover is concentrated mainly in unskilled categories so that benefits from training of labour and technology transfer are minimal. Only part of the production process is usually transferred to the Third World so that local linkages are insignificant. Moreover the very limited investment which the TNCs undertake make host countries very vulnerable to withdrawal should conditions change. Finally the footloose character of such plants and the availability of cheap labour in many Third World countries severely weakens the bargaining power of states which base their development strategy on attracting foreign investment to exploit cheap labour, compared to cases where foreign investment is in mineral extraction or production for the domestic market. Consequently there is a danger of an incentives war as host countries compete amongst themselves to offer the most attractive terms to the TNCs.

Neo-imperialist writers broadly concur with the above analysis but go further in detailing the consequences for local labour of the development of export processing activities. The rapid growth of manufactured exports from Third World countries is seen as a consequence of the 'needs of capital'. This is seen either as a consequence of developments in the labour process leading to fragmentation, and deskilling, and developments in transport and communications which have led to the constitution of a world market for labour power and production sites (Frobel et al. 1980) or as a result of a profit squeeze created by rising wages in the advanced capitalist countries (A. G. Frank 1980, 1981).

TNC export production is therefore based on super-exploitation of labour in the Third World. Detailed studies have documented the low wages, long hours of work, short holidays, high level of intensity of labour, poor working conditions and rapid rates of labour turnover which characterize 'world market factories' (Frobel et al. 1980, 350–60; A. G. Frank 1981, ch. 5). Low wages are seen as a consequence of 'super-exploitation' whereby capital is not required to pay the full cost of reproduction of labour power which is borne in part by pre-capitalist sectors. Competition between workers faced with the existence of a vast industrial reserve army enables capital to impose long hours, short holidays and high work rates in poor conditions. These factors contribute to high labour turnover as a result of the mental and physical exhaustion of the workers. Indeed this practice has been compared to that of shifting cultivation whereby farmers move on once the soil is exhausted.

In order to guarantee the conditions for profitable accumulation in the host country, measures to control or suppress workers' rights and trade union activity are often necessary. This may extend to a generalization of repression involving the installation of a military regime. A. G. Frank goes as far as to claim that:

Demonstrably, this repressive political policy has the very clear economic purpose and functions of making these economies more competitive on the world market by lowering wages and by suppressing those elements of the local bourgeoisie who are tied to the internal market.
(A. G. Frank 1981, 134)

The overall effect of these developments has been graphically summed up in the phrase 'Banana republics becoming pyjama republics' (quoted in Adam 1975, 102).

Before embarking on a more detailed discussion of these issues, let us first look at the magnitude of the phenomena under consideration. Despite the rapid growth of manufactured exports from Third World countries, they still account for a relatively small proportion (about a tenth) of world trade in manufactures. The share of all Third World countries in the total consumption of manufactured goods in North America, the EEC and Japan increased from less than 1 per cent in the late 1960s to 2 per cent in the early 1980s and only in clothing did the Third World's share reach more than 10 per cent (UNCTAD, *Handbook of International Trade and Development* 1981 and 1984 supplements).

The exact proportion of such trade which comes from export processing zones is difficult to gauge. There are indications however that it is quite limited. Evidence from four important Third World exporters of manufactures (South Korea, India, Philippines and Taiwan) indicates that in each case less than 10 per cent of all manufactured exports come from export processing zones (OECD 1984, table 15). Similarly, total employment in export processing zones in the Third World has been estimated at around 650,000 in the late 1970s (Samuelson 1982, table 1). In individual Third World countries employment in such zones rarely accounts for more than 5 per cent of total industrial employment (OECD 1984, table 12).

Not all exports from free trade zones are supplied by TNC subsidiaries and there is a significant and growing involvement of local capital in such zones in a number of countries including Bataan in the Philippines, Masan in South Korea and the Mexican–US border (OECD 1984, 41; Luna 1984). Moreover there is evidence of specialization by sectors with, for example, local firms being more conspicuous in clothing and foreign subsidiaries dominating the electrical and electronic industries.

The internationalization of capital approach offers important insights into the questions raised above. It has been argued that:

> The process of internationalization of production of labour-intensive manufactures cannot be reduced to the rational application of corporate planning by MNCs on a worldwide basis; nor to the emergence of a new more efficient international division of labour based on some rational principle, such as specialisation according to comparative advantage. Instead it is a contradictory process – uneven, conflictual, and potentially crisis-ridden – tending to undermine its own basis. It is the result of a complex interaction between international and national capitals as they each seek to overcome the limits posed by labour to the making of profit; an interaction which is necessarily mediated by the exercise of state power.   (Elson and Pearson 1980, 9)

The relocation of production to export processing zones in the Third World is not a general tendency of capital. Historically capital accumulation in the advanced capitalist countries has been based on increasing relative surplus value through rising productivity, and not on reducing wages through industrial relocation. It is only at certain times and in certain branches where there are major obstacles to increasing relative surplus value that relocation has emerged as a specific response. In the 1960s and 1970s such conditions existed in clothing and electronics, where economic and technological considerations made increased mechanization difficult with existing technologies. These considerations related to the rapid devaluation of fixed capital in these industries as a result primarily of changing technology in electronics and fashion changes in clothing. Not surprisingly three-quarters of employment in a sample of export processing zones was in the textile and clothing and electrical/electronics industries in the mid-1970s (Frobel et al. 1980, table III.10).

This explains the limited extent of industrial relocation noted above. It also suggests a further source of instability facing Third World countries which base their development strategy on this type of export promotion. Technological breakthroughs in those branches which have relocated to the Third World may undermine the very basis of that relocation by making it possible to mechanize rapidly and shift production back to the advanced capitalist countries. There is indeed growing evidence that such a process is already under way in the early 1980s (Kaplinsky 1984).

The uneven and contradictory nature of the process of internationalization may also explain why, at the same time as certain firms are relocating production to export processing zones, there has been a resurgence of protectionism in the advanced capitalist countries. The so-called 'New Protectionism' based on quotas, voluntary export restraints (VER) and orderly marketing agreements (OMA) has expanded markedly since the early 1970s. By 1980 over a sixth of OECD imports were subject to non-tariff barriers, compared to only 4 per cent in 1974 (Greenaway 1983). Commodities which have been particularly affected by increased protectionism are iron and steel, ships, clothing and footwear, all of which are important Third World exports, but not ones in which TNCs are heavily involved. Indeed it has been claimed that 'governmental barriers against "disruptive" imports into the North are more likely when they emanate from firms which are truly "foreign" than when they originate in subsidiaries or affiliates of firms within the importing country' (Helleiner 1982, quoted in Kaplinsky 1984). This provides an interesting new twist to the argument that TNCs can provide access to developed country markets for Third World manufactures.

Many of the criticisms made of export processing zones in terms of their impact on development are valid. The point, however, is not to bemoan the existence of such zones and hope that they will go away, but to try and analyse their dynamic and the new contradictions to which they give rise.[1] It is here that the critics find themselves on weak ground. At best they claim that the export processing zones will create a working class in the host countries, thus sowing the seeds of the system's destruction (Landsberg 1979; Frobel et al. 1980, 405-6). And though they recognize the obstacles in the way of such a development, they singularly fail to relate it to their own detailed (sometimes) analysis of the nature of the labour processes transferred and labour force being created.

Although it is frequently mentioned that the bulk (80 per cent or more) of the labour force is made up of young, women workers, it is only recently that attention has been focused on the implications of this fact, beyond a belief that the docility of female labour makes it particularly suitable for employment in these zones. A moment's thought should make it clear that the overwhelming predominance of female labour in these industries raises questions not only about the viability of traditional conceptions of the development of an industrial proletariat and the appropriate forms of workers' struggle, but also wider issues of the implications for gender relations in society as a whole (see Elson and Pearson 1980 for a discussion of these issues).

STRATEGIES FOR LABOUR

The growth of world-wide sourcing poses in a particularly sharp way the problems created for labour by the internationalization of capital. The neo-classical view is quite sanguine, suggesting that TNC expansion does not pose any threat to labour which is able to share in the gains from increased efficiency as a result of TNC operations. In so far as there are any problems, for example from industrial relocation, these are temporary, frictional difficulties affecting specific groups of workers or particular regions. These can best be dealt with by adjustment assistance policies, retraining programmes, etc., by home country governments, a view that is shared by the TNCs themselves. Interestingly, the American Chamber of Commerce, representing large US TNCs, has proposed adjustment assistance measures which were far more generous than those which the government was prepared to offer (Barnet and Müller 1974, 132).

Critics of the TNCs view these problems much more seriously. They recognize that the implications of the growth of TNCs extend beyond their impact on employment levels in different parts of the world. The organization of capital on an increasingly international scale, while labour continues to be primarily nationally based, has major implications for the bargaining power of workers.

Within national boundaries trade unions have to a considerable extent succeeded in strengthening the position of labour by eliminating competition between workers. The internationalization of capital tends to re-create competition between workers by taking advantage of the national divisions of the working class. There are a number of ways in which the TNCs weaken the working class. First, the international mobility of capital renders national unions subject to blackmail by threats to transfer production overseas or to locate future expansion of capacity in other countries. Secondly, TNCs are able to resort to multiple sourcing of particular parts or products in two or more countries so that if a strike in one subsidiary threatens to disrupt production, output of similar products can be stepped up elsewhere. Thirdly, unions are faced with problems of incomplete information where the companies with which they negotiate are subsidiaries of a TNC. Decisions concerning the local subsidiary are made in the light of the TNC's global rationality, but without considerable knowledge of the way in which the local subsidiary fits into the international operations of the parent company, union negotiators find themselves at a considerable disadvantage. The possibility of manipulating transfer prices in order to disguise the true profitability of the subsidiary is an example of the kind of problem that can exist. In the absence of an international organization of labour to match the internationalization of capital these factors tend to weaken the working class both in the TNCs' home countries and overseas.

The identification of these problems leads to consideration of ways in which labour can defend itself against the power which TNCs derive from the international scope of their operations and the greater international mobility of capital. One study categorizes possible strategies for countervailing the power of TNCs in the following way:

Tactic	Reducing TNC power	Increasing labour's power
National effort	National state regulation	Labour control over TNC's decisions
International effort	International state regulation	International labour co-operation

(Adapted from Bergsten *et al.* 1978, table 4.2)

In other words labour can either find ways of putting pressure directly on TNCs or alternatively attempt to put pressure on governments and international organizations to control TNC operations.

National efforts to reduce TNC power

These focus on measures which reduce the international mobility of capital which is seen as a fundamental factor in the power of TNCs, and controls on some of the restrictive business practices employed by TNCs internationally. A frequently cited example is the Burke–Hartke bill, developed and sponsored by the AFL–CIO in the United States in the early 1970s. This proposed less favourable tax treatment for foreign investment, presidential licensing of all direct foreign investment and technology transfer (with the effect on US jobs as one of the criteria on which decisions should be based); more disclosure of information on foreign operations of TNCs; and protectionist measures to limit world-wide sourcing. These proposals failed to become law.

In Britain the planning agreements which were an important element of the Labour Party and TUC's Alternative Economic Strategy, also represent an attempt to control TNCs. Measures to increase disclosure of information by TNCs have also been proposed as part of the AES (CSE London Working Group 1980, 107–8). In Third World countries there have been numerous efforts at controlling foreign corporations, ranging from nationalization to more limited control measures on technology transfer, profit remittances and so on. These measures have often been supported by organized labour in the countries concerned.

International efforts to reduce TNC power

Trade unions have lent support to attempts to develop international codes of conduct governing the operations of TNCs. They have also tried to use existing codes of conduct, in particular the OECD 'Guidelines for Multinational Enterprises' of 1976 and the ILO's 'Tripartite Declaration of Principles concerning Multinational Enterprises and Social Policy' (1977), to further the interests of labour. However, these efforts have not been very successful over the past decade (Robinson 1983; Enderwick 1985, ch. 6). Both these codes are voluntary and enforcement is likely to be particularly difficult in Third World countries.

A rather different approach has been adopted within the EEC. The proposed Vredling Directive made extensive disclosure of information and consultation with employees mandatory for all TNCs with subsidiaries employing at least 100 people in the EEC. However, opposition by the TNCs and particularly by the British government led to a substantial watering down of the original proposals so that TNCs could easily give the appearance of conforming and run little risk of provoking sanctions (Haworth and Ramsay 1986).

National efforts to increase labour's power

A different approach which has been used in some countries is for labour to attempt to directly influence the decisions of TNCs by participating in the decision-making process. This is institutionalized in West Germany through workers' representation on the supervisory boards of companies – referred to as codetermination. This was used to some effect by Volkswagen workers whose opposition to VW's plans to invest in the United States led to a delay in the implementation of the project. However, this has not been widely adopted.

International efforts to increase labour's power

A constant theme in much of the discussion of labour's response to the TNCs is that the internationalization of labour lags behind the internationalization of capital. Just as labour had to organize itself nationally at an earlier stage of capitalist development, now it needs to organize internationally in response to the growth of TNCs. Sometimes, the analogy between the internationalization of business and the growth of international trade unionism is taken to the extreme of seeing them evolving through a three-stage process – ethnocentric, polycentric and geocentric (Levinson 1972, ch. 4). Thus trade union strategy is seen as evolving from an initial stage in which a national union in dispute with a TNC is given international assistance through international federations such as the International Metalworkers' Federation, International Food and Allied Workers, etc., via co-ordinated negotiations in different countries at the same time, to a final stage of integrated or centralized bargaining with parent and subsidiaries around common demands.

Although there has been a substantial growth in international co-operation between trade unions, this has been mainly at the level of information and one-off solidarity actions by national trade unions. By the mid-1970s a quarter of US firms and 40 per cent of non-US firms among a sample of TNCs reported that they had encountered some types of union solidarity (quoted in Bergsten *et al.* 1978, 116). These include financial aid to a striking subsidiary, refusal of other workers to increase production to make up for lost output and public information campaigns and threats of a consumer boycott.

Another aspect of the internatioinal response of labour to the TNCs has developed outside the formal structure of international trade union-ism. The growth of International Combine Committees for individual firms and the promotion of international consultations between workers in the same industry, or the same TNC in different countries, are examples of this type of development. So, too, are more broadly based coalitions formed around specific issues such as divestment in South Africa, or the activities of companies such as Coca Cola in Guatemala (TIE 1985). Nevertheless the internationalization of labour still demon-strably lags behind the internationalization of capital.

Global Reach critics differ in their evaluation of the viability of the different strategies proposed. Most attention has been focused on national efforts to reduce TNC power and international efforts to increase labour's power. Although there is general agreement that in the end labour must organize internationally to develop its countervailing power against the TNC, some writers are sceptical about the viability of this strategy in the immediate future. Obstacles to trade union inter-nationalization such as language differences, distance, organizational differences (e.g. the basis on which unions are organized – plant, craft, industry) and ideological differences (e.g. between Socialist, Com-munist and Christian Unions) are often cited. In the short run there-fore they believe that the TNCs can be most effectively challenged by labour through its influence on government policies (Bergsten *et al.* 1978, 118–19; Cox 1976).

On the other hand some critics, most notably Levinson (1972), point to the ability of TNCs to escape the controls of individual nation states, because of their international flexibility, and therefore stress the need for international trade unionism as a top priority for labour. The focus of such internationalism is seen as collective bargaining over wages and working conditions. This is not only seen as a necessity, but it is also argued that the growth of TNCs has created the objective conditions for such trade union internationalism (Levinson 1972, 141).

Neo-imperialist writers share this emphasis on the need to build international working-class solidarity. The other alternatives mentioned above are all the products of dangerous illusions. Not only is the capacity of the national state to control the TNCs questionable, as some non-Marxist critics have pointed out, but the nature of the capitalist state renders it unlikely to attempt to control TNCs in the interests of the working class (Altvater 1973, 13). Controls where they do exist are more likely to be applied in the interests of other fractions of capital or capital as a whole than in the interests of labour. It is not surprising to find therefore that proposals for such controls have not been effectively implemented in either the United States or Britain.[2]

At the level of international state regulation the prospects are even more limited. Such institutions as do exist are even less subject to working-class pressures than national governments. The success of the TNCs in blocking the Vredling proposal for greater disclosure by TNCs in the EEC is a clear illustration of this. Similarly codetermination does not offer an effective means of controlling TNCs. In practice by making workers' representatives partly responsible for the decisions of management, they serve to co-opt labour rather than to control capital. In the case of Volkswagen's investment in the US discussed above, which incidentally has been described as 'the most concrete success to date of codetermination *vis-à-vis* foreign investment' (Bergsten et al. 1978, 113), the workers were only able to *delay* implementation and force the resignation of the management which proposed it. That workers were not able to fundamentally affect the 'logic of capital' is shown by the fact that the new management went ahead with the investment.

Thus the weaknesses of the proposed alternatives, as well as Marx's own exhortation, point in the direction of uniting the workers of the world. However, neo-imperialist writers also follow Levinson in seeing the growth of the TNCs as creating the objective conditions for internationalizing labour. In other words, 'just as the national organization of capital has led to the national organization of those dependent on it for employment, so the MNC as the modern form of the international capitalist economy will bring about the internationalization of the trade union movement' (Phiehl, quoted in Olle and Schoeller 1977, 72). A similar conclusion is drawn from the analysis of the relocation of industrial production to the Third World (Frobel et al. 1980, 406; Landsberg 1979, 62).

The problems now facing trade union internationalization can be overcome by appropriate organizational forms and overcoming the reluctance of national unions to develop more meaningful international co-operation.

It is on this question that the internationalization of capital approach differs from the neo-imperialist view, arguing that there is nothing inevitable about the internationalization of labour. The observed weakness of labour's response to the internationalization of capital has been explained at two levels. First, it has been argued that there is a fundamental asymmetry between labour and capital (Haworth and Ramsay 1984, 1986). Capital regards labour power as a commodity. One labourer is equivalent to another of equal skill in that they create the same value. From the point of view of capital, labour is substitutable irrespective of national origin. It is therefore the logic of capital to operate on an international scale. The solidarity of workers, however, is based on their experience of community and identity, of which the workplace is a central focus. There is no inherent tendency for this experience to be internationalized, indeed the tendency is for labour's struggles to be locationally specific, while capital expands across the world economy.

Secondly, it is denied that the internationalization of capital tends to equalize wages and working conditions internationally (Olle and Schoeller 1977). This is particularly noticeable where the internationalization of capital has been to Third World countries. Thus far from the TNCs creating similar conditions and therefore common interests amongst their workers, they in fact exploit national differences in wages and working conditions in order to further their own expansion. That they do not provide a direct economic basis for international solidarity is clear from the conflicts which are generated as a result of the relocation of industry to Third World countries, e.g. the conflict within the International Union of Food and Allied Workers' Associations (IUF) between the affected unions when Nestlé shifted production from France to Madagascar (Olle and Schoeller 1977, 73).

A number of more specific criticisms have been made of the forms of international trade union organization which have been adopted on the basis of the conventional view.

a) The emphasis of the International Trade Secretariats on the organization of World Company Councils covering individual TNCs leads to the 'segmentation' of the working class along the lines of single international capitals (Altvater 1973, 13). This is a source of strength to capital which can use the threat of competition from other capitals in order to discipline and control labour.

b) The belief that TNCs create the objective conditions for the inter-
    nationalization of labour has also led to an economistic response on
    the part of labour. In fact, however, international solidarity does not
    develop out of a defence of immediate economic interests, and it is
    necessary to struggle against working class economism (Elson 1982).
    This is particularly difficult within the current framework of inter-
    national trade union organization.

c) The previously discussed asymmetry of capital and labour also
    accounts for the widely noted fact that international trade union
    organizations tend to be bureaucracies (often located in Geneva) far
    removed from shop-floor influence and control (Thomson and
    Larson 1978, ch. 8).

d) It also leads to the restriction of internationalism to the employees of
    TNCs.[3] Thus the strategy has been seen by some as uniting élite
    groups of workers, and therefore having regressive implications for
    workers as a whole. Moreover it offers little prospect for workers in
    export processing zones in the Third World whose governments
    guarantee low wages and freedom from strikes in order to attract
    foreign capital (Cox 1976).

e) International trade unionism focuses on wages and working con-
    ditions but historically many of labour's gains nationally have been
    at the political level in health, education, welfare and social security
    (Hymer 1979, 269).

More detailed consideration of the history of international trade unionism in the post-war period confirms that existing structures do not in any
way represent an internationalization of labour in response to the growth
of the TNCs. The two major international trade union confederations –
the International Confederation of Free Trade Unions and the World
Federation of Trade Unions – were a reflection not of the growth of
TNCs, but of the Cold War and competition for control of trade union
movements in the Third World. The State Department and the CIA saw
the ICFTU as a bulwark against the development of Communist Trade
Unions, while in the Third World the State Department finances the
American Institute for Free Labor Development, the Inter-American
Regional Labour Organization and similar organizations in Africa and
Asia as a means of ideological penetration of the local labour movement
(Thomson and Larson 1978).

  The WCCs, which were first set up at General Motors, Ford and
Chrysler in 1966 and spread rapidly in the motor vehicle, chemical and
electrical industries, were not a reflection of trade union internationalism
either. They were first promoted by the UAW in the United States, with

the aim of establishing wage parity between the American and European plants of the US car companies. The underlying motive of the UAW was essentially protectionist in that it sought to deprive the European plants of their competitive advantage which was leading to acceleration of foreign production. Subsequently with the growth of foreign production by Western European firms they also began to take an interest in the formation of WCCs.

> From this it can be seen that the trade-union WCCs were not some quasi-offshoot of the multinational corporation, but arose under specific historical conditions at precisely that point in time at which the *protectionist interests of the American unions corresponded with those of the West European (and in particular the West German) trade unions.*
>
> (Olle and Schoeller 1977, 66–7, emphasis in original)

It should not be concluded from the above analysis that it is impossible to build up an effective counter force to the TNCs at the international level. Indeed it might well be concluded that it implies an even greater need for conscious struggle to achieve international solidarity since this will not come about automatically as a result of the growth of TNCs. Certainly the obstacles are more fundamental than has been recognized by some of the proponents of international trade unionism, and the existing forms of organization internationally are inappropriate. However this should not lead to abandoning all such efforts. Increased information about the international operations of TNCs is a prerequisite for any labour strategy and there is still a lot to be done here. The critical perspective outlined above also has further implications. The need to go beyond a purely economistic approach, developing a political strategy, to counter the TNCs is one such implication (Elson 1982). The bureaucratic nature of existing international trade union organization makes it necessary to develop new forms of co-operation based on links between shopfloor activists. It has also been argued that it is necessary to broaden the analysis beyond the factory gate or union office to develop new forms of international solidarity (Haworth and Ramsay 1984).

NOTES

1   When critics of export processing zones in Sri Lanka tried to warn potential workers of the disadvantages of such zones, the first question they were asked was how to go about getting a job there.
2   Such a strategy also runs the risk of developing a reactionary and chauvinistic line within the working class (Babson 1973).

3   Note the case of Brooke Bond which was forced to negotiate with the IUF and the International Federation of Plantation, Agricultural and Allied Workers (IFPAW) over working conditions in their tea plantations in Sri Lanka. These negotiations were terminated with the nationalization of the plantations.

FURTHER READING

The ILO has undertaken a number of empirical studies of the impact of TNCs on employment in Third World countries. A summary of the results of some of these studies can be found in Sabolo and Trajtenberg (1976) and ILO (1981b). A paper prepared for the ILO (Vaitsos 1976) provides one of the most detailed theoretical and empirical accounts from a critical perspective of the impact of TNCs on employment. For a general discussion of TNCs and labour, not specifically directed at Third World issues, see Enderwick (1985).

The classical presentation of the 'labour aristocracy' thesis is Arrighi (1970). For a critique see Waterman (1975). For a very different interpretation of high wages in TNC subsidiaries see Humphrey (1980/81).

There is a rapidly growing literature on export processing zones in the Third World. For a recent empirical survey, see OECD (1984). A major Marxist theoretical statement and empirical study is Frobel, Heinrichs and Kreye (1980). For a brief presentation from a similar standpoint, see Frank (1981, 96–111). For a critique of these views and a presentation of the internationalization of capital approach to the new international division of labour see Jenkins (1984b). For a discussion of the role of TNCs in Third World exports of manufactures generally see Nayyar (1977).

Strategies for labour are discussed from a non-Marxist standpoint by Bergsten, Horst and Moran (1978, ch. 4) and Cox (1976). A useful collection of articles is Waterman (1984), particularly the papers by Olle and Schoeller, Haworth and Ramsay and Elson and Pearson. A brief description of the major international trade union organizations can be found in TIE Bulletin, no. 13/14, 63–7. For a polemical attack on international trade union organizations and their role in the Third World, see Thomson and Larson (1978). A useful source of current information on international labour struggles is *International Labour Reports*.

7

Transnational corporations and local capital in the Third World

INTRODUCTION

One of the major issues raised by the operations of transnational corporations in the Third World is their impact on local capital in host countries. There are sharply contrasting views on this question. For some, TNCs pose a major threat to local firms while for others they complement and encourage local capital. This chapter considers the main perspectives on the relationship between foreign and local capital, before discussing in some detail the comparative behaviour of local firms and TNC subsidiaries. The chapter concludes with an analysis of the internationalization of Third World firms which has attracted considerable attention in the past few years.

Consider first the case of the orthodox defence of TNCs. As has already been seen, a crucial assumption here is that foreign investment is a supplement to domestic resources. Thus the operations of TNCs complement those of local capital. Frequently foreign investment is seen as presenting new challenges and new opportunities for local firms, leading to improved efficiency as a result of externalities and new markets through backward linkages (Reuber 1973, ch. 7; see also the views of the TNCs themselves reported in I. Frank 1980, 437–47). The overall effect on local capital is benign not threatening. Although generally, because for instance they tend to concentrate in different sectors, TNCs and local firms are not alternatives, where they do coexist the performance of TNCs will be at least as favourable (and in some areas such as exports more so) in terms of its impact on economic development as that of local firms. There is no essential difference between this position and that of certain Marxists who stress the progressive impact of TNCs. They also argue that compared to traditional (locally owned) firms the specific character of the TNC tends to promote development (Emmanuel 1976, 763).

This benign view of the impact of TNCs on local capital is challenged by those writers who emphasize the market power of TNCs. They stress the way in which foreign investment competes with local capital and excludes it from the most dynamic sectors of the economy. The displacement of local capital leads to a denationalization of the economy and the transfer of decision centres overseas. Since this is attributed to the market power of the TNCs rather than to greater efficiency compared to local firms, the overall impact is negative. Indeed it is argued that local capital represents a superior alternative to the TNCs and that an 'infant entrepreneur' argument (analogous to the 'infant industry' justification for tariff protection) makes it necessary for the state to support the development of local entrepreneurs (Hymer 1979, ch. 7).

This can be contrasted to the position of neo-imperialist writers. Although they concur with the view that foreign investment leads to a denationalization of the host economy, they do not share the bourgeois critics' optimism concerning the possibilities of national capitalist development in the Third World. They reject the view of a potential national bourgeoisie implicit in many non-Marxist critiques of TNCs, emphasizing the 'comprador', 'dependent' or 'auxiliary' nature of the local bourgeoisie in the Third World and seeing local capital as subordinated to international capital. Thus the only alternative to the TNCs is socialism.

The internationalization of capital approach, while emphasizing the integration of local capital to a model of capital accumulation led by the TNCs, does not see the local bourgeoisie as totally subordinate to foreign capital. The crucial departure of this approach is to recognize the local bourgeoisie as a distinct social force. The interconnections of the circuits of capital at the national and international level give rise to complex relations between foreign and local capital. These form the bases for the alliance of foreign and local (both private and state) capital which characterize 'dependent development' (Evans 1979). While there is an overall common interest in a particular model of accumulation there are also possible conflicts between foreign and local capital which are by no means always resolved in favour of the TNCs. A further implication of this approach is that static comparisons of the behaviour of TNCs and local firms are largely irrelevant to the main issue which is the dynamic impact of the internationalization of capital as reflected in the behaviour of both foreign and local firms.

This brief review of alternative views of the relationship between TNCs and local capital raises two issues for more detailed consideration. First, what is the nature of the relations between foreign and local capital and secondly, do TNCs behave differently in important ways from locally owned firms? Before examining these issues however, it is necessary to consider briefly the economic organization of local capital in the Third World.

THE ECONOMIC GROUPS

A characteristic of local capital in many Third World countries, particularly the more industrialized ones (many Latin American countries, India, Pakistan, South Korea, the Philippines, etc.), is the existence of a number of large 'economic groups'. The economic group has been defined as 'a multicompany firm which transacts in different markets but which does so under common entrepreneurial and financial control' (Leff 1978, 663).

They are distinguished from the traditional family firm by their broader management and ownership base. Their activities are often highly diversified and may involve quite unrelated products. They also frequently include banks and other financial institutions able to tap outside sources of funds. These groups can be extremely large and control a significant number of the largest local firms in the country (see Jenkins 1984a, 148 for empirical evidence from a number of Latin American countries).

Alongside these economic groups, there may also be a section of local capital made up of independent, mainly medium and small firms which correspond more closely to the image of the weak, subordinated local bourgeoisie found in some writing. On the other hand in the less industrially advanced economies, particularly those where political independence came late and the emergence of a local bourgeoisie is an extremely recent phenomenon, it seems that economic groups are not so common and small and medium-scale enterprises and family firms are much more characteristic of local capital (as for example in Africa).

RELATIONS BETWEEN TNCS AND LOCAL CAPITAL

Relations between TNCs and local capital in the Third World are many and varied. In some branches TNCs and local firms are in direct competition, while in others local firms have been largely displaced by the competitive advantages of the TNCs. In other areas there is collaboration and integration between foreign and local capital (see the discussion of Brazil in Evans 1979, ch. 3).

There are a number of links which form the basis of a symbiotic relationship between local and international capital. Joint-ventures have become increasingly common in recent years (UNCTC 1983, 46). Already by the 1970s a majority of manufacturing subsidiaries in the Third World were less than wholly-owned and a significant proportion involved at least 50 per cent local share-holdings (Table 7.1). Licensing agreements are also common particularly amongst the largest local firms (UNCTAD 1980). Local capital may also be integrated into the circuit of international capital through commercial relationships as a supplier, sub-contractor or customer.

Table 7.1 Ownership patterns of manufacturing affiliates of TNCs in Third World countries

	US TNCs (1975)		Non-US TNCs (1970)	
	Number	*%*	*Number*	*%*
Wholly-owned	523	50.1	392	25.1
Majority-owned	204	19.5	428	27.5
50–50	95	9.1	298	19.1
Minority-owned	222	21.3	441	28.3
TOTAL	1,044	100.0	1,559	100.0

Source: UNCTC (1978), table III.26.

The existence of a considerable number of joint-ventures and licensing agreements between foreign and local capital cannot be regarded as an indication that the latter is subordinated to the former. These relationships frequently involve the economic groups which because of their size and widely diversified interests can establish links with a number of foreign firms. They are not therefore subordinated to the interest of any one foreign capital. Although such agreements tend to unify the long-term strategic interests of the TNCs and local large capital around a particular development model, they also create new areas of conflict between local and foreign capital. For example, the establishment of a licensing agreement can give rise to conflict over the level of royalty payments or restrictive clauses in the technology contract; however there is no conflict over issues such as the type of production technology to be used, or the strategy of product differentiation.

From the above discussion it can be seen that foreign capital is by no means always complementary to local capital. There are important areas where foreign and local capital compete and coexist. Although in some branches the TNCs are able to displace local capital, this should not lead to the conclusion that the local bourgeoisie is uniformly weak and subordinated to the interest of international capital. A situation of mutual dependence often exists which is by no means free of conflict.

The question which now arises is, in the light of the coexistence of local and foreign capital in the Third World countries, can anything be said about their relative merits as agents of economic development? Is the nationality of ownership largely irrelevant to the performance of capital as some Marxists have argued? Do the size, flexibility, technology and management skills of the TNC make it a more effective promoter of development as claimed by some apologists for the TNCs? Or does the global rationality of the TNC conflict with the needs of economic development in the Third World as argued by the critics? It is to this question that we now turn.

COMPARISONS OF TNCS AND LOCAL FIRMS

A number of the debates concerning the impact of TNCs, as was seen in earlier chapters, revolve around the likely alternatives to TNCs and in particular the probability that local firms could replace TNC subsidiaries. Global Reach critics argue that such alternatives do exist and that the behaviour of local capital is more conducive to development than that of the TNCs which is determined by global rather than national considerations. In particular it is claimed that TNCs use capital-intensive techniques, centralize R & D in their home countries, restrict exports, use imported inputs, advertise and differentiate their products and transfer profits abroad to a much greater extent than local firms.

Evaluating these claims is much more difficult than might at first sight appear. Aggregate comparisons of local firms and foreign subsidiaries in a particular country are of limited use because of differences in the distribution of the two groups of firms in terms of size and sector, so that it is impossible to separate out the effect of foreign ownership from other factors. To separate out these influences it is necessary to have information on a firm-by-firm basis. One such approach involves choosing 'matched pairs' of foreign and local firms which are usually similar in terms of size and product line and then finding any systematic differences between the two types of firms. This approach, however, tends to underestimate differences between firms because it is often applied to small samples of firms so that differences may not prove to be statistically significant, and because by focusing on only those products which are produced by both types of firm, it may not be representative of the economy as a whole. Careful interpretation of empirical results is therefore particularly important in this area.

Choice of technique

There is considerable evidence to support the view that, on average, TNC subsidiaries are more capital-intensive than local firms in Third World countries (Jenkins 1986c). But is this because they are foreign owned or because of the industries in which they operate, or by virtue of their greater size? Studies comparing foreign subsidiaries with local firms producing the same products on a similar scale show that there is little difference in capital intensity between the two types of firm (Jenkins 1986c). In other words, when local firms are in direct competition with TNCs and are producing at similar levels of output, the technologies which they choose are likely to be just as capital-intensive as those of the foreign firms.

Taken together with the observation that TNCs tend to make only limited adaptation to the lower cost of labour in Third World countries, these findings suggest the following interpretation. In general TNCs tend to locate in the more capital-intensive branches of industry (except where foreign investment is largely export oriented). They also tend to be considerably larger than the average local firm. Since large firms are often more capital-intensive than small firms the difference in size distribution between foreign and local firms may also contribute to the greater capital intensity of TNCs within industries. In addition TNCs may be more capital-intensive than local firms within industries, even when account is taken of size, because they produce different products within a dualistic industry. Thus for instance it has been noted in Nigeria that foreign firms in the textile industry tend to be more capital-intensive than local firms, but this probably reflects the fact that TNCs produce synthetic textiles while local firms are concentrated in cotton (Biersteker 1978). Similarly the finding that TNCs tend to be more capital-intensive in the Bazilian auto parts industry (Morley and Smith 1977) is not that surprising in the light of the fact that subsidiaries tend to produce relatively sophisticated parts for the car assemblers, while local firms are more likely to be engaged in producing simple parts for the replacement market.

Where, however, local firms and TNCs are in direct competition, producing similar products for the same market, there is a tendency for local firms to adopt similar production techniques to those of the TNCs. Indeed this is part of a general survival strategy, whereby in order to compete successfully with the TNCs local capital attempts to imitate the behaviour of the TNCs. It is not surprising therefore that those studies based on matched pairs of local and foreign firms have failed to show significant differences in behaviour.

The fact that foreign and local firms producing similar products do not differ significantly in terms of capital intensity cannot be interpreted as indicating that foreign penetration of Third World economies is irrelevant in terms of its effects on the overall capital intensity of the economy or on the level of employment. It is in fact quite consistent with foreign investment leading to a substantial rise in capital intensity. First, in so far as entirely new branches of industry are established in the host country, this tends to be towards the more capital-intensive end of the spectrum of industries. Secondly, where foreign capital enters existing industries, it does so with the capital-intensive techniques of the home country. The tendency then is for local capital either to be displaced since it is unable to compete with the TNCs, or for it to become more capital-intensive in response to the competition.

A number of industry case studies have illustrated this phenomenon. Thus Langdon discussing the Kenyan soap industry writes, 'the first machine-made laundry soap in Kenya was MNC produced and that initiative was central in forcing many local firms to mechanize' (Langdon 1975, 25). A similar situation was found in the Kenyan footwear industry (Langdon 1981, 88–9). Similarly in the Latin American cigarette industry, licensing of 'international' brands by local firms has led to the import of more capital-intensive machinery by local firms (Shepherd 1985). There is therefore a tendency for the whole industrial structure to become more capital-intensive as a result of the internationalization of capital.

Research and development

As was seen in chapter 4, TNCs tend to centralize their R & D activities in their home countries and undertake relatively little R & D in the Third World. The question therefore arises: do local firms perform better than foreign subsidiaries in terms of undertaking local R & D? Unfortunately the empirical evidence on this is rather limited. What it does show is that *both* foreign subsidiaries and local firms spend very little on R & D – typically less than 1 per cent of their sales – and that even in industries which are usually regarded as very R & D intensive such as pharmaceuticals and electronics, in Third World countries such as Argentina and Hong Kong with a skilled labour force and relatively well developed scientific infrastructure, local R & D is less than 2 per cent of sales (Chudnovsky 1979b; Chen 1983, table 3.3). There is no clear evidence that local firms do more R & D that foreign subsidiaries (Jenkins 1986c).

Export performance

It is often asserted that the promotion of exports is a major contribution which TNCs can make to economic development in the Third World. There is no doubt that TNC subsidiaries enjoy a number of advantages relative to local firms when it comes to exporting. The fact that they produce internationally known brand names and can take advantage of the distribution networks of the parent company overseas places them in a favourable position *vis-à-vis* local firms who would need to develop their own brand name image and distribution system. In fact it has been argued that the marketing skill of the TNC is a vital factor in enabling exports from less developed countries to penetrate advanced country markets (De la Torre 1972). An often quoted statistic (from the Council for Latin America, a pressure group for US TNCs in Latin America) is that US subsidiaries accounted for more than 40 per cent of Latin American exports of manufactured goods in 1966, although their share of manufacturing value added was less than 10 per cent. Commenting on this Vernon states that 'without multi-national links, the subsidiaries would probably not have increased their exports on anything like the same scale' (Vernon 1973, 107).

Against this, TNC critics have argued that the global rationality of TNCs tends to militate against their playing a major role in promoting exports of manufactures. With the exception of the relatively small investments in export processing zones, subsidiaries continue to produce primarily for the domestic market. As a result less than 10 per cent of the sales of US manufacturing subsidiaries located in Third World countries are directed to overseas markets. The frequently found clauses in technology transfer contracts which restrict export production are cited as further evidence of the limited contribution of TNCs in this area, and may even indicate that TNCs have a negative impact on export performance. It is claimed that TNCs are reluctant to let their subsidiaries in the Third World compete with established operations in their home countries, either directly or through exports to third markets.

There is no clear evidence that TNCs have performed systematically better or worse in terms of exports than local capital, either in countries which have emphasized import substitution (Latin American countries and India) or those that have applied more export-oriented development strategies (East Asia) (Jenkins 1986c). There is some evidence that in Latin America TNCs tend to export a higher proportion of their total exports to regional markets (Jenkins 1979) and they may perform better than local firms in this respect. This is not surprising in view of the fact that the international spread of their operations enables them to take advantage of regional integration schemes to a much greater extent than their local competitors (Vaitsos 1978, 4–7). Different industries show different patterns of export performance although again it is difficult to discern any systematic pattern (Jenkins 1986c). In some cases differences have been found in the performance of TNCs from different countries. Thus in Brazil it was found that West European and Japanese TNCs tended to export a higher proportion of output than US TNCs reflecting, it was suggested, the more limited extension of their international networks (Newfarmer and Marsh 1981).

The relative performance of TNCs and local firms cannot be derived from the possession of some general 'advantage' on the part of the TNCs. It is the outcome of a complex interaction of the internationalization of capital in particular branches of industry and local capitalist development in specific Third World countries. However, it is clearly not the case either, that TNCs are implacably opposed to exports by their Third World subsidiaries. Under certain circumstances they have taken an active role in promoting manufactured exports through the relocation of labour-intensive processes and products. In other cases, under pressure from host governments, they have undertaken to export capital-intensive manufactures in return for certain local privileges. The capacity of local firms to compete in international markets varies from country to country. In general, however, it is precisely those countries in which local firms have shown the greatest capacity to compete internationally that TNCs have tended to concentrate their exports.

Imports

As was pointed out in chapter 5, there are a number of reasons for expecting TNCs to rely more heavily on imported inputs than locally owned firms. Empirical studies have consistently shown foreign subsidiaries to be more import-intensive than local firms both on an aggregate basis and when samples of firms are compared (Jenkins 1986c). Thus it can be concluded that even when TNCs and local firms are producing similar products, the former are likely to rely more heavily on imported inputs.

This is the only aspect of performance on which clear evidence exists to support the view that local firms have more beneficial effects on economic development. However, as was pointed out in chapter 5, differences in import propensities are often rather small and factors other than ownership, such as the level of industrial development in the host country and government policies, are likely to be more important determinants of the level of imports.

Advertising and marketing strategies

The impact of TNCs on consumption patterns in the Third World was discussed in chapter 4 where the importance of advertising was examined. Is there a significant difference between TNCs and local firms in terms of their marketing strategies, particularly advertising? In aggregate there is little doubt that TNCs spend more heavily on advertising than local firms, but they also tend to be concentrated in industries generally characterized by high levels of advertising (Jenkins 1986c).

Case studies of individual industries show a mixed pattern. In some cases it has been shown that foreign firms tend to spend substantially more on advertising than their local competitors. In the Kenyan soap industry, for instance, TNCs spent six times as much (in relation to sales) on advertising (Langdon 1975). Similarly in the Mexican yoghurt industry the major TNCs, Danone and Chambourcy, advertised heavily, while the major local firm did no advertising (Montavon 1979, 55). In contrast in the Argentinian pharmaceutical industry a rather different pattern prevailed. Whereas in aggregate foreign subsidiaries spent slightly more on advertising than local firms, amongst the largest pharmaceutical companies the situation was reversed (Chudnovsky 1979b).

These case studies suggest that where TNCs and local firms compete directly in the same industry, then the latter are faced with a choice. They may adopt similar competitive strategies (advertising, product differentiation) to those of the TNCs in order to maintain their market share as in the case of the larger Argentinian pharmaceutical companies. Not surprisingly it has been noted that acquisition of foreign trade-marks through licensing agreements is an important element in the competitive strategy of local capital (Sercovich 1974; Mytelka 1979, 121–2; Kaplinsky 1979, 91). Alternatively they may choose (or have no alternative but) to continue to advertise much less than their TNC competitors. In this case the prospects are bleak and they are likely to be squeezed by the growing market share of the TNCs as in the case of the Kenyan soap and Mexican yoghurt industries.

As in the case of the discussion of capital intensity then, the more relevant question is what is the impact of foreign penetration on the overall economic structure and marketing strategies, rather than whether TNCs spend more or less on advertising than local firms. The results of static comparisons will depend on the point in time at which the comparison is made and the dominant response of local capital. However, it can be seen that in a dynamic context the internationalization of capital is contributing to a growing emphasis on the production of differentiated products and the reproduction of the competitive strategies of capital in the advanced capitalist countries.

Profit remittances

At first sight it might appear obvious that foreign subsidiaries are more likely to repatriate profits, since their owners are overseas, than local firms, whose owners are by definition nationals. The problem is that local owners may also export part or their profits, whether to Swiss bank accounts or to buy property in the United States. Whatever else it may have done, the current debt crisis of countries such as Mexico should have dispelled the illusion that the local bourgeoisie patriotically invests in the national economy while foreign capital 'drains surplus' from the country.

Any empirical analysis of this issue is unfortunately virtually impossible. Transfers of capital by local firms must often be carried out by illegal means and are therefore by definition not reflected in published statistics. One must therefore rely on fragmentary and anecdotal evidence such as the statement by an accountant with a large multinational accounting firm in Kenya that 'the indigenous capitalists were more guilty of transfer pricing than the foreign subsidiaries' (Kaplinsky 1980, 92). Even the remittances of foreign subsidiaries are difficult to estimate completely because of the use of transfer pricing mechanisms. The evidence that local firms perform any better than foreign subsidiaries in this respect is unclear.

Conclusion

The general picture that emerges from this brief survey is that when local firms and TNCs produce similar products on the same scale, there is very little difference in their behaviour in most respects. It is true that foreign subsidiaries are likely to use slightly more imported inputs, but their behaviour even in this regard only modifies the overall pattern which is determined by the level of development of the productive forces locally and the policy of the host government rather than ownership.

From an internationalization of capital standpoint, however, such static comparisons obscure rather than reveal the processes at work. TNC penetration in many sectors has led local firms to mechanize in order to meet foreign competition; to import foreign trade-marks and advertise heavily, or to be increasingly marginalized by TNC brand names and to rely heavily on imported technology and as a result find their exports just as limited by restrictive clauses as those of TNC subsidiaries and often just as dependent on imported inputs. Not surprisingly, in imitating the TNCs in order to compete with them in their domestic markets, some firms in the more industrialized Third World countries have themselves begun to expand internationally.

THIRD WORLD TNCS

In the past few years a much commented-on phenomenon has been the emergence of 'Third World TNCs'. Initially identified with the 'American Challenge', TNCs subsequently came to be identified with the advanced capitalist countries generally, with the international expansion of European and Japanese capital. Now 'Third World TNCs', which would have been unthinkable a decade ago, are receiving growing attention. What does this new phenomenon amount to? Undoubtedly a substantial number of firms based in LDCs have set up subsidiaries overseas. The most comprehensive estimate indicates that by 1980, 963 Third World firms had established 1964 overseas subsidiaries and branches of which 938 were in manufacturing (Wells 1983, 2). The total direct foreign investment by LDCs at this time was estimated at between $5 billion and $10 billion (ibid., 2), which compares to a total stock of direct foreign investment in LDCs of $119 billion (UNCTC 1983, table II.5).

However, despite the recent international expansion of firms based in Third World countries, it is difficult to avoid the conclusion that they have been the subject of academic and media hype. Despite constant references to 'Third World multinationals', the term is only justified by adopting the broadest possible definition of what constitutes a 'multinational'. In other words any Third World firm which has any foreign subsidiaries is immediately classified as a Third World multinational. The significance of this elastic definition becomes immediately apparent if one compares it with the stricter definition used in many studies of developed country multinationals. Thus on the Harvard Business School's Multinational Enterprise Project definition that a firm must have manufacturing subsidiaries in six or more foreign countries in order to qualify as a multinational, only six of the 963 Third World firms should be included (Wells 1983, 9).

The point is not to deny the significance of the recent international expansion of Third World firms. There is little doubt that as capitalism develops in different parts of the Third World, capital finds it necessary to expand beyond national frontiers. As Table 7.2 indicates, a number of large economic groups and state enterprises have invested abroad. However, it is necessary to be cautious in assuming that so-called Third World

Table 7.2 Largest Third World firms with overseas investments

Company	Country	1983 mn $ sales	Sector
Hyundai Group	S. Korea	9,300	Machinery/equipment
Petrobras*	Brazil	8,810	Oil
Samsung Group	S. Korea	7,167	Construction/electronics
Lucky Group	S. Korea	7,159	Construction/plastics/ textiles
Daewoo Group	S. Korea	6,313	Construction/machinery/ textiles
Sunkyong Group	S. Korea	6,210	Trade and general manufacturing
Chinese Petroleum*	Taiwan	5,352	Oil
Ssangyong Cement Industries Corp.	S. Korea	3,257	Cement/petroleum
Birla Group	India	2,843	Industrial group
YPF*	Argentina	2,421	Oil
Tata Group	India	2,369	Industrial group

Source: South, July 1985 and own investigation.

* State enterprises.

multinationals are comparable to developed country multinationals that have been defined according to quite different criteria.

Third World foreign investors come mainly from the small group of countries often classified as NICs (newly industrializing countries). Between them, Hong Kong, India, South Korea, Brazil, Argentina, Singapore, the Philippines and Mexico accounted for over 60 per cent of all the foreign subsidiaries owned by LDC firms (Wells 1983, table 1.2). Taiwan, another leading source of foreign investment, is not included in the table. They invest mainly (but not exclusively) in other less developed countries, particularly those in the same geographical region.

The growth of foreign investment by LDC based firms raises a number of issues. What factors have led to their international expansion? Are they significantly different from traditional TNCs from the advanced capitalist countries in certain key respects? If so what are the implications of these differences? What are the future prospects for the foreign investors based in the Third World? What are the implications of their growth for development in the Third World? Do they provide a material basis for 'collective self-reliance' among Third World countries which many leaders have called for? Do they indicate a fundamental shift in the centres of world economic power? In what follows we shall try to answer some of these questions.

Characteristics

Despite (or perhaps because of) the limited empirical evidence that has so far become available on Third World TNCs, there is a widely held conventional wisdom about the characteristics of such firms and the ways in which they differ from traditional TNCs. Their first characteristic is the use of technology which has been adapted to the specific conditions of the less developed countries. In particular, because of their relatively small home markets these firms have experience in operating small-scale technologies. As a result, it is argued, subsidiaries of Third World firms tend to be smaller than those of developed country TNCs. A concomitant of this small-scale technology is a tendency for production to be more labour-intensive than that of developed country subsidiaries. Another form of adaptation of technology which has been identified is to make greater use of locally available raw materials and other inputs which means that LDC subsidiaries tend to be less dependent on imported inputs.

Not only is the technology supplied by Third World firms adapted to the conditions of the LDCs but so are the types of products produced. While developed country TNCs tend to concentrate on high quality, highly differentiated products, firms from LDCs tend to focus on standardized products which compete on the basis of price. As a result they tend to spend substantially less on advertising than developed country subsidiaries.

A further characterisitic of Third World foreign investors is their tendency to make extensive use of joint-venture arrangements with local firms rather than insist on majority ownership which has often been the case with TNCs. The pattern of using joint-ventures is similar to that which has been observed for smaller TNCs from developed countries. A lower level of equity participation also tends to be accompanied by a higher degree of autonomy for the local subsidiary in the case of a Third World owned firm.

The foreign exchange costs associated with investors from less developed countries are also regarded as being lower than those of developed country investors. As already mentioned, greater use of locally available inputs means lower import costs. There is also some evidence that both royalty payments and profit remittances by firms from LDCs tend to be lower than those of developed country TNCs.

Finally, two further differences have been noted compared to the traditional TNCs. First, there is a tendency to rely much more heavily on expatriate manpower in the subsidiaries. Secondly, the traditional TNCs tend to export on a more significant scale than do LDC investors.

It is only on these last two points that the conventional wisdom establishes significant differences between Third World and traditional TNC investors which are more favourable to the latter.

Given the heated debate over almost every other issue related to the impact of TNCs in the Third World, it is surprising to find such widespread agreement concerning the nature and impact of Third World TNCs. They have been welcomed from such different points of the ideological spectrum as the *Harvard Business Review* (Heenan and Keegan 1979) and President Nyrere of Tanzania who is quoted as wanting 'Third World multinational corporations owned by us and controlled by us to serve our purposes' (Wells 1983, 137). There is a clue here of course. Basically, they are welcomed by the neo-classicals because they are TNCs and by Third World nationalists because they are *Third World* TNCs.

A reflection on the major non-Marxist theoretical approaches to TNCs will help to clarify the point. Much of the work on Third World TNCs has, in fact, been written from a neo-classical internalization view of the TNCs (particularly Wells 1983; Kumar 1982; and Chen 1983, ch. 8). The writers have therefore been particularly concerned to identify the intangible assets which have enabled LDC firms to compete internationally. Whereas TNCs from the advanced capitalist countries enjoy intangible assets such as advanced technology and marketing skills, these are believed to be inadequate to explain the success of Third World firms as foreign investors. Instead, it is held that their advantages derive primarily from their adaptation of technology to local conditions, their lower overheads and their familiarity with operating in a Third World environment. It is thus but a small step to conclude that Third World TNCs are particularly 'appropriate' for other Third World countries and 'that investors from other developing countries offer, on average, more net benefits for most host countries than do the traditional multinationals' (Wells 1983, 142).

On the other hand, the Global Reach approach emphasizes that local firms behave better than TNCs in precisely these ways – the use of more appropriate technology, less reliance on imports, less advertising. It is thus entirely consistent with this view to argue that Third World firms when they extend their operations to neighbouring countries will continue to perform better in these respects than developed country TNCs. It also has a wider ideological appeal. If the growth of Third World TNCs is welcomed from a neo-classical point of view as leading to a more 'realistic' attitude towards incoming foreign investment from states which are now both home and host countries (Heenan and Keegan 1979, 108), for critics of developed country TNCs and existing North–South relations generally they hold out the prospect of South–South co-operation and the development of the strategy of 'collective self-reliance' (Agrawal 1981). Their emergence, moreover, has 'considerably enhanced Third World bargaining power in negotiating with multinational enterprises of the developed world in obtaining capital and relevant technology' (Agrawal 1981, 121).

While non-Marxist writers have devoted considerable attention to the rise of Third World TNCs, it has been largely neglected by Marxists. This is not entirely surprising as far as the neo-imperialist view is concerned since their emphasis on the 'comprador' character of the local bourgeoisie is hardly compatible with vigorous international expansion. On the other hand it does fit in well with the argument of neo-fundamentalist Marxists, who argue that substantial capitalist development is taking place in the Third World, and it is more surprising to find no discussion of the phenomenon in these writings.

A critique of the conventional wisdom

The convergence of neo-classical and Global Reach thinking on Third World TNCs and the lack of serious Marxist discussion has meant a paucity of critiques of the conventional wisdom on the subject. One direction in which such a critique might be developed has already been suggested. Are these firms really TNCs at all, and if not is it valid to compare them with developed country TNCs?

A number of other problems can also be raised. Since most of the technology transferred by Third World firms was originally imported from the advanced capitalist countries, the conventional wisdom implies that only local firms adapt imported technology and that TNC subsidiaries do not, despite considerable experience of operating in LDC markets. If this were not the case Third World TNCs would have no competitive advantage over the traditional TNCs. However, there is considerable evidence that the major form of market adaptation undertaken by traditional TNCs in Third World countries is the down-scaling of plant in response to the smaller market size. This is of course precisely the form of adaptation by Third World TNCs which is most emphasized by Wells. It is also questionable whether Third World firms are more likely to adapt imported technology in order to make greater use of labour (see above).

The evidence that is used to support these propositions often amounts to little more than casual empiricism (Lall 1984a, 12). For instance the smaller size both of parent companies and of subsidiaries of Third World investors compared to traditional TNCs is the main evidence for the existence of 'down-scaling' of technology. However, this is at best a very indirect indicator and it is quite compatible with a situation in which the LDC firm has carried out no technological adaptation of its own. In fact, those studies which have looked in detail at the process of technological adaptation by Third World firms show a very varied pattern with no tendency for down-scaling to be particularly prominent (Lall 1984b, 50–61); Katz and Kosacoff 1984, appendix IIb).

There is even less evidence to support the view that Third World firms generally adapt their technology in a labour-intensive direction. As Lall has commented on the basis of Indian evidence, '*the classic spur to technical change in economic theory turned out to be of no practical significance whatsoever*' (Lall 1984b, 56–7, emphasis in the original). Comparisons which purport to show that the subsidiaries of Third World firms are less capital-intensive than those of traditional TNCs are subject to the criticism that they are not comparing like with like. Much more sophisticated comparisons are required before it can be accepted that Third World subsidiaries are in fact more labour-intensive.

The view that Third World investors tend to produce more appropriate products than traditional TNCs is also open to similar questioning (Lall 1984a, 17). There is evidence that a higher proportion of subsidiaries owned by Third World firms do operate in industries in which advertising levels are relatively low (Wells 1983, tables 5.5–5.8). However, the evidence that Third World subsidiaries operating in the same industries tend to produce more appropriate products is much less clear. In some cases Third World firms whose strategy has involved imitating the product differentiation strategies of traditional TNCs have led the way in international expansion. A case in point is the leading Argentinian pharmaceutical firm Laboratorio Bago SA with investment in five other Latin American countries (Chudnovsky 1979b).

Not only are there problems of comparability in discussing Third World investors and traditional TNCs in terms of their technology because of their tendency to concentrate in different industries, but there are also problems of interpretation which arise from our earlier questioning of the validity of referring to Third World investors as TNCs at all. This is very clear in the context of the argument that Third World firms tend to adapt technology in order to use locally available inputs and that as a result they will import a lower proportion of their inputs than traditional TNCs. Even if the evidence shows that Third World investors have a lower propensity to import than developed country TNCs, this is open to different interpretations. It may reflect not the fact that Third World firms adapt their technology, but rather that because the subsidiary is not part of an integrated international operation, the pressure to buy from other affiliates is much less. In other words it is the fact that the Third World investor is *not* a TNC which accounts for its lower import propensity. This obviously has very different implications from the view that emphasizes technological adaptation to use local inputs. In particular it suggests that if Third World firms continue to expand internationally so that they do become genuine TNCs, then their behaviour is likely to be similar to that of the traditional TNCs and their imports will increase.

A similar point can be made in relation to the apparent preference of Third World investors for joint-ventures. The contrast is most marked when comparisons are made with large US TNCs. The ownership patterns are much more similar when Third World firms are compared with smaller investors from other countries (Wells 1983, 111) or with Japanese TNCs. Thus it is possible to conclude that the use of joint-ventures is not a characteristic of Third World firms *per se*, but rather that it reflects their small scale and recent development. Similarly the greater autonomy given to subsidiaries by Third World firms can also be explained by the fact that they do not form part of an integrated global network.

In summary, then, three points can be made in criticism of the conventional wisdom regarding Third World TNCs. First, some of the arguments are based on invalid comparisons which do not compare like with like. Secondly, some of the empirical evidence that is used does not necessarily indicate what it purports to show, particularly regarding the nature of technological adaptation by Third World firms. Finally, some of the differences which do exist reflect not specific characteristics of *Third World* TNCs but the fact that these firms are not TNCs at all.

The internationalization of capital

The inadequacy of the conventional wisdom concerning Third World TNCs requires the development of an alternative theoretical approach, although so far no such approach has emerged to challenge the conventional wisdom. One possible line of approach would be to attempt to explain foreign investment by Third World firms along the same lines as have been used in the Global Reach approach to analyse the expansion of traditional TNCs, namely as an aspect of the oligopolistic strategy of large firms. At first sight there appears to be some evidence to support such an interpretation. In India for instance it has been noted that many of the leading foreign investors are in fact 'dominant' or 'monopoly' firms under the Monopoly and Restrictive Trade Practices Act, which are subject to certain limitations on their expansion in India. By the late 1970s two-thirds of all Indian joint-ventures had been carried out by such firms and the largest twenty Indian business houses were responsible for 60 per cent of all ventures (Encarnation 1982, tables 1 and 2). The tendency for foreign investors to be large firms operating in concentrated sectors has also been noted in Argentina (Katz and Kosacoff 1984, 162–3), while in Brazil many of the major foreign investors belong to large economic groups (Villela 1984).

However, while such an oligopolistic theory of foreign investment appears promising in the context of Indian and Latin American investors, it seems less relevant in the case of Asia. Although the evidence is a little sketchy it appears that in both Hong Kong (Chen 1983) and South Korea (Jo 1981), foreign investment has been mainly undertaken by medium-sized firms, often operating in industries characterized by low levels of concentration. It seems, therefore, to be more akin to the early pattern of Japanese foreign investment.

Thus while restrictions on growth at home, either because of anti-monopoly legislation as in India, or because of slow-growing oligopolistic markets as in Argentina, appear to have played a part in the international expansion of some Third World firms, it does not offer a general explanation of foreign investment by such firms. As capitalism develops in the Third World competition increases, in the sense that capital becomes more mobile. It is hardly surprising that it no longer remains tied to particular local or national markets, since this has been the experience of capitalist development everywhere. The drive of competition forces firms to look for new markets and given suitable conditions these are found overseas. The internationalization of Third World capital is then simply a likely step in the development of Third World capitalism. Not surprisingly those parts of the Third World where capitalism is most developed, the NICs, became first of all major exporters of manufactures and then foreign investors and exporters of technology.

Not surprisingly the defence of export markets has been a major motive for foreign investment (Wells 1983, 67–73; Katz and Kosacoff 1984, appendix IIb; Lall 1984a, 70–3; Chen 1984, table 3.10). With many Third World countries pursuing import substituting policies, firms from other LDCs which had developed export markets in these countries then found it necessary to set up local production facilities in order to maintain their position. In the case of firms from Hong Kong, an additional important consideration has been to gain access to developed country markets by relocating to other countries and thus avoiding the limitations which developed country quotas placed on direct exports from Hong Kong (Chen 1984). There has also been relocation from Hong Kong in the face of rising land and labour costs.

The internationalization of capital gives further opportunities to capital in terms of overcoming the restrictions which being confined within national boundaries inevitably imposes upon it. A large national firm is in a very exposed postion *vis-à-vis* the state. It is also subject to the vagaries of the national market. International expansion can diminish both political risks and fluctuations associated with national recessions (Lecraw 1977). Particularly in view of the stringent foreign exchange controls operated by many Third World states, foreign investment may be an important means of obtaining greater flexibility *vis-à-vis* foreign exchange controls (White 1981).

Implications for the future

It is now time to draw out some of the implications of the growth of foreign investment from the Third World in relation to the questions which were raised at the beginning of this section. It has been my contention that in so far as Third World firms are any different from the traditional TNCs, this is because they are at an incipient stage of their development and are not yet 'real' TNCs at all. There is, however, no reason to suppose that such firms, particularly those belonging to the large economic groups within the major NICs, will not internationalize further in the future. If they do so, then it is to be expected that they will tend to behave in ways which become increasingly similar to the traditional TNCs.

As far as the LDCs are concerned there is no reason to believe that they will be significantly better or worse than traditional TNCs as agents of development. They will, however, probably contribute to further undermine the ability and willingness of Third World states to control TNCs. In the case of India, for example, the internationalization of local firms is intimately linked to policy towards inward investment (Encarnation 1982, 54–6). In addition the growth of international operations may also undermine the state's ability to exercise control over the national economy.

If Third World TNCs are basically similar to those from the advanced capitalist countries, it is highly contradictory to welcome joint-ventures with Indian or Argentinian firms in the name of 'collective self-reliance' while at the same time vilifying the traditional TNCs. It is not surprising then that some of the smaller neighbours of the leading NICs have viewed their enthusiasm for 'collective self-reliance' with some scepticism (Encarnation 1982, 56–8).

Finally, then, does the emergence of foreign investors from the Third World indicate a major shift in world economic power? Probably not. It does, however, lay the basis for a more symmetrical relationship between capitals. Thus the growing interpenetration of capital which is likely to proceed will give rise to a more complex interweaving of capitalist interests on an international scale.

FURTHER READING

There is a considerable literature on the relationship between foreign capital and the local bourgeoisie particularly in the context of Latin America and Kenya. On Latin America in general see Jenkins (1984a, 145–63). Evans (1979, ch. 3) is an excellent case study of Brazil. On Kenya see the debate between Kaplinsky, Henley and Leys (all 1980) and the references therein.

A general review of the literature comparing foreign and local firms can be found in Newfarmer (1985a). Reviews of studies which compare the choice of technique by foreign and local firms are White (1978, 42–5) and Lall (1980, 47–51). Some of the methodological problems of such comparisons are discussed in Ingles and Fairchild (1977).

Case studies of the relationship between foreign capital and local capital within a particular industry which illuminate a number of the points discussed in this chapter are Langdon (1975) on the Kenyan soap industry, Chudnovsky (1979a) on the Argentinian pharmaceutical industry and Evans (1979, 121–43) on the Brazilian pharmaceutical and textile industries.

There is a rapidly growing literature on Third World TNCs. Two recent books, Wells (1983) and Lall (1984a), provide a wealth of empirical material. Shorter summaries are Kumar (1982) and O'Brien (1980). Encarnation (1982) provides an interesting case study of the political economy of foreign investment by Indian firms.

8

Transnational corporations and the state

The growth of TNCs documented in earlier chapters poses major questions in relation to the state and state policy. Has the internationalization of capital made the nation state obsolete? Have TNCs tended to undermine national sovereignty? Can, should and will Third World governments exercise control over the TNCs? In so far as the state represents the interest of particular classes or class fractions, will it be dominated by foreign or national capital?

There are two ways of approaching the question of the state and transnational corporations. The first views the state largely as a neutral instrument, which intervenes in the economy in the 'national interest' and asks whether the growth of the TNCs has undermined national sovereignty and rendered the traditional instruments of national economic policy ineffective. This is the approach adopted by most non-Marxists and some Marxists (e.g. Murray 1975; Warren 1975).

The second approach addresses the political economy of state–TNC relations and explicitly recognizes the class nature of the capitalist state. It therefore poses the question of whose interest does the state represent and what are the factors which contribute to accommodation or conflict between host governments and TNCs. In terms of analysing the likelihood and significance of Third World states controlling TNCs, it is necessary to address both these issues since it will depend on both the *ability* of the state to control TNCs and its *willingness* to do so.

TNCS AND THE POWER OF NATION STATES

In 1969 Charles Kindleberger wrote 'the nation state is just about through as an economic unit'. It was a widely held view amongst orthodox economists at the time that the growth of the transnational corporation had rendered the nation state obsolete. The international flexibility of the TNCs enabled them to move funds and goods around the world, freeing them from national economic controls. This also meant that traditional fiscal and monetary policies were rendered increasingly ineffective and that balance of payments problems were exacerbated by the ability of TNCs to escape exchange controls through manipulating transfer prices (Barnet and Müller 1974, ch. 10; Holland 1975, ch. 3). The view that the power of the nation state and the feasibility of national Keynesian policies has declined as a result of the internationalization of capital has been shared by some Marxists (Murray 1975; Radice 1984).

Neo-classical writers welcomed the decline of the power of nation states, contrasting the global rationality of the TNCs to the parochial interests of national governments. The growth of TNCs was seen as a contribution to a more rational worldwide allocation of resources to which existing nation states had tended to pose an obstacle. While irrational nationalism might lead certain governments to attempt to impose controls and restrictions on the operations of TNCs, this was unlikely to persist in the long run, because of the economic and technological benefits to be obtained from the unfettered operation of TNCs and the fact that attempts by individual states to regulate the TNCs, taken in isolation, were likely to prove ineffective or counterproductive.

Critics of the TNCs see a real conflict between the global maximization strategies of the companies and the interest of host countries, as for example when restrictions are imposed on exports by subsidiaries. Paradoxically, these writers, despite their portrayal of the immense power of the TNCs and their ability to undermine national economic policy, are surprisingly optimistic about the ability of the nation state not only to survive but to exercise countervailing power *vis-à-vis* the TNCs.

The view of the TNC sweeping all before it, of the late 1960s and early 1970s, has been challenged from a number of quarters. Some orthodox writers have predicted on the basis of the 'obsolescing bargain' model of state–TNC relations that as competition among TNCs intensifies and the capacity of host countries to participate in management grows, then the ability of host governments to control the TNCs and extract better terms from them has tended to increase (Bergsten, Horst and Moran 1978, 341).

Arguing from a Marxist perspective, Warren has pointed to a number of factors which have increased the power of nation states to control TNCs. The contradictions of capitalist development have led to the expansion of state intervention in economic life. This, together with the concentration and centralization of capital (which makes it easier for a state to control capital because there are a few large firms and not the myriad of small ones) and growing interdependence between national economies (which forces the state to take a more active role) have according to Warren tended to strengthen the power of the state *vis-à-vis* individual capitals.

Warren also believes that the power of the state in the Third World has tended to increase *vis-à-vis* the TNCs. Political independence, East–West rivalry and increasing inter-imperialist rivalry have given Third World states much more room for manoeuvre than in the past. As a result they have been able to carry out a significant number of nationalizations of foreign subsidiaries, to obtain better bargains from TNCs, e.g. in the area of technology transfer, and to exercise more control over the activities of foreign corporations (Warren 1973; Warren 1980, 170–6).

THE POLITICAL ECONOMY OF STATE–TNC RELATIONSHIPS

The problem with the approach discussed in the last section is that it emphasizes the independent power of the state *vis-à-vis* the TNCs and tends to ignore the class nature of the capitalist state and the implications that this has for state intervention. The state has been a major area of debate in recent years and there is no unified Marxist theory of the state (see Gold *et al.* 1975; Jessop 1977; and Holloway and Picciotto 1977, for surveys of these debates). Not surprisingly therefore there are a number of different perspectives concerning state–TNC relations within the Marxist tradition.

The neo-imperialist view of the relationship between state and capital sees the home states of the TNCs representing the interests of their 'own' capital and particularly that of the most internationalized sector of capital. In the Third World, on the other hand, as many dependency writers have argued, the state is usually dominated by foreign capital (Frank 1981, 230–1).

The explanation of why the state acts in the interest of its own capital in the advanced capitalist countries is often premised on an 'instrumentalist' theory of the state, which emphasizes the close links between members of the state apparatus and the ruling class. Thus the US state acts in the global interest of US capital because of the common background of corporate managers and government officials (Bergsten, Horst and Moran 1978, 314–23). A similar view also underlies the analysis of the state in the Third World (Leys 1980).

Foreign capital is seen as forming a 'reactionary alliance' with conservative forces in the host economy (Moran 1978). Those who staff the state apparatus are frequently closely linked to foreign capital.

Moreover the vast financial resources of the TNCs together with the widespread state involvement in economic affairs have given rise to considerable scope for bribery and corruption of government officials (a practice which of course is not confined to TNCs). The TNCs are also able to mobilize their home states to bring pressure to bear on Third World governments when this proves necessary (Moran 1978).

On this view international capital not only controls and manipulates the dependent state in the Third World, but it also structures the form of the state. Thus the emergence of authoritarian regimes in Latin America and other parts of the Third World since the mid-1960s are explained in terms of the 'needs' of international capital. Indeed for some the military rulers of these countries are identified as 'the political party of the multinational corporations' (Petras, quoted in Serra 1979, 100).

This approach tends to minimize the impact of measures taken by Third World states to nationalize or control the TNCs. Although recent writings recognize the existence of Third World economic nationalism as a result of the attempts of the local bourgeoisie and the state bureaucracy to redefine their relations with the international economy, these are not seen as fundamentally threatening the position of international capital. Indeed economic nationalism in the Third World has been co-opted by the TNCs who are able to use increased raw material prices as a justification for raising their product prices and increasing downstream profits; to negotiate favourable terms in compensation for the nationalization of their operations; and to specialize in the provision of services such as management, purchasing and marketing to state enterprises. In addition the main requirement of capital for a reliable supply of raw materials can be better guaranteed without wholly owned subsidiaries in the Third World (Girvan 1975).

Warren, in contrast, takes a diametrically opposed position, seeing the state in Third World countries intervening to promote national capital accumulation even in the absence of a local bourgeois ruling class (Warren 1973, 42–3). He rejects the instrumentalist position which emphasizes the need for a national bourgeoisie to control the state apparatus in order to bring about authentic capitalist development and which considers the lack of such a bourgeoisie and the domination of the state by foreign capital to be major problems in the Third World today.

Thus Warren considers that Third World states are both able and willing (in the interests of promoting capitalist development) to control the TNCs. However, it is clearly in the interest of host countries to avoid 'nationalistic excesses' and measures that would tend to reduce the flow of foreign investment (Warren 1980, 176).

INTERNATIONALIZATION OF CAPITAL AND
THE NATION STATE

A major weakness of the approaches to state–TNC relations discussed so far is their inadequate conceptualization of the state. A number of Marxist writers on the state have sought to relate the nature of the capitalist state to the essentially competitive nature of the capitalist mode of production. This can be seen in relation to all three levels of competition: between capital and labour; between capitals; and among workers. Poulantzas sees the state as countering the threat to the unity of the capitalist class posed by competition over the appropriation of surplus value, and at the same time fragmenting the working class, channelling its political action into economistic interest group struggles (Gold *et al.* 1975, 37). German Marxists have also attempted to derive the nature of the capitalist state from the existence of capital in the form of individual capitals, while others have sought to relate it to the conflict between capital and labour in the labour process (Holloway and Picciotto 1977).

This stress on the competitive nature of capitalism leads them to emphasize the '*relative autonomy*' of the state, in the sense that the state is independent of the particularistic interests of individual capitals or fractions of capital. This is seen as necessary if the state is to act in the interests of capital as a whole and to perform its role in maintaining social cohesion. In contrast the approaches reviewed above tend to assume either *absolute* autonomy of the state which is seen as independent of, and opposed to, the transnationals, or a total lack of autonomy with the state under the control of transnational capital.

Once the relative autonomy of the state is recognized, it is quite possible for conflicts to develop between the state and particular TNCs or TNCs as a group. However, it is equally possible that, at particular times, the state, in order to promote capitalist development, will take steps that are particularly favourable towards TNCs in order to attract foreign capital. In other words there is no reason to expect the state to be consistently 'nationalist' nor consistently 'comprador' (Evans 1979, 214–16).

It is also important not to conceive of the state as a monolithic entity pursuing a single coherent strategy. Competition and conflict between different capitals and class fractions are often reproduced within the state apparatus (Hirsch, quoted in Picciotto 1978, 224). It has been argued that this competition is particularly characteristic of Third World states, leading to the establishment of a large number of public organizations each with its specific objectives and criteria and with little prospect of collaborating among themselves to achieve common goals.

Such fragmentation of the state apparatus tends to be accompanied by the 'capture' of certain sections of the state by particular interests (Evers 1979, 169–71).

The policies pursued by a particular state at a certain point in time towards TNCs will be governed by a number of factors. First, it will depend on the overall pattern of capital accumulation and the requirements that this imposes for capitalist development. Secondly, it will be influenced by the overall balance of forces between different classes and class fractions at the time. Thirdly, it will depend on the evolution of international economic conditions and the possibilities and constraints which these impose on the country concerned. These factors will be illustrated by the discussion of the Chilean case below.

The question of the disappearance of the nation state as a result of the growth of the TNC can also be approached in a different light once it is recognized that the state plays a particular role in the reproduction of capitalist social relations. Murray (1975) notes that as capital expands internationally there arises a problem of 'territorial non-coincidence' between capital and the nation state. This does not however imply that the system of atomistic nation states is outdated or that the TNC and the nation state are fundamentally opposed to each other. Rather the TNCs are politically opportunist and take advantage of the national divisions in the world economy, e.g. in exploiting the advantages offered by tax havens.

Murray focuses on the economic interventions of the state. His conclusion that although the power of the nation state may be weakened by the internationalization of capital, it is not about to disappear, is reinforced by Poulantzas' (1975) analysis of the state as a factor of cohesion in society. The nation state continues to play a crucial role in the reproduction of capitalist relations of production because of its role in legitimating the interests of the ruling class. Despite the internationalization of capital, the class struggle continues to be primarily nationally based, so that the legitimating functions of the state must also be performed at the national level. This explains why, despite the internationalization of capital, national state apparatuses are not being replaced by international state apparatuses.

However, it has also been argued that Poulantzas has tended to underestimate the significance of international state apparatuses (Fine and Harris 1979, 159–69). These have continued to grow in importance precisely because they are more distant from the immediate pressures of the class struggle and much less constrained than the nation state in acting on behalf of capital, particularly internationalized capital. Thus international organizations, such as the IMF, are able to exert what appears as external pressure on nation states in the interests of internationalized capital. Again the point can be made that there is no necessary conflict between TNCs and nation states or inevitable coincidence between the internationalization of capital and the growth of supranational institutions, but rather that the TNCs are politically opportunist in their relations with states.

INTERNATIONAL CONTROLS ON TNCS

If then TNCs are able to exploit the fragmentation of the world economy into nation states to their own advantage, do international controls over TNCs offer a solution? The history of attempts to introduce such controls suggest not. Despite years of discussion, little has been achieved in this area. After World War II the Havana Charter which was to have established an International Trade Organization included provisions for the protection of investment and the control of restrictive business practices. This was never ratified, however, so that the post-war international economic order was characterized by a complete lack of international regulation of foreign investment and the operations of TNCs.

The 1970s, with the emergence of a generally more critical climate towards TNCs, saw a number of initiatives aiming towards an international code of conduct on TNCs. The first off the mark was the International Chamber of Commerce, an organization representing internationalized capital which adopted its Guidelines for International Investment in 1972. The flavour of these guidelines is captured in the recommendation that 'the government of the host country should place no restrictions on the remittance of loan interest . . . licence fees, royalties and similar payments'.

This was followed four years later by the OECD Declaration on International Investment and Multinational Enterprises. This has been described as a 'Pre-emptive Western strike emphasizing business responsibility' (Robinson 1983). It was an attempt by the governments of the advanced capitalist countries to respond to growing Third World criticism of the TNCs, while at the same time making it clear that the West was not prepared to see excessive controls imposed on the TNCs. Like the ICC Guidelines before it, the OECD's code was voluntary and not legally binding.

A number of international organizations have drawn up codes of conduct covering different aspects of TNC operations. These include the International Labour Office (on Social Policy), UNCTAD (on Restrictive Business Practices and the Transfer of Technology) and the

World Health Organization (on the Marketing of Breast-Milk Substitutes). The most comprehensive, however, has been the UN Code of Conduct on Transnational Corporations, being negotiated under the auspices of the Commission on Transnational Corporations.

This is still under discussion and a number of key areas of disagreement have emerged during the course of the negotiations. One is whether or not the code should be legally binding or simply voluntary as in the case of the OECD code. Second there has been some disagreement over the definition of TNCs, particularly over whether or not state-owned firms should be included as well as private corporations. A third area of considerable disagreement is the insistence of the advanced capitalist countries that TNCs should be guaranteed equality of treatment with national firms, a demand about which Third World states have considerable reservations. There is also some debate over the specification of the terms on which compensation should be paid in the event of nationalization of a TNC subsidiary. The disagreements are largely those that might be expected with the advanced capitalist countries playing the role mainly of home countries for the TNCs, while Third World states are still almost exclusively host countries. Although final agreement has yet to be reached, it seems unlikely, in view of the general move towards more liberal treatment of foreign capital in many Third World countries, that a tough, legally binding code will eventually be agreed.

NATIONAL LEGISLATION

A number of countries have introduced legislation covering areas in which TNCs are allowed to operate, permitted shareholding, and aspects of TNC behaviour in recent years. Foreign capital is often excluded from sectors such as public utilities, mining, iron and steel, retailing, insurance and banking. A recent example has been the decision of the Brazilian government to exclude IBM from the local micro computer industry. A number of countries, including Brazil, India, Indonesia, South Korea, Malaysia, Mexico, Pakistan, the Philippines and Sri Lanka, also require majority local shareholdings in joint-ventures with foreign firms, particularly where these are in what are regarded as low priority areas (UNCTC 1983, 60).

A number of Third World countries mainly in Latin America and India have imposed limitations on profit remittances and technology payments by TNC subsidiaries. These seek to limit the outflow of foreign exchange associated with the operations of the TNCs. In addition recent laws in Brazil (1975), Zambia (1977), the Philippines (1978), South Korea (1981) and Mexico (1982) seek to outlaw many of the restrictive business practices typically associated with technology transfer. These include tying of inputs, restrictions on the volume of output or prices at which it can be sold, export restrictions and 'grant-back' clauses whereby the licensee is required to make any improvements in technology available free of charge to the licensor (UNCTC 1983, 69).

Trade related performance requirements are often imposed by Third World countries to reduce the adverse impact of TNC subsidiaries on their balance of payments. It has been estimated that 29 per cent of US subsidiaries operating in the Third World are subject to this kind of performance requirement (UNCTC 1983, 124, n. 7).

Another widespread requirement is for indigenization of the labour force of the local subsidiary. The extent of indigenization rises with the level of development of the local economy so that this has proved to be a particularly important issue in countries at a relatively low level of development where considerable expatriate labour is still employed. There have also been some attempts in the more industrially advanced Third World countries to require TNCs to undertake some local research and development. Finally, in some countries (Brazil, Kenya, the Philippines) limits have been placed on the access of TNCs to local sources of loan funds in order to avoid their pre-empting the limited supply of capital available locally (UNCTC 1983, 65).

Has tighter regulation of TNCs had the effects their proponents claim, of substantially reducing costs to host countries, or is it the case as the TNCs themselves argue, that they serve to dry up the supply of foreign capital and technology? One of the most ambitious attempts to control foreign capital was Decision 24 of the Andean Pact group of countries (Bolivia, Chile, Colombia, Ecuador, Peru and, after 1973, Venezuela) on the 'Common Treatment for Foreign Capital, Trademarks, Patents, Licensing Agreements and Royalties', adopted in December 1970. It provides a useful test of the competing views in this area.

Among the principal features of Decision 24 were the establishment of national agencies to screen direct foreign investment and technology transfer; prohibition of any new foreign investment in utilities, insurance, commercial banking and finance, transport, advertising and communications; requirements that majority foreign-owned firms should divest over a period of time; a limit on profit repatriation of 14 per cent of registered capital per annum; limits on the access of foreign firms to medium- and long-term local loans; prohibition on restrictive clauses in technology transfer agreements (see Mytelka 1979, ch.3 for more details). In other words Decision 24 included most of the ownership and behavioural controls on TNCs recommended by their critics.

Despite problems of implementation, there is little doubt that Decision 24 did have some impact in controlling foreign capital in the region. The most noticeable results were achieved in the field of technology transfer where contracts were renegotiated to reduce the restrictive clauses and the level of royalty payments. It has been estimated that in Venezuela, for instance, technology payments were reduced by over 20 per cent in 1978, as a result of renegotiation (UNCTAD 1980, table 4). Substantial savings have also been reported in Colombia (Vaitsos 1974a, 129). Less significant changes have been found in terms of the dilution of the share of foreign ownership in subsidiaries. Nevertheless, there was a small increase in the proportion of minority-owned affiliates and a reduction in the proportion of wholly-owned subsidiaries in the first five years of the implementation of Decision 24 (Mytelka 1979, tables 3.5 and 3.6). It is also worth noting that the share of manufacturing production accounted for by foreign subsidiaries declined between 1971 and 1974 in both Colombia and Peru, the two countries for which data are available (Mytelka 1979, table 1.6; and UNCTC 1983, table II.24).

There are two diametrically opposed views concerning the effects of Decision 24 on foreign investment in the Andean Pact countries. The TNCs themselves reacted with considerable hostility. The Council of the Americas prepared a critical report on their behalf arguing that business interests were adversely affected and that a number of new investment projects were held up because of the adoption of Decision 24 (Jenkins 1984a, 192). This view has been supported by some academic analysts of Decision 24 who argue that it led to a significant decline in US investment in the area in the early and mid-1970s (Grosse 1980).

On the other hand, it has been argued that Decision 24 was not intended to impede the flow of foreign investment to the region. 'Indeed, despite the initial hostility of American businessmen and the sometimes negative evaluations of Decision 24 made by the Andean corporate managers, it is now quite clear that Decision 24 has not been an obstacle to continued direct foreign investment' (Mytelka 1979, 111). Similarly it has been argued that there has been a continuing or even growing transfer of technology to the main Andean Pact countries (UNCTAD 1980, 8–12).

Evaluation of these two positions is difficult given the available empirical information. This is particularly scanty as far as technology transfer is concerned, but even information on foreign investment is inadequate. Given large-scale divestment by TNCs in the extractive industries in the region in this period, as part of a worldwide trend, the most relevant indicator is investment in manufacturing. Unfortunately data are only available on US investment in manufacturing. While Mytelka (1979, table 3.13) cites the growing absolute level of US DFI in manufacturing in the region in the 1970s, Grosse (1980) compares growth in the Andean Pact countries with other Latin American countries to argue that Decision 24 had a negative effect. While it is true that US DFI in the region continued to grow after the passing of Decision 24, the share of the Andean Pact countries in the increase in the stock of US DFI in Latin America was lower after the passing of Decision 24.[1] However, there is some evidence that non-US investment was not negatively affected. Data on German DFI indicate the share of investment in Latin America going to the Andean Pact countries as increasing between 1965–70 and 1971–6.[2] Moreover the total stock of direct foreign investment in the Andean Pact countries increased only slightly more slowly than all DFI in developing countries between 1971 and 1977.[3] Thus by concentrating exclusively on US investment it appears that Grosse paints an unduly pessimistic picture.

On balance, therefore, it seems that Decision 24 did not have a major negative impact on the total amount of foreign investment in the Andean Pact countries and that it did achieve some of the expected benefits which the proponents of control of TNCs have identified. However, it is also important to bear in mind who the principal beneficiaries of such controls have been. It has not been some abstract notion of national welfare, but rather large local capital whose bargaining strength *vis-à-vis* foreign capital has been increased, and which has been able to participate in the profit from joint-ventures with the TNCs.

BARGAINING

In addition to legislation to control the behaviour of TNC subsidiaries, governments have also resorted to case-by-case negotiation with companies to establish the terms for their operations. Not surprisingly in the case of large-scale extractive operations host governments have tended to negotiate specific terms with investing TNCs rather than enacting general legislation to cover the operations of all TNCs. Over time these contracts have been renegotiated, often reflecting changes in the relative bargaining strengths of the participants. More recently there has also been a growing emphasis on bargaining in the manufacturing sector, particularly in relation to technology transfer and exports. A notable example is the Brazilian BEFIEX system whereby TNC subsidiaries, particularly in the motor industry, have negotiated individual export targets with the government.

The growing importance of direct negotiations between TNCs and host governments has led a number of writers to develop a bargaining framework for analysing state–TNC relations. This was initially applied to the division of extractive industry rents (Mikesell 1970; Vernon 1977, ch. 2) but subsequently extended by TNC critics from the special case of natural resource rents to the general case of monopoly rents on foreign investment.

A brief consideration of the neo-classical view shows why bargaining can only be a special case within this framework. In the normal case there is a direct and continuous relationship between the flow of foreign investment and the rate of return. Government attempts to increase its share of the output from foreign investment, through, for example, taxation, will lead to a reduction in the inflow of investment because of the lower post-tax rate of return. Where investment takes place under non-competitive conditions, however, the existence of monopoly rents implies that the host government can tax part of those rents without having any adverse effect on the inflow of foreign capital (see Streeten 1981, ch. 15 for a diagrammatic exposition).

The bargaining approach as generally conceived is premised on a number of assumptions. Bargaining takes place between two independent parties (TNC and government) each having well-defined objectives. Each party has particular advantages to offer the other, e.g. advanced technology in the case of the TNC; access to the local market or the supply of minerals in the case of the government. It is then a matter of evaluating the bargaining strengths of the parties concerned in order to determine the outcome of the negotiation. Bargaining strengths may change over time, either because of the investment cycle in natural resource industries, so that the TNCs' bargaining power is at a maximum in the pre-investment stage, or because of general developments such as changing competitive conditions in the market for a particular technology, or growing knowledge and experience on the part of host country negotiators.

While this model has provided several useful insights to the analysis of host-government–TNC relations, particularly in extractive industries, it suffers from a number of weaknesses. It is premised on a view of the state as the embodiment of the 'national interest' of the host country, and fails to recognize the existence of conflicting class interests within the host country. The internal structure of the host country and in particular its class structure are not incorporated into the general model and can only be included in an *ad hoc* manner (Fortin 1979, 220, n. 2). Following on from this perspective, it assumes that the state is a coherent body with clearly defined aims. While this is a reasonable assumption to make in the case of the TNC with centralized management and a relatively small number of simple objectives, it is hardly adequate in the case of the state. The aims of state policy are likely to be considerably more complex than those of the TNCs, while, as was pointed out above, the state apparatuses of Third World countries are often characterized by high levels of fragmentation and incoherence. Case studies of TNC–state relations illustrate the difficulties of pursuing any consistent policy towards foreign capital (Philip 1976, on Peruvian policies towards IPC) and the internal conflicts within the state apparatus over such policies (Bennett and Sharpe 1979).

A further problem of this approach is the view that the TNC and the state are two independent parties with conflicting objectives. Once it is recognized that the state is not a monolithic body, then attention must be given to the channels of influence which the TNCs enjoy within the state apparatus. These extend from direct bribery and corruption of government officials and ministers to more subtle forms of influence whereby particular departments come to see things from the point of view of the companies concerned. Although by its very nature, information on the extent of bribery and corruption by TNCs is incomplete, there is ample evidence to illustrate its existence. Major US TNCs which are known to have made illegal or questionable payments in the 1970s include Exxon, ITT, United Brands, General Tire, Goodyear, American Home Products, Johnson and Johnson, Merck and Warner Lambert (Jacoby et al. 1977, table 3). Such payments are particularly prevalent in industries such as aerospace, pharmaceuticals, tobacco, oil, rubber and chemicals, reflecting the considerable government regulations in many of these industries (ibid., table 4).

That some bribery can affect government control of and bargaining with TNCs is vividly illustrated by the case of United Brands in Honduras. This is of particular interest because it relates to the attempt of the banana exporting countries to repeat the success of OPEC. In 1974 the Union de Paises Exportadores de Banano (UPEB) was formed and three of its members (Honduras, Costa Rica and Panama, which accounted for over half of United Brands' banana supplies) imposed a tax of $1 on every forty-pound box of bananas, which would have cost the company $20 million a year. In order to undermine this effort United Brands paid the Honduran Economics Minister $1.25 million to have the tax cut to 25 cents a box (ibid., 105–6). As a result of this, and other company pressures, no member country of UPEB succeeded in levying the full $1 tax (Burbach and Flynn 1980, 217).

Even discounting the possibility that TNCs exercise direct influence on the state, there is often considerable convergence of interest between the TNCs and the state. In other words bargaining, far from indicating a fundamentally antagonistic relationship between TNCs and the state, takes place at the margins of a broadly defined common interest.

Finally, there is a tendency for the analysis of bargaining to be undertaken in a vacuum. It is seen as a technical issue abstracted from politics, so that changes in bargaining outcomes are related to technical/economic variables not to political changes. State policies towards foreign investment are divorced from the general context of government policies and the nature of the state that is implementing them. They are also divorced from the general context of world capitalist development.

NATIONALIZATION

The most extreme form of control of ownership consists of the nationalization of foreign owned subsidiaries. Nationalization in Third World countries reached a peak in the mid-1970s with 68 cases in 1974 and 83 in 1975. Subsequently the rate declined to an annual average of only 16 in 1977–9 (UNCTC 1983, 11). A number of points are worth making about nationalization. It has been used by a large number of Third World countries, not simply a few whose orientation might be defined as socialist. Indeed most cases of nationalization in the 1960s and 1970s were selective (Kobrin 1980).

A significant proportion of the firms nationalized received compensation (see Williams 1975, for details on the period 1956–72). Thirdly, nationalization does not always involve a complete break with the TNCs, and they may well continue after nationalization to be involved in running the nationalized enterprise, through a management contract, or in marketing its output. Finally, nationalization has been particularly heavily concentrated in the primary sector with mining, oil and agriculture accounting for a large share of both firms and value of assets taken over (Williams 1975; Kobrin 1980).

Orthodox economists tend to view the question of nationalization in cost-benefit terms, unless on the extreme right they invoke the sanctity of private property. It is then a question to be settled in each individual case whether the benefits of nationalization outweigh the costs. Neoclassical writers tend to expect the costs to exceed the benefits, while the reverse is true of those writers who emphasize the market power of the TNCs. The cost-benefit calculation may also differ from country to country and sector to sector.

The possible benefits of nationalization include the appropriation of profits which would otherwise have accrued to foreign capital, a reduction in the outflow of foreign exchange, the development of an integrated national industry through forward and backward linkages, increased employment, replacement of expatriate managers and technicians by nationals and the potential for greater control over the national economy, i.e. increased autonomy.

On the other hand, a number of costs must be set against the potential benefits. Most obviously these are the direct costs of compensation to be paid to the companies affected. Unless compensation which is regarded as adequate by the companies is paid they are in a position to exacerbate a number of other costs which may occur. These include marketing problems, and a lack of adequate financial resources for new investment. Other costs often cited by critics of nationalization include the inherent inefficiency of state enterprises which are not governed by market criteria and the increased opportunities for corruption which are believed to be associated with nationalization (Sigmund 1980, 271–4).

This cost-benefit approach to nationalization sees it as one of a whole range of policy options facing Third World governments ranging from outright expropriation without compensation through joint-ventures to screening and control of foreign investment and special tax regimes. In other words nationalization can be seen as one government option within a broader framework of state–TNC bargaining. A not infrequent conclusion of this approach is that host governments can often get better terms without resorting to full-scale nationalization (Caves 1982, 123).

The problems with this type of approach, as with all cost-benefit analysis, is that it isolates the particular firm or industry under consideration from its wider context, and that it assumes the existence of a government attempting to maximize national welfare (see Lall and Streeten 1977, ch. 12, for a critique). It is this which distinguishes orthodox approaches from Marxist approaches to nationalization.

Nore, analysing the oil nationalizations of the 1970s, distinguishes two diametrically opposed views:

One claims nothing fundamental has changed in the relationship between producer states and imperialism. Dependence and imperialist domination have simply taken on new forms. The other interpretation sees the nationalization as part of a struggle waged by the people of the Third World against imperialism.   (Nore 1980, 69)

What both these approaches suffer from is an excessive level of generalization. In practice any nationalization can only be analysed in the context of the specific character of the state concerned, the class structure on which it is based and the development project being implemented, as well as the specific pattern of capital accumulation in the industry concerned (Fortin 1979).

Nationalization of foreign subsidiaries in Third World countries has been carried out by a variety of different regimes in very different industries. In some cases a capitalist state has sought to acquire control of a key sector in order to promote capitalist development. Thus nationalization is seen as a response to the need for a foreign controlled export sector to play a more dynamic role in the capital accumulation process, either through reduced outflows of foreign exchange, increased output, forward and backward integration or increased state control over surpluses which can then be redirected for accumulation. Nationalization can not only promote accumulation, but it may also prove very important as a means of legitimizing a particular regime in view of the prevalence of nationalist sentiments. In these cases nationalization can often be fairly amicably negotiated and compensation paid to the companies. Examples of nationalization along these lines include the Christian Democrats' Chileanization of copper in the 1960s and the Venezuelan oil nationalization in the 1970s.

Particularly where there is a large surplus available from a foreign owned industry and the state has begun to tap this through taxation or profit-sharing and where local capitalist development is very limited, it is possible that a state bureaucracy may nationalize foreign capital in order to strengthen its own position rather than to promote capitalist development.

Finally, nationalization may form part of a thorough-going attempt at a socialist transformation of society following a major (probably revolutionary) political change. The weakness of a cost-benefit approach to nationalization is particularly clear in such a case, since the whole social framework on which conventional cost-benefit analysis is based is being challenged, and what is at issue is not marginal changes in ownership but fundamental changes in the social relations of production. Nationalization has to be seen then as part of a project to redirect the whole economy and to introduce national economic planning. In these circumstances it is extremely likely that the nationalization process will prove to be conflictual, not simply because of the opposition of the firms affected but because of the wholesale opposition of their home states, particularly the USA, to any project of socialist transformation. In these circumstances the government will gain little from attempting to negotiate acceptable terms for compensation with the companies since this will not reduce the hostility of US imperialism. Consequently it is much more likely that in these cases compensation will not be paid.[4]

US TNCS AND CHILEAN COPPER

The history of relations between the two US copper TNCs, Anaconda and Kennecott, and the Chilean state illustrates many of the issues discussed in previous sections. The relationship evolved from one of *laissez-faire*, through increased government taxation and other policies to redistribute natural resource rents, to joint-ventures and finally total nationalization. It also brings out the complex of internal and external forces which influence state–TNC relations.

The growth of the modern copper industry dates from the last two decades of the nineteenth century. In the United States there was a phase of concentration and centralization of capital in the early twentieth century and by 1910 four major groups dominated the industry. In the next two decades the industry expanded internationally into Latin America and Africa. The industry came to be dominated by a handful of TNCs. By the late 1940s, seven companies (Kennecott, Anaconda, Phelps Dodge, Union Minere, Anglo American, Roan-AMC and Inco) accounted for 70 per cent of copper production in the capitalist world (UNCTC 1981b, 29).

Chile was a major copper producer in the second half of the nineteenth century, at one stage accounting for almost two-thirds of world production. However, with the exhaustion of high-grade ores, the industry declined. US capital entered the Chilean copper industry in the period immediately before World War I and for the first two decades the mines operated as a classic enclave sector, with only about a quarter to a third of the total value of production staying in Chile, made up mainly of labour costs (Girvan 1976a, table 3; Reynolds 1965, statistical appendix).

A number of factors gave rise to increased government pressure on the companies from the 1930s onwards. Until the 1920s nitrates had been the major source of revenue for the Chilean government, but the industry went into decline in the 1920s and it became necessary to look for new sources of income. This was further stimulated by the Great Depression and the resulting collapse of export earnings. However, it would be misleading to see increased financial requirements as the sole cause of increasing pressure on the companies. Major social changes were taking place in Chile at this time. The middle class was becoming an increasingly important political force. Moreover there was also a growing working class which the governments of the day attempted to incorporate through a series of social concessions.

At the same time the economic crisis led to a need for much greater state intervention. This culminated with the Popular Front government which emerged from the 1938 elections. The government established a national development corporation (CORFO) to expand the country's productive capacity, financed by an additional 15 per cent tax on the profits of the copper industry. The combined effect of increasing state economic intervention and growing social expenditure led to government expenditures increasing more than fourfold in real terms between the early 1930s and the early 1950s. In order to replace declining revenue from other sources and to maintain an increased level of state expenditure, the Chilean government increased its share of the surplus generated in copper mining (i.e. of profits plus taxes) more than threefold, from 18 per cent in 1925–34 to 63 per cent in 1945–54. By the early 1950s, copper taxes paid for more than a fifth of all government expenditure.

By the mid-1950s, however, it was clear that these policies were proving counterproductive. The production of the US companies was falling, Chile's share of world copper output was down from over 21 per cent in 1948 to less than 14 per cent in 1953, and there was a need for new investment. These developments coincided with a shift to the right in Chilean politics in the second half of the Ibanez presidency, which was consolidated with the election of Alessandri in 1958. The Chilean bourgeoisie began to become concerned at the degree of state intervention in the economy and saw the establishment of a 'good investment climate' for foreign capital as part of their own campaign to restrain government intervention (Moran 1974, 89).

This led in 1955 to the 'Nuevo Trato' for the copper companies which reduced taxes and abolished the special exchange rate which the industry had had to pay since the 1930s. Despite the much more favourable treatment received by the companies, which led to a substantial increase in profits, there was no significant increase in production and the response of investment was lukewarm, while the share of copper which was refined locally fell by half.

The period of concessions to the US copper companies was fairly short-lived. The failure of the 'Nuevo Trato' and disillusion on the right with US support for agrarian reform under the Alliance for Progress, made them a target for a broad spectrum of political groups in the early 1960s. The Minister of Mines in the Alessandri government sparked off a political crisis by announcing a compulsory programme of increased production and refining for Anaconda and Kennecott. The left, whose candidate, Salvador Allende, had been runner-up in the 1958 presidential elections, advocated wholesale nationalization of the US companies. The Christian Democrats under Frei offered a reformist alternative to socialism – the 'Revolution in Liberty'. This alternative involved Chileanization of the copper companies, whereby the government would negotiate a shareholding in the mines. The motives which lay behind Chileanization were twofold. First, it was designed to encourage large new investments in the copper industry which would generate a substantial increase in export earnings. Secondly, it was an important element in presenting the Christian Democrats as a radical alternative to the left in the 1964 elections, which the US government in its Alliance for Progress phase of promoting reform in order to forestall revolution, looked on favourably. Frei himself also saw the copper programme as the main plank of his development plan which would help him finance agrarian reform, urban welfare and economic development (Moran 1974, 127).

The Frei Chileanization was a classic example of a non-conflictual government takeover of some of the assets of US TNCs. The companies emerged rather well from it. Indeed the apparently most radical part of the programme, the acquisition of a 51 per cent government share in Kennecott's subsidiary, was in fact proposed by the company itself. The agreement left the company far better off than before with a 49 per cent shareholding in a company valued at four times its previous worth. Without putting in any new money, Kennecott would be getting 49 per cent of the profits on an output increased by almost two-thirds at a tax rate which had been cut from over 80 per cent to 44 per cent. The company also obtained a ten-year management contract. It succeeded in creating a web of international links involving US AID, the US EXIM Bank and a consortium of European banks and Japanese institutions, which subsequently created major problems for the Allende government when it nationalized the company. Initially Anaconda, the other major company, agreed only to sell 25 per cent of the small new Exotica mine to the government. In 1969, however, it came under pressure to accept Chileanization but the company asked for full nationalization with compensation. By that date, with a prospect of a left victory in the elections the following year, the company preferred to divest in Chile and concentrate on its newly discovered deposits in the United States and Australia.

Despite these strategies by the companies, the victory of Popular Unity in the 1970 presidential elections led to the outright nationalization of the companies without compensation, as part of a broader programme of transition to socialism. In determining the compensation to which the companies were entitled, the government deducted excess profits made by the companies in previous years from the book value of their investment, so that Anaconda was left owing the government $78 million and Kennecott, $310 million. Clearly the companies' and the

US government's response to the Allende nationalizations was quite different from their response to Frei's Chileanization programme. Kennecott in particular pursued the Chilean government in US and European courts, creating difficulties for the sale of Chilean copper and the government was forced to accept all the subsidiary's international obligations. The US government cut off aid to Chile, put pressure on multilateral agencies to do likewise and engaged in political destabilization. Although Anaconda received no compensation during the three years in which Popular Unity was in power, after the 1973 military coup it did receive generous compensation.

It would be too simplistic to attribute US hostility towards the Popular Unity government to the latter's nationalization of Anaconda and Kennecott, and to believe that had the companies been offered more generous terms, the opposition of the US would have disappeared. US policy was not dictated by the immediate interests of a handful of foreign investors but by a much broader strategic assessment of the influence which a successful socialist experiment would have in Latin America and elsewhere. As Girvan points out, 'The Chilean copper expropriations became an issue not so much for their intrinsic as for their symbolic significance' (Girvan 1976, 92).

It is very difficult to evaluate the success of the nationalization of the Chilean copper industry given the difficult internal and external conditions of the time. While some critics have pointed to the problems posed by declining labour discipline, sectarian struggles within the nationalized mines and the departure of qualified workers, both North Americans and Chileans, the most intractable problems facing the nationalized copper industry were in its relations to the world market. This involved not only the problems posed by the companies' attempts to secure compensation, but also the constraints which producing for the world market imposes on the nationalized producer. The tendency for the major copper TNCs to diversify internationally and to integrate vertically to obtain secure sources of supply or markets threatens to push the Third World state enterprises into suppliers of last resort and carriers of world excess capacity. The alternative is for the state companies to join the international oligopoly and play according to its rules (Moran 1974, 242). There could scarcely be a more telling illustration of the constraints which the world market places on nationalized producers.

Until the Popular Unity government (1970–3) Chilean policy towards the US copper companies had been determined by the need to promote capital accumulation and to reproduce capitalist relations of production. From the 1930s until the mid-1950s, this involved increased pressure on the companies in order to increase the government's share of rents from the mines. From the mid-1950s to 1970 the emphasis switched to attempts to increase investment by the companies, first through reduced taxation and subsequently by establishing joint-ventures.

Chilean copper policy has never been a coherent expression of a well defined 'national interest'. Rather it has been the outcome of struggle between different classes and class fractions, which has depended partly on the balance of forces at any particular time, as with the shift to more liberal policies in the mid-1950s, and partly on changing positions adopted by particular groups. An example of the latter is the hostility of landowners to the US companies from the early 1960s, in marked contrast to their pro-company position in earlier years. Such conflicts have even manifested themselves within the state apparatus as in the case of the dispute between Alessandri and his Minister of Mines over the programme for compulsory expansion of production in the early 1960s.

The international system has also placed major constraints on Chilean policy towards the copper industry. This is most obvious in the period since 1970. However, it is also evident in the decade after World War II which culminated in the 'Nuevo Trato' of 1955. These pressures derive from the insertion of Chile in the world economy and are both directly political and economic.

NOTES

1 Between 1965 and 1970 Colombia, Peru and Venezuela accounted for 19.1 per cent of the increase in US DFI in Latin American manufacturing. This fell to 11.8 per cent in the period 1970 to 1976 (calculated from US Department of Commerce, Survey of Current Business, various issues).

2 The same three countries mentioned above increased their share of German foreign investment flows to Latin America from 2.4 per cent to 4.5 per cent (Billerbeck and Yasugi 1979, table SI.22).

3 7.4 per cent per annum in the Andean Pact compared to 9.6 per cent in all developing countries (UNCTAD 1980, table 3; UNCTC 1983, annex table II.13).

4 Williams (1975) notes that those countries which have carried out the most extensive nationalizations which he characterizes as 'socialist' countries, have compensated a far lower proportion of the assets nationalized. A similar conclusion can be drawn from data on Latin America in Sigmund (1980, table 1), which shows only Cuba and Chile under Allende having carried out substantial nationalization of US firms without paying compensation.

FURTHER READING

Different views on the relationship between the growth of TNCs and the power of nation states are surveyed in Bergsten, Horst and Moran 1977, ch. 9). Holland (1975, ch. 3) documents the way in which TNCs tend to reduce the effectiveness of national economic policies. Murray (1975) and Warren (1975) debate from a Marxist perspective whether internationalization has reduced or increased the power of nation states.

Valuable case studies of the political economy of state–TNC relationships are found in Lall (1980, ch. 9) on pharmaceuticals in Sri Lanka, and Evans (1979, ch. 5) on Brazil.

For general accounts of national and international attempts to regulate TNCs see Hood and Young (1979, 238–81) and UNCTC (1983, ch. III). For a more detailed discussion of the Andean Pact countries' policies, see Mytelka (1979).

The bargaining framework for analysing state–TNC relations is presented in Mikesell (1970, ch. 2) and the notion of the 'obsolescing bargain' in natural resources is discussed in Bergsten, Horst and Moran (1977, 130–40). Critiques of the bargaining model are found in Fortin (1979) and Bennett and Sharpe (1985, ch. 4).

Recent trends in nationalization in Third World countries are described in Williams (1975) and Kobrin (1980). For an early attempt to identify the benefits to host countries of nationalization see Bronfenbrenner (1955). Two volumes of case studies of nationalization from opposite ends of the ideological spectrum provide interesting reading – Sigmund (1980) and Girvan (1976a).

There is an extensive bibliography on the Chilean copper industry of which Moran (1974) is outstanding. Also worth consulting are Girvan (1976a, ch. 2) and Reynolds (1965).

9

Conclusion: future prospects

Prediction is always a risky business and speculation concerning the future of the transnational corporation is no exception to this rule. The predictions of the 1960s that 'the nation state is just about through as an economic unit' (Kindleberger 1969, 207) and that 'the nation state is becoming obsolete: tomorrow it will in any meaningful sense be dead – and so will the corporation that remains essentially national' (*Business International* quoted in Barnet and Müller 1974, 19) seem rather dated in the 1980s. Claims that by 1985, between 200 and 300 global corporations would control 80 per cent of productive assets in the non-Communist world (Perlmutter quoted in Barnet and Müller 1974, 26) have proved to be extremely exaggerated. Nevertheless analysts of the TNCs continue to make predictions about their future. By way of conclusion therefore we shall consider the alternative scenarios sketched out for each of the major approaches to the TNCs discussed in this book.

NEO-CLASSICAL THEORY

The global neo-classical vision of the dynamic growth of the TNC sweeping away the nation state and leading to the creation of a world federal government (Johnson 1970) has been substantially tempered in more recent neo-classical discussions. The contemporary view is that some of the ownership advantages of the TNCs have been eroded, while at the same time increasing international competition and the operation of the 'obsolescing bargain' in the extractive industries have led to increased bargaining power of host governments, which has in turn led to a decline in the internalization advantages of TNC operations. For some the consequence is that 'the multinational tide is ebbing' (Rose 1977). More generally, however, what is predicted is that the traditional TNCs involved in extracting raw materials and in producing technologically standardized products will decline in importance, as will the extent of majority owned subsidiaries. On the other hand, TNCs will

continue to grow in importance in industries in which there are important economies from international integration and optimization, both
through the use of export platforms and regional integration (Dunning
1983). There will also be a continued growth of joint-ventures, often
involving state firms in the Third World, and licensing. TNCs which
are willing and able to adapt to these new conditions will continue to
expand, but other firms are likely to become less multinational (Buckley
and Casson 1976, ch. 5).

As far as the Third World is concerned, TNCs are likely to play a continuing role in the future. Despite the increased bargaining power of host
governments this is unlikely to be used to exclude foreign capital (Vernon
1981). TNCs will still have an important role to play where they can
provide access to developed country markets (Vernon 1973, 246), and
where they have specialized skills in the adaptation of products to Third
World environments (Buckley and Casson 1976, 104). A number of
factors will prevent the environment for TNCs in Third World
countries from becoming unduly restrictive. In addition to the economic
advantages which the TNCs can offer, their ability to circumvent
controls also limits the viability of restrictive measures. Finally, the
growth of Third World TNCs tends to reduce hostility towards foreign
TNCs and leads to less restrictive policies. Providing then that host
countries do not impose excessive restrictions on TNCs in the future,
they can make a major contribution to Third World development, particularly through their contribution to establishing a new international
division of labour in which the Third World becomes a major exporter
of manufactured goods.

GLOBAL REACH

In contrast the Global Reach approach maintains that increasing
competition will not dilute the market power of the TNCs in the foreseeable future. What is foreseen, however, is that the very power of the
TNCs will generate hostile reactions. Barnet and Müller (1974, 21–5)
identify three groups of opponents of the TNCs: labour, government
bureaucrats and young people. As awareness of the power of the TNCs,
and the monopoly rents which they appropriate, grows, new forms of
countervailing power against the TNCs emerge. For most writers in this
tradition, the major countervailing force to the TNC will be the state.

In some respects therefore the projected scenario can be described as
one of benign mercantilism (cf. Gilpin 1975). This involves a major shift
away from the liberal economic order that characterized the quarter
century after World War II, to an international system with much

greater state control of international economic relations on either a national or regional (e.g. EEC) scale. For these writers the shift to less nationalistic policies towards the TNCs in many countries in the late 1970s and early 1980s, is not an indication of a new era of peaceful coexistence in TNC–host country relations (as the neo-classical approach suggests) but rather a temporary lull brought about by a weakening of the bargaining power of many host countries as a result of increased international indebtedness (Newfarmer 1983).

A second countervailing force which some authors have argued will emerge in response to the growth of the TNCs, is international trade union organizations (Levinson 1972). In the same way as the growth of state controls is predicted as a response to the conflict between the global interests of the TNCs and the national interest of individual states, so the undermining of purely national trade union organization by the growth of TNCs is predicted to bring about the establishment of international organizations.

In the Third World measures to control TNCs are likely to involve a more significant role for the state in the economy, including the growth of national economic planning. Again although some role will still be played by TNCs in the Third World this is likely to be much less dominant than in the past, with a correspondingly enhanced role for state and private local capital.

NEO-IMPERIALIST THEORIES

The neo-imperialist view foresees further concentration and centralization of capital on a world scale in the form of continued TNC expansion. This is associated with a continuation of US hegemony and the reinforcing of the hierarchy of nation states through a corporate international division of labour in which the Third World is assigned the role of 'hewers of wood and drawers of water' while R & D and management and the associated high-skill and high-income jobs are concentrated in the advanced capitalist countries (Hymer 1979, ch. 2). Some Third World countries may be able to improve their position relatively, differentiating themselves from the majority of Third World countries to form a semi-periphery, an intermediate stratum between the advanced capitalist countries and most of the Third World (Girvan 1975). However, the hierarchy of development is maintained and these countries will never be able to form part of the developed centre (Frank 1981, ch. 1).

Within the Third World countries, the prospect is of growing polarization between a small minority of 'haves' who are integrated into the international system and the vast majority of 'have nots' who are increasingly marginalized. The counterpart of transnational integration is national disintegration in the Third World (Sunkel 1973). Two alternative scenarios are offered for the world economy – world empire or world revolution (Sweezy and Magdoff 1969, 13). Continued growth of the TNCs involves the main instrument of the TNCs in the world today, the US government, doing its best to maintain a world of obedient satellites.

An alternative socialist path of development independent of the TNCs is often postulated, but rarely spelt out in detail. Consistent with the implicit voluntarism of much of this tradition, the mechanisms by which this alternative might be brought about are rarely spelt out.

NEO-FUNDAMENTALIST

The main predictions of this approach are of continued inter-capitalist competition on an international scale and rapid capitalist development in the Third World. Extrapolating the tendencies of the 1950s and 1960s, it is expected that the bargaining power of host governments in the Third World will continue to grow. The role of TNCs in the Third World will probably decline with increasing indigenous control and ownership of previously foreign-owned domestically located assets (Warren 1973, 41).

The most controversial prediction is that far from reinforcing a stable hierarchy of capital accumulation in favour of the metropolitan countries, uneven development of the capitalist mode of production leads to changing hierarchies of development and the emergence of new power centres throughout the Third World (Warren 1973, 43). In so far as the TNCs have played an important role in promoting capitalist development in the Third World, then the implication must be that they have planted the seeds of their own destruction through the creation of new centres of competition (including possibly Third World TNCs).

INTERNATIONALIZATION OF CAPITAL

The earlier approaches discussed differ over whether in the future internationalizing or nationalizing tendencies will dominate in the world economy. The neo-classicals and the neo-imperialists expect the dominant trend to be internationalization, whereas the Global Reach approach and the neo-fundamentalists view the future in terms of the dominance of nationalizing tendencies. Perhaps, however, this is again a false polarity, and the future should be viewed more in terms of the dialectic between internationalization and nationalization. The internationalization of capital approach predicts that continuing concentration and centralization of capital on an international scale will lead to intens-ified competition. But it has also been argued that intensified inter-national competition leads capital to seek support from the state (Rowthorn 1975, 177). Thus internationalization and nationalizing tendencies are not opposed trends but two sides of the same process (cf. Bukharin 1917).

Another aspect of this process is that although the internationalization of capital is leading to the demise of the national economy (Radice 1984), this is not the same as the demise of the nation state. In this situation tensions are bound to arise in the future between TNCs and nation states, and between states. Such conflicts should be seen, however, as a manifestation of the inherently contradictory nature of the international-ization of capital, rather than as a result of a fundamental opposition between the TNC and the nation state (Radice 1975, 18).

Within this perspective, it is entirely possible that the forms taken by the internationalization of capital may change in the future, and TNCs as currently constituted may even decline in importance. What is predicted, however, is that the internationalization of capital (of which the TNCs as we have argued before are only an institutional manifesta-tion) will continue to characterize the world economy in the future. In contrast to current neo-classical thinking with its stress on the form of international involvement (DFI, licensing, exports), the international-ization of capital approach is more concerned with the processes at work in the world economy rather than the precise institutional form in which they manifest themselves.

In the Third World it is predicted that uneven development will lead to increasing differentiation of the periphery. New centres of accumulation may well emerge in the Third World. However, this does not necessarily mean that the geographical hierarchy of accumulation can be substantially changed as Warren argues. There are strong forces attracting new capital accumulation to existing areas where the forces of production are highly developed (Murray 1972). The much heralded new international division of labour is proving to be a mirage as the objective conditions which gave rise to selective relocation to the Third World in the 1960s and 1970s are changing (Jenkins 1984b). Moreover there are serious doubts concerning the ability of the international economic order to absorb a significant number of new Japans (OU 1983, 111).

Finally, it is impossible to make any unambiguous predictions concern-ing future relations between TNCs and the state in the Third World. That both will continue to play a role in accumulation seems probable. Indeed there may be a growing convergence of interest as an alliance between state capital and the TNCs is consolidated in some Third World countries. However, relations are likely to vary over time (between periods of growth and recession) and over space (between countries depending on class structure and the nature of the regime in power). Even where socialist governments come to power in the Third World it is unlikely that they will totally exclude the TNCs, as the experience of Angola and the recent attempts of China and Cuba to attract foreign investment illustrate.

CONCLUSION

Despite the fact that concern over the impact of TNCs on the Third World, which was such a prominent feature of the development discussions of the 1970s, has receded somewhat in the 1980s with the burgeoning debt problem moving into the headlines, the issues discussed in this book will continue to be hotly debated in the foreseeable future. In an area where the ratio of heat to light generated in the past has often been high, it is my hope that this book has contributed both to shedding more light on the activities of TNCs, and to understanding why so much heat has been generated.

In their own ways each of the perspectives discussed in this book has contributed to understanding certain aspects of the impact of TNCs in the Third World. It is my belief that the internationalization of capital approach provides the richest understanding of these issues because it recognizes the fact that TNCs are bearers of wider forces within the capitalist mode of production and cannot be analysed in isolation, but only as a manifestation of these forces. In particular the TNCs are a manifestation of the competitive nature of the capitalist mode of production at three levels: the competition of capital and labour over the production of surplus value, the competition between capitals over the distribution of surplus value and the competition among workers. By way of conclusion, then, I shall briefly summarize the main insights into the impact of TNCs in the Third World which this perspective provides.

In chapter 3, having distinguished between different conceptions of competition and monopoly, I argued that the international expansion of capital should be seen as an outcome of competition rather than monopoly as some critics have argued. I also showed that both at the international and the national levels the growth of TNCs involves a dialectic of competition and monopoly since the competitive struggle takes the form of a search for quasi-monopolistic positions which generate surplus profits.

Chapter 4 brings out a number of ways in which the development and commercialization of technology is conditioned by competition.

Capital–labour competition within the labour process makes mechanization the dominant tendency of technological change under capitalism as capital seeks to secure control over production, while competition between capitals ensures that the technique which has the lowest unit cost will be introduced. This explains the prevalence of capital-intensive techniques and Fordist or Taylorist labour processes in many TNC subsidiaries in the Third World. The cost of technology and the restrictive clauses so frequently found in technology contracts are a reflection of the existence of surplus profits and attempts to reproduce those surplus profits which characterize modern capitalism.

Seeing competition in terms of the mobility of capital within the TNC leads to new insights into the much discussed questions of the 'drain of surplus' from Third World countries and the 'enclave' nature of much TNC activity. I showed in chapter 5 that these derive primarily from the logic of capital accumulation rather than the institutional form of the TNC. Similarly, the prevalence of intra-firm trade and the extent of transfer pricing were shown to be a consequence of the contradiction between the socialization of production and the continued private appropriation of profit which accompanies the development of capitalism. These factors lie behind the much discussed transfer pricing strategies of TNCs which are so often discussed in institutionalist terms.

The internationalization of capital raises major questions for labour. The most fundamental is undoubtedly how to respond to the intensified competition between workers which it brings about. At the national level, trade union organizations have operated to reduce such competition, but internationally capital has found enormously expanded opportunities to divide and rule, which labour has as yet been able to do little to counter (see chapter 6).

Institutional approaches to the TNC have often counterposed the 'bad' TNC to the 'good' national firm, in terms of their impact on development in the Third World. Viewing TNCs as a particular form taken by competitive capital leads to a more critical approach. In chapter 7, I show how competition between foreign and local capital often leads to very similar behaviour by both types of firm. It also brings out more clearly the real significance of the internationalization of capital from Third World countries themselves.

Finally, in chapter 8, I argued that the relative autonomy of the state derives from various aspects of competition within the capitalist mode of production. This helps explain why the state in Third World countries sometimes apparently intervenes in favour of the TNCs and sometimes against them. Furthermore, competition is often reproduced within the state apparatus, making it difficult to conceive of any coherent state policy *vis-à-vis* the TNCs, contrary to the assumptions of simplistic bargaining theories.

The picture that we get of the TNCs in the Third World is complex and contradictory. There is no doubt that the pictures of the TNC as a knight on a white charger coming to the rescue of Third World countries, or as the evil genius behind all their problems are more appealing. But since capitalist development is itself both uneven and contradictory, it is hardly surprising that the impact of the TNC is also uneven and contradictory.

FURTHER READING

A useful introduction to alternative models of the future of TNCs is Hood and Young (1979, ch. 9). For particular views of the future of TNCs see Buckley and Casson (1976, ch. 5), Vernon (1977, ch. 9), Hymer (1979, ch. 2) and Sunkel (1973). The last two focus particularly on the implications for the Third World.

Glossary

Concentration and centralization of capital – the twin processes by which firms grow larger. Concentration of capital refers to the internal growth of firms and the elimination of weaker firms; centralization of capital to the merger of firms under common control.

Constant capital – the value of raw materials, intermediate inputs and machinery (depreciation) used up in the production of a commodity.

Cost-benefit analysis – a technique for evaluating the returns to an investment project using prices other than market prices where the latter are either unavailable or do not reflect the social costs and benefits of certain inputs or outputs.

Direct foreign investment – investment overseas where the investing firm acquires *control* over the firm in which it invests. This is usually regarded as requiring ownership of a certain minimum percentage, say 10 per cent, of the shares of the foreign subsidiary.

Isoquant – a curve showing the different combinations of capital and labour which can be used by a firm to produce a given output of a particular good.

Net present value – the value of the excess of future benefits over costs during the lifetime of a project discounted to the present.

Oligopoly – a situation in which there are a small number of firms in an industry, so that each firm is conscious of the mutual interdependence of their actions.

Pareto Optimality – an economic situation in which no one can be made better off without making someone else worse off.

Portfolio investment – acquisition of foreign securities without any control over, or participation in, the management of the companies concerned.

Public good – goods which cannot be divided up and consumed individually, but which are available to additional consumers at no extra cost. The classic example is a lighthouse.

Social marginal cost – the additional cost to society of producing an additional unit of a good.

Socially necessary labour time – the amount of labour of average efficiency required to produce a commodity under the normal technological conditions of the time.

Surplus value – the excess of value created by labour over the value equivalent of the wage received, which is the basis of profit in capitalist society.

Value – exchange value. The quantity of socially necessary labour time required for the production of a commodity.

Variable capital – that part of capital which is used to hire workers.

Bibliography

Adam, G. (1975) 'Multinational corporations and worldwide sourcing', in H. Radice (ed.), *International Firms and Modern Imperialism*, Harmondsworth, Penguin.

Agmon, T. and Hirsch, S. (1979) 'Multinational corporations and the developing economies: potential gains in a world of imperfect markets and uncertainty', *Oxford Bulletin of Economics and Statistics*, November.

Agrawal, R. G. (1981) 'Third world joint ventures: Indian experience', in K. Kumar and R. G. McLeod (eds), *Multinationals from Developing Countries*, Lexington, Mass., Lexington Books.

Altvater, E. (1973) 'Multinational corporations and labour class', in K. Tudyka (ed.), *Multinational Corporations and Labour Unions*, Nijmegen, SUN.

Amin, S. (1977) *Imperialism and Unequal Development*, Hassocks, Harvester.

Arrighi, G. (1970) 'International corporations, labour aristocracies and economic development in tropical Africa', in G. Arrighi and J. S. Saul, *Essays on the Political Economy of Africa*, New York, Monthly Review Press, 1973.

Arrow, K. (1962) 'Economic welfare and the allocation of resources for invention', in *The Rate and Direction of Inventive Activity: Economic and Social Factors*, National Bureau of Economic Research, Special Conference Series no. 13, Princeton University Press.

Arruda, M. *et al.* (1975) *Multinationals and Brazil: The Impact of Multinational Corporations in Contemporary Brazil*, Toronto, Brazilian Studies, Latin American Research Unit.

Babson, S. (1973) 'The multinational corporation and labour', *Review of Radical Political Economics*, 1.

Baer, W. (1976) 'Technology, employment and development: empirical findings', *World Development*, 4, 2.

Balasubramanyam, V. N. (1980) *Multinational Enterprises and the Third World*, London, Trade Policy Research Centre, Thames Essay no. 26.

Baran, P. (1973) *The Political Economy of Growth*, Harmondsworth, Penguin.

Baran, P. and Sweezy, P. (1966) *Monopoly Capital: An Essay on the American Economic and Social Order*, Harmondsworth, Penguin.

Barnet, R. and Müller, R. (1974) *Global Reach: The Power of the Multinational Corporations*, New York, Simon & Schuster.

Barratt Brown, M. (1974) *Economics of Imperialism*, Harmondsworth, Penguin.

Bennett, D. and Sharpe, K. (1979) 'Agenda setting and bargaining power in the Mexican automobile industry: the Mexican state vs transnational automobile companies', *World Politics*, 32(1).

Bennett, D. and Sharpe, K. (1985) *Transnational Corporations versus the State*, Princeton University Press.

Benviganti, A. (1985) 'An empirical investigation of international transfer-pricing by U.S. manufacturing firms', in A. Rugman and L. Eden (eds), *Multinationals and Transfer Pricing*, London, Croom Helm.

Bergsten, F., Horst, T. and Moran, T. (1977) *American Multinationals and American Interests*, Washington, The Brookings Institution.

Bernal Sahgun, V. (1976) *The Impact of Multinational Corporations on Employment and Income: The Case of Mexico*, Geneva, International Labour Office.

Biersteker, T. (1978) *Distortion or Development? Contending Perspectives on the Multinational Corporation*, Cambridge, Mass., MIT Press.

Billerbeck, K. and Yasugi, Y. (1979) *Private Direct Foreign Investment in Developing Countries*, Washington, World Bank Staff Working Paper, 348.

Blair, J. (1976) *The Control of Oil*, New York, Pantheon Books.

Blaug, M. (1971) 'A survey of the theory of process-innovation', in N. Rosenberg (ed.), *The Economics of Technological Change*, Harmondsworth, Penguin.

Braverman, M. (1974) *Labour and Monopoly Capital*, New York, Monthly Review Press.

Brewer, A. (1980) *Marxist Theories of Imperialism: A Critical Survey*, London, Routledge & Kegan Paul.

Bronfenbrenner, M. (1955) 'The appeal of confiscation in economic development', *Economic Development and Cultural Change*, III, 3.

Brooke, M. S. and Remmers, H. L. (1973) *The Strategy of Multinational Enterprise*, London, Longman.

Bryan, R. (1985) 'Monopoly in Marxist method', *Capital and Class*, 26.

Buckley, P. and Casson, M. (1976) *The Future of Multinational Enterprise*, London, Macmillan.

Bukharin, N. (1917) *Imperialism and World Economy*, London, Merlin.

Burbach, R. and Flynn, P. (1980) *Agribusiness in the Americas*, New York, Monthly Review Press/NACLA.

Burkett, P. (1986) 'A note on competition under capitalism', *Capital and Class*, 30.

Business Monitor (1983) *Overseas Transactions 1983*, London, HMSO.

Caputto, O. and Pizarro, R. (1970) *Desarrollismo y Capital Extranjero*, Santiago de Chile, Ediciones de la Universidad Tecnica del Estado.

Cardoso, F. H. (1972) 'Dependency and development in Latin America', *New Left Review*, 74.

Casson, M. (1979) *Alternatives to the Multinational Enterprise*, London, Macmillan.

Caves, R. (1982) *Multinational Enterprise and Economic Analysis*, Cambridge University Press.

Caves, R., Porter, M. and Spence A. with J. T. Scott (1980) *Competition in the Open Economy. A Model Applied to Canada*, Cambridge, Mass., Harvard University Press.

Chen, E. (1983) *Multinational Corporations, Technology and Employment*, London, Macmillan.

Chen, E. (1984) 'Multinationals from Hong Kong', in S. Lall (ed.), *The New Multinationals: The Spread of Third World Enterprises*, Chichester, John Wiley & Sons.

Chudnovsky, D. (1979a) 'Foreign Trademarks in Developing Countries', *World Development*, 7.

Chudnovsky, D. (1979b) 'The challenge by domestic enterprises to the transnational corporations' domination. A case study of the Argentine pharmaceutical industry', *World Development*, 7, 1.

Chudnovsky, D. (1981a) *Las subsidiarias en America Latina y el financamiento de la inversion de las ET manufacturas de EUA*, Mexico City, ILET, DEE/D/159/e.

Chudnovsky, D. (1981b) 'Pricing of intra-firm technological transactions', in R. Murray (ed.), *Multinationals Beyond the Market*, Brighton, Harvester.

Chudnovsky, D. (1982) 'The changing remittance behaviour of United States manufacturing firms in Latin America', *World Development*, 10, 6.

Chudnovsky, D. (1983) 'Patents and Trademarks in Pharmaceuticals', *World Development*, 11, 3.

Chudson, W. (1981) 'Intra-firm trade and transfer pricing', in R. Murray (ed.), *Multinationals Beyond the Market*, Brighton, Harvester.

Clairmonte, F. (1981) 'Conglomerate and oligopolistic power in the 1980s', *Raw Materials Report*, 1, 1.

Clark, N. (1975) 'The multinational corporation: the transfer of technology and dependence', *Development and Change*, VI, 1.

Clifton, J. (1977) 'Competition and the evolution of the capitalist mode of production', *Cambridge Journal of Economics*, 1.

Cohen, B. (1973) *The Question of Imperialism: the Political Economy of Dominance and Dependence*, London, Macmillan.

Connor, J. (1977) *The Market Power of Multinationals: A Quantitative Analysis of U.S. Corporations in Brazil and Mexico*, New York, Praeger.

Contreras, G. (1976) *Technology Transfer: A Survey and Some Policy Proposals*, Lima, Office of the Field Co-ordinator, STPI Project, mimeo.

Cooper, C. (1973) 'Choice of techniques and technological change as problems in political economy', *International Social Science Journal*, XXV, 3.

Cooper, C. and Hoffman, K. (1981) *Transactions in Technology and Implications for Developing Countries*, Science Policy Research Unit, University of Sussex, mimeo.

Cox, R. (1976) 'Labour and the multinationals', *Foreign Affairs*, 54, 2.

CSE London Working Group (1980) *The Alternative Economic Strategy*, London, CSE Books.

Curhan, J., Davidson, W. and Suri, R. (1977) *Tracing the Multinationals: A Sourcebook on US-based Enterprises*, Cambridge, Mass., Ballinger Publishing Co.

Cypher, J. (1979) 'The internationalization of capital and the transformation of social formations: a critique of the Monthly Review School', *The Review of Radical Political Economics*, 11, 4.

De la Torre, J. (1972) 'Marketing factors in manufactured exports from developing countries', in L. T. Wells, Jr (ed.), *The Product Life Cycle and International Trade*, Cambridge, Harvard University Press.

Donsimoni, M. P. and Leoz-Arguelles, V. (1980) 'Profitability and international linkages in the Spanish economy', unpublished manuscript, Université Catholique de Louvain.

Dos Santos, T. (1968) 'Foreign investment and the large enterprise in Latin America: the Brazilian case', in J. Petras and M. Zeitlin (eds), *Latin America: Reform or Revolution?* Greenwich, Fawcett Publications.

Dos Santos, T. (1970) 'The structure of dependence', *American Economic Review*, Papers and Proceedings, May.

Dunning, J. (1981) *International Production and the Multinational Enterprise*, London, George Allen & Unwin.

Dunning, J. (1983) 'Changes in the level and structure of international production: the last one hundred years', in M. Casson (ed.), *The Growth of International Business*, London, George Allen & Unwin.

Dunning, J. and Pearce, R. (1985) *The World's Largest Industrial Enterprises 1962–83*, Aldershot, Gower.

ECLA (Economic Commission for Latin America) (1976) *Exportacion de Manufacturas en Mexico y la Politica de Promocion*, CEPAL/MEX/-76/10/Rev. 1.

Edwards, C. (1985) *The Fragmented World*, London, Methuen.

Ellis, F. (1981) 'Export valuation and intra-firm transfers in the banana export industry in Central America', in R. Murray (ed.), *Multinationals Beyond the Market*, Brighton, Harvester.

Elson, D. (1982) 'The Brandt Report: a programme for survival?' *Capital and Class*, 16.

Elson, D. and Pearson, R. (1980) *The Latest Phase of the Internationalization of Capital and its Implications for Women in the Third World*, Brighton, Institute of Development Studies, DP 150.

Emmanuel, A. (1976) 'The multinational corporations and inequality of development', *International Social Science Journal*, XXVIII.

Emmanuel, A. (1982) *Appropriate or Underdeveloped Technology?* Chichester, Wiley/IRM Series on Multinationals.

Encarnation, D. (1982) 'The political economy of Indian joint industrial venture abroad: a study of domestic policies and transnational linkages', *International Organization*, Winter.

Enderwick, P. (1985) *Multinational Business and Labour*, London, Croom Helm.

Erdilek, A. (1982) *Direct Foreign Investment in Turkish Manufacturing. An Analysis of the Conflicting Objectives and Frustrated Expectations of a Host Country*, Kieler Studien, 169, Tübingen, JCB Mohr.

Evans, J., James, D. and Hoffel, P. (1985) 'Labour in the Argentine motor vehicle industry', in R. Kronish and K. Mericle (eds), *The Political Economy of the Latin American Motor Vehicle Industry*, Cambridge, Mass., MIT Press.

Evans, P. (1977) 'Direct Investment and Industrial Concentration', *Journal of Development Studies*, 13, 4.

Evans, P. (1979) *Dependent Development: the Alliance of Multinational, State and Local Capital in Brazil*, Princeton University Press.

Evers, T. (1979) *El Estado en la Periferia Capitalista*, Mexico City, Siglo XXI.

Fajnzylber, F. (1976) 'Oligopolio, Empresas Transnacionales y Estilos de Desarrollo', *El Trimestre Economico*, 171.

Fajnzylber, F. and Martinez Tarrago, T. (1975) *Las Empresas Trans-nacionales, Expansion a Nivel Mundial y Proyeccion en la Industria Mexicana (Version Preliminar)*, Mexico City, CIDE/CONACYT.

Fine, B. (1975) *Marx's Capital*, London, Macmillan.

Fine, B. and Harris, L. (1979) *Rereading Capital*, London, Macmillan.

Forsyth, D., McBain, N. and Solomon, R. (1980) 'Technical rigidity and appropriate technology in less developed countries', *World Development*, 8, 5/6.

Fortin, C. (1979) 'The state, multinational corporations and natural resources in Latin America', in J. Villamil (ed.), *Transnational Capitalism and National Development*, Hassocks, Harvester.

Frank, A. G. (1969) *Capitalism and Underdevelopment in Latin America*, New York, Monthly Review Press.

Frank, A. G. (1972) *Lumpenbourgeoisie: Lumpendevelopment*, New York, Monthly Review Press.

Frank, A. G. (1980) *Crisis in the World Economy*, London, Heinemann Educational Books.

Frank, A. G. (1981) *Crisis in the Third World*, London, Heinemann Educational Books.

Frank, I. (1980) *Foreign Enterprise in Developing Countries*, Baltimore, Johns Hopkins University Press.

Franko, L. G. (1974) 'The origins of multinational manufacturing by Continental European firms', *Business History Review*, XLVIII, 3.

Franko, L. G. (1976) *Multinational Enterprise, The International Division of Labour in Manufactures and the Developing Countries*, Geneva, ILO, WEP 2–28/WP4.

Franko, L. G. (1978) 'Multinationals: the end of U.S. dominance', *Harvard Business Review*, November–December.

Fransman, M. (1985) 'Conceptualizing technical change in the Third World in the 1980s: an interpretative survey', *Journal of Development Studies*, 21, 4.

Freeman, C. (1974) *The Economics of Industrial Innovation*, Harmonds-worth, Penguin.

Friedman, A. (1977) *Industry and Labour*, London, Macmillan.

Frobel, F., Heinrichs, J. and Kreye, O. (1980) *The New International Division of Labour*, Cambridge University Press.

Fung, S. and Cassiolato, J. (1976) *The International Transfer of Technology to Brazil through Technology Agreements – Characteristics of the Government Control System and the Commercial Transactions*, Cambridge, Mass. Centre for Policy Alternatives, MIT.

Gereffi, G. (1983) *The Pharmaceutical Industry and Dependency in the Third World*, Princeton University Press.

Gereffi, G. (1985) 'The global pharmaceutical industry and its impact in Third World countries', in R. Newfarmer (ed.), *Profits, Progress, Poverty: studies of International Industries in Latin America*, Notre Dame University Press.

Germidis, D. (1977) 'Transfer of technology by multinational corporations and absorptive capacity of the developing countries: a synthesis', in D. Germidis (ed.), *Transfer of Technology by Multinational Corporations*, Paris, OECD Development Centre.

Germidis, D. and Brochet, C. (1975) *The Price of Technology Transfer in Developing Countries*, Paris, OECD Development Centre, Industry and Technology, Special Study, 5.

Gilpin, R. (1975) *U.S. Power and the Multinational Corporation*, New York, Basic Books.

Girvan, N. (1971) *Foreign Capital and Economic Underdevelopment in Jamaica*, Institute of Social and Economic Research, University of the West Indies.

Girvan, N. (1975) 'Economic nationalists v. multinational corporations: revolutionary or evolutionary change?', in C. Widstrand (ed.), *Multinational Firms in Africa*, Uppsala, Scandinavian Institute of African Studies.

Girvan, N. (1976a) *Corporate Imperialism: Conflict and Expropriation*, New York, Monthly Review Press.

Girvan, N. (1976b) *The Impact of Multinational Enterprises on Employment and Income in Jamaica – Preliminary Report*, Geneva, ILO WEP2–28, Working Paper 8.

Gold, D., Lo, C. and Wright, E. (1975) 'Recent developments in Marxist theories of the capitalist state', *Monthly Review*, October and November.

Gorecki, P. (1976) 'The determinants of entry by domestic and foreign enterprises in Canadian manufacturing industries: some comments and empirical results', *Review of Economic Statistics*, 58.

Graham, R. (1982) *The aluminium industry and the Third World*, London, Zed Books.

Greenaway, D. (1983) *International Trade Policy: From Tariffs to the New Protectionism*, London, Macmillan.

Griffin, K. (1970) 'Foreign capital, domestic savings and economic development', *Bulletin of the Oxford University Institute of Economics and Statistics*, May.

Griffin, K. (1978) *International Inequality and National Poverty*, London, Macmillan.

Grosse, R. (1980) 'Foreign investment regulation in the Andean Pact: the first ten years', *Inter-American Economic Affairs*, XXXIII.

Grubel, H. (1977) 'The case against the new international economic order', *Weltwirtschaftliches Archiv*, 113.

Guimaraes, E. (1980) *Industry, Market Structure and the Growth of the Firm in the Brazilian Economy*, Ph.D. Thesis, University of London.

Harris, L. (1977) 'The balance of payments and the international economic system', in F. Green and P. Nore (eds), *Economics: An Anti-Text*, London, Macmillan.

Haworth, N. and Ramsay, H. (1984) 'Grasping the nettle: problems in the theory of international labour solidarity', in P. Waterman (ed.), *For a New Labour Internationalism*, The Hague, ILERI.

Haworth, N. and Ramsay, H. (1986) 'Workers of the world untied', in R. Southall, *Third World Trade Unions and the Changing International Division of Labour*, London, Zed Books.

Heenan, D. and Keegan, W. (1979) 'The rise of Third World multinationals', *Harvard Business Review*, January–February.

Helleiner, G. K. (1975) 'The role of multinational corporations in the less developed countries trade in technology', *World Development*, 3, 4.

Helleiner, G. K. (1976) 'Multinationals, manufactured exports and employment in the less developed countries', in International Labour Office, *Tripartite World Conference on Employment, Income Distribution and Social Progress and the International Division of Labour*, Background paper, *Vol. II*, Geneva.

Helleiner, G. K. (1979) 'Structural aspects of Third World trade: some trends and some prospects', in S. Smith and J. Toye (eds), *Trade and Poor Economies*, London, Frank Cass.

Helleiner, G. K. (1981) 'Intra-firm trade and the developing countries an assessment of the data', in R. Murray (ed.), *Multinationals Beyond the Market*, Brighton, Harvester.

Helleiner, G. K. (ed.) (1982) *For Good or Evil: Economic Theory and North–South Negotiations*, University of Toronto Press.

Henley, J. (1980) 'Capitalist accumulation in the periphery – straw men rule OK?' *Review of African Political Economy*, 17.

Hirata, H. (1981) *Firmes multinationales au Brasil: technologie et organisation du travail*, paper presented to 2nd Seminario Internacional, Crisis, Nuevas Tecnologias y Procesos de Trabajo, UNAM, Mexico City.

Hirschman, A. O. (1968) 'The political economy of import substituting industrialization in Latin America', *Quarterly Journal of Economics*, 82, 1.

Hirschman, A. O. (1969) 'How to divest in Latin America and why', *Essays in International Finance*, 76, Princeton University Press.

Holland, S. (1975) *The Socialist Challenge*, London, Quartet.

Holloway, J and Picciotto, S. (1977) 'Introduction: towards a materialist theory of the state', in J. Holloway and S. Picciotto (eds), *State and Capital: A Marxist Debate*, London, Edward Arnold.

Hood, N. and Young, S. (1979) *The Economics of Multinational Enterprise*, London, Longman.

Hoogvelt, A. (1982) *The Third World in Global Development*, London, Macmillan.

Huggins, H. (1965) *Aluminium in Changing Communities*, London, André Deutsch.

Humphrey, J. (1979) 'Auto workers and the working class in Brazil', *Latin American Perspectives*, 23, Winter.

Humphrey, J. (1980/81) 'Labour use and labour control in the Brazilian automobile industry', *Capital and Class*, 12.

Humphrey, J. (1982) *Capitalist Control and Workers' Struggle in the Brazilian Auto Industry*, Princeton University Press.

Hymer, S. (1976) *The International Operations of National Firms: A Study of Direct Foreign Investment*, Cambridge, Mass., MIT Press.

Hymer, S. (1979) *The Multinational Corporation: A Radical Approach* (papers by S. Hymer, edited by R. Cohen, N. Felton, M. Nkosi and J. van Liere), Cambridge University Press.

Illich, I. (1973) 'Outwitting the "developed" countries', in H. Bernstein (ed.), *Underdevelopment and Development*, Harmondsworth, Penguin.

ILO (International Labour Office) (1981a) *Employment Effects of Multinational Enterprises in Industrialised Countries*, Geneva, ILO.

ILO (1981b) *Employment Effects of Multinational Enterprises in Developing Countries*, Geneva, ILO.

ILO (1984) *Technology Choice and Employment Generation by Multinational Enterprises in Developing Countries*, Geneva, ILO.

IMF (International Monetary Fund) (1985) *Foreign Private Investment in Developing Countries*, Washington DC, IMF.

Ingles, J. and Fairchild, L. (1977) 'Evaluating the impact of foreign investment: methodology and evidence from Mexico, Colombia and Brazil', *Latin American Research Review*, 12, 3.

INTI (Instituto Nacional de Tecnologia Industrial) (1974) *Aspectos Economicos de la Importacion de Tecnologia en la Argentina en 1972*, Buenos Aires, INTI.

IRS (Internal Revenue Service) (1984) *Internal Revenue Service Study of International Cases Involving Section 482 of the Internal Revenue Code*, Washington, Department of the Treasury.

Jacoby, N. (1974) *Multinational Oil*, New York, Macmillan.

Jacoby, N., Nehemkis, P. and Eells, R. (1977) *Bribery and Extortion in World Business. A Study of Corporate Political Payments Abroad*, New York, Macmillan.

James, J. and Stewart, F. (1981) 'New products: a discussion of the welfare effects of the introduction of new products in developing countries', *Oxford Economic Papers*.

Jenkins, R. O. (1977) *Dependent Industrialization in Latin America*, New York, Praeger.

Jenkins, R. O. (1979) 'The export performance of multinational corporations in Mexican industry', *Journal of Development Studies*, 15, 3, April.

Jenkins, R. O. (1984a) *Transnational Corporations and Industrial Transformation in Latin America*, London, Macmillan.

Jenkins, R. O. (1984b) 'Divisions over the international division of labour, *Capital and Class*, 22.

Jenkins, R. O. (1986a) *Transnational Corporations, Competition and Monopoly*, University of East Anglia, mimeo.

Jenkins, R. O. (1986b) *Transnational Corporations and the Latin American Motor Industry*, London, Macmillan.

Jenkins, R. O. (1986c) *Comparing Foreign Subsidiaries and Local Firms in Less Developed Countries: Theoretical Issues and Empirical Evidence*, mimeo, University of East Anglia.

Jessop, B. (1977) 'Recent theories of the capitalist state', *Cambridge Journal of Economics*, 1.

Jo, S. (1976) *The Impact of Multinational Firms on Employment and Incomes: The Case of South Korea*, World Employment Programme Research, WEP 2–28, Geneva, ILO.

Jo, S. (1981) 'Overseas direct investment by South Korean firms: direction and pattern', in K. Kumar and M. G. McLeod (eds), *Multinationals from Developing Countries*, Lexington, Lexington Books.

Johnson, H. G. (1970) *International Economic Questions Facing Britain, the United States and Canada in the 1970s*, London, British–North American Research Association.

Kaplinsky, R. (1979) 'Inappropriate products and techniques: breakfast foods in Kenya', *Review of African Political Economy*, no. 14.

Kaplinsky, R. (1980) 'Capitalist accumulation in the periphery – the Kenyan case re-examined', *Review of African Political Economy*, January–April.

Kaplinsky, R. (1984) 'The international context for industrialization in the coming decade', *Journal of Development Studies*, 21, 1.

Katz, J. (1984) 'Domestic technological innovations and dynamic comparative advantage', *Journal of Development Economics*, 16.

Katz, J. and Kosacoff, B. (1984) 'Multinationals from Argentina', in S. Lall (ed.), *The New Multinationals: The Spread of Third World Enterprises*, Chichester, John Wiley & Sons.

Kennedy, C. and Thirlwall, A. P. (1973) 'Technical progress', in Royal Economic Society, *Survey of Applied Economics*, vol. 1, London, Macmillan.

Kindleberger, C. (1969) *American Business Abroad: Six Lectures on Direct Investment*, New Haven, Yale University Press.

Kirim, A. (1984) 'Do patents really block industrial development in LDCs?' Development Studies Occasional Paper 24, University of East Anglia.

Kirkpatrick, C., Lee, N. and Nixson, F. (1984) *Industrial Structure and Policy in Less Developed Countries*, London, George Allen & Unwin.

Knickerbocker, F. (1973) *Oligopolistic Reaction and Multinational Enterprise*, Cambridge, Mass., Harvard Graduate School of Business Administration.

Knickerbocker, F. (1976) 'Market structure and market power consequences of foreign direct investment by multinational companies', Occasional Paper 8, Washington Center for Multinational Studies.

Kobrin, S. (1980) 'Foreign enterprise and forced divestment in LDCs', *International Organization*, 34, 1.

Kronish, R. and Mericle, K. (eds) (1984) *The Political Economy of the Latin American Motor Vehicle Industry*, Cambridge, Mass., MIT Press.

Kumar, K. (1982) 'Third World multinationals: a growing force in international relations', *International Studies Quarterly*, 26.

Lal, D. (1978) 'On the multinationals', *ODI Review*, 2.

Lall, S. (1974) 'Less-developed countries and private foreign direct investment: a review article', *World Development*, 2, 4 and 5.

Lall, S. (1980) *The Multinational Corporation: Nine Essays*, London, Macmillan.

Lall, S. (1981) *Developing Countries in the International Economy*, London, Macmillan.

Lall, S. (1984a) 'The theoretical background', in S. Lall (ed.), *The New Multinationals: The Spread of Third World Enterprise*, Chichester, John Wiley & Sons.

Lall, S. (1984b) 'Multinationals from India', in S. Lall (ed.), *The New Multinationals: The Spread of Third World Enterprise*, Chichester, John Wiley & Sons.

Lall, S. and Streeten, P. (1977) *Foreign Investment, Transnationals and Developing Countries*, London, Macmillan.

Landsberg, M. (1979) 'Export-led industrialization in the Third World: manufacturing imperialism', *The Review of Radical Political Economics*, 11, 4.

Langdon, S. (1975) 'Multinational corporations, taste transfer and underdevelopment: a case study from Kenya', *Review of African Political Economy*, November.

Langdon, S. (1978) 'The multinational corporation in the Kenya political economy', in R. Kaplinsky (ed.), *Readings on the Multinational Corporation in Kenya*, Nairobi, Oxford University Press.

Langdon, S. (1981) *Multinational Corporations in the Political Economy of Kenya*, London, Macmillan.

Lecraw, D. (1977) 'Direct investment by firms from less developed countries', *Oxford Economic Papers*, November.

Lecraw, D. (1985) 'Some evidence on transfer pricing by multinational corporations', in A. Rugman and L. Eden (eds), *Multinationals and Transfer Pricing*, London, Croom Helm.

Leff, N. (1978) 'Industrial organization and entrepreneurship in the developing countries: the economic groups', *Economic Development and Cultural Change*, 26, July.

Lenin, V. I. (1917) *Imperialism: the Highest Stage of Capitalism*, Moscow, Progress Publishers.

Levinson, C. (1972) *International Trade Unionism*, London, George Allen & Unwin.

Leys, C. (1980) 'Kenya: What does dependency explain?' *Review of African Political Economy*, 17.

Leys, C. (1984) 'Relations of production and technology', in M. Fransman and K. King (eds), *Technological Capability in the Third World*, London, Macmillan.

Lim, L. (1980) 'Women workers in multinational corporations: the case of the electronics industry in Malaysia and Singapore', in K. Kumar (ed.), *Transnational Enterprises: Their Impact on Third World Societies and Cultures*, Boulder, Colorado, Westview Press.

Lipietz, A. (1982) 'Towards global Fordism?' *New Left Review*, 132.

Lipsey, R., Kravis, I. and Roldan, R. (1982) 'Do multinational firms adapt factor proportions to relative factor prices?', in A. Krueger (ed.), *Trade and Employment in Developing Countries, vol. 2, Factor Supply and Substitution*, University of Chicago Press.

Little, I. (1982) *Economic Development*, New York, Basic Books.

Little, I., Scitovsky, T. and Scott, M. (1976) *Industry and Trade in Some Developing Countries*, London, Oxford University Press.

Litvak, I and Maule, C. (1984) 'Assessing industry concentration: the case of aluminium', *Journal of International Business Studies*, Spring/-Summer.

Lucena, H. (1979) 'Nacionalizacion del petroleo y relaciones laborales en Venezuela', in J. Somavia, R. Trajtenberg and J. G. Valdes (eds), *Movimiento Sindical y Empresas Transnacionales*, Mexico City, Editorial Nueva Imagen.

Luiz Possas, M. (1979) *Employment Effects of Multinational Enterprise in Brazil*, Research on Employment Effects of Multinational Enterprise, Working Paper 7, Geneva, ILO.

Luna, M. (1984) 'Industria maquiladora en Mexico. La presencia extranjera', in CIDE, Departamento de Economia Internacional, *Mexico en la Division Internacional del Trabajo*, Mexico City, CIDE.

Lustig, N. (1979) 'Distribucion del ingreso, estructura del consumo y caracteristicas del crecimiento industrial', *Comercio Exterior*, 29, 5.

Madeuf, B. and Michalet, C. A. (1978) 'A new approach to international economics', *International Social Science Journal*, XXX, 2.

Magee, S. (1977) 'Technology and the appropriability theory of the multinational corporation', in J. Bhagwati (ed.), *The New International Economic Order*, Cambridge, MIT Press.

Mamalakis, M. (1970) 'The American copper companies and the Chilean government, 1920–1967', in R. F. Mikesell (ed.), *Foreign Investment in the Petroleum and Mineral Industries: Case Studies of Investor–Host Country Relations*, Baltimore, Johns Hopkins University Press.

Mandel, E. (1975) 'International capital and supranationality', in H. Radice (ed.), *International Firms and Modern Imperialism*, Harmondsworth, Penguin.

Mandel, E. (1976) *Late Capitalism*, London, New Left Books.

Mansfield, E. and Romeo, A. (1980) 'Technology transfer to overseas subsidiaries by US-based firms', *Quarterly Journal of Economics*, 15.

Mansfield, E., Romeo, A. and Wagner, S. (1979) 'Foreign Trade and U.S. Research and Development', *Rev. Econ. Statist*, 61.

Marcussen, H. and Torp, J. (1982) *Internationalization of Capital: prospects for the Third World*, London, Zed Books.

Marx, K. (1867) *Capital*, vol. I, Harmondsworth, Penguin.

May, H. (1970) *Impact of U.S. and Other Foreign Investment in Latin America*, New York, Council of the Americas.

May, H. (1975) *Multinational Corporations in Latin America*, New York, Council of the Americas.

Meier, G. (1972) 'Private foreign investment', in J. Dunning (ed.), *International Investment*, Harmondsworth, Penguin.

Merhav, M. (1969) *Technological Dependence, Monopoly and Growth*, New York, Pergamon Press.

Mericle, K. (1984) 'The political economy of the Brazilian motor vehicle industry', in R. Kronish and K. Mericle (eds), *The Political Economy of the Latin American Motor Vehicle Industry*, Cambridge, Mass., MIT Press.

Mikesell, R. F. (ed.) (1970) *Foreign Investment in the Petroleum and Mineral Industries: Case Studies of Investor–Host Country Relations*, Baltimore, Johns Hopkins University Press.

Minian, I. (1983) 'Internacionalizacion y crisis financiera en America Latina', in I. Minian (ed.) *Transnacionalizacion y Periferia Semindustrializada*, Mexico City, Libros del CIDE.

Montavon, R. (1979) *The Role of Multinational Companies in Latin America: A Case Study in Mexico*, Farnborough, Saxon House.

Moran, T. (1974) *Multinational Corporations and the Politics of Dependence: Copper in Chile*, Princeton University Press.

Moran, T. (1978) 'Multinational corporations and dependency: a dialogue for dependentistas and non-dependentistas', *International Organization*, Winter.

Morley, S. and Smith, G. (1973) 'The effects of changes in the distribution of income on labour, foreign investment and growth in Brazil', in A. Stepan (ed.), *Authoritarian Brazil*, New Haven, Yale University Press.

Morley, S. and Smith, G. (1977) 'The choice of technology: multinational firms in Brazil', *Economic Development and Cultural Change*, vol. 25, no. 2.

Moxon, R. (1979) 'The cost, conditions and adaptation of MNC technology in developing countries', in R. G. Hawkins (ed.), *The Economic Effects of Multinational Corporations*, Greenwich, Conn., JAI Press.

Muller, J. (1984) 'Facilitating an indigenous social organization of production in Tanzania', in M. Fransman and K. King (eds), *Technological Capability in the Third World*, London, Macmillan.

Murray, R. (1972) 'Underdevelopment, the international firm and the international division of labour', in Society for International Development, *Towards a New World Economy*, Rotterdam University Press.

Murray, R. (1975) 'The internationalization of capital and the nation state', in H. Radice (ed.), *International Firms and Modern Imperialism*, Harmondsworth, Penguin.

Murray, R. (ed.) (1981a) *Multinationals Beyond the Market*, Brighton, Harvester.

Murray, R. (1981b) 'Transfer pricing and its control: alternative approaches', in R. Murray (ed.), *Multinationals Beyond the Market*, Brighton, Harvester.

Mytelka, L. (1979) *Regional Development in a Global Economy*, New Haven, Yale University Press.

Nadal, A. (1977) 'Multinational corporations and transfer of technology: the case of Mexico', in D. Germidis, *Transfer of Technology by Multinational Corporations*, Paris, OECD Development Centre.

Nayyar, D. (1977) 'Transnational corporations and manufactured exports from poor countries', *Economic Journal*, 88, March.

Newfarmer, R. (1979) *Transnational Conglomerates and the Economics of Dependent Development*, Greenwich, Conn., JAI Press.

Newfarmer, R. (1983) 'Multinationals and marketplace magic in the 1980s', in C. P. Kindleberger and D. B. Audretsch (eds), *The Multinational Corporation in the 1980s*, Cambridge, Mass., MIT Press.

Newfarmer, R. (1985a) 'International industrial organization and development: a survey', in R. Newfarmer (ed.), *Profits, Progress, Poverty: Studies of International Industries in Latin America*, Notre Dame University Press.

Newfarmer, R. (1985b) 'International oligopoly and uneven development: an introduction to the issues', in R. Newfarmer (ed.), *Profits, Progress, Poverty: Studies of International Industries in Latin America*, Notre Dame University Press.

Newfarmer, R. (ed.) (1985c) *Profits, Progress, Poverty: Studies of International Industries in Latin America*, Notre Dame University Press.

Newfarmer, R. and Marsh, L. (1981) 'Industrial interdependence and development: a study of international linkages and industrial performance in Brazil', University of Notre Dame, mimeo.

Newfarmer, R. and Mueller, W. (1975) *Multinational Corporations in Brazil and Mexico: Structural Sources of Economic and Non-Economic Power*, Report to the Subcommittee on Multinational Corporations of the Committee on Foreign Relations, United States Senate, Washington DC, US Government Printing Office.

Nore, P. (1980) 'Oil and the state: a study of nationalization in the oil industry', in P. Nore and T. Turner (eds), *Oil and Class Struggle*, London, Zed Books.

Nore, P. and Turner, T. (eds) (1980) *Oil and Class Struggle*, London, Zed Books.

Nun, J. (1979) 'Dismissals in the Argentine motor industry: a case study of the floating surplus population', *Labour, Capital and Society*, 12, 1.

O'Brien, P. (1974) 'Developing countries and the patent system: an economic appraisal', *World Development*, September.

O'Brien, P. (1980) 'The new multinationals: developing country firms in international markets', *Futures*, August.

O'Connor, J. (1970) 'International corporations and economic underdevelopment', *Science and Society*, 32.

OECD (Organization for Economic Cooperation and Development) (1983) *Aluminium Industry: Energy Aspects of Structural Change*, Paris, OECD.

OECD (1984) *Investing in Free Export Processing Zones*, Paris, OECD, Development Centre Studies.

Olle, W. and Schoeller, W. (1977) 'World market competition and restrictions upon international trade union policies', *Capital and Class*, 2.

Olle, W. and Schoeller, W. (1982) 'Direct investment and monopoly theories of imperialism', *Capital and Class*, 16.

Oman, C. (1984) *New Forms of International Investment in Developing Countries*, Paris, OECD.

OU (1983) *Third World Studies, Block 4. The International Setting*, Milton Keynes, The Open University Press.

Ozawa, T. (1979) 'International investment and industrial structure: new theoretical implications from the Japanese experience', *Oxford Economic Papers*, 31.

Pack, H. (1981) 'Fostering the capital-goods sector in LDCs', *World Development*, 9, 3.

Palloix, C. (1975) 'The internationalization of capital and the circuit of social capital', in H. Radice (ed.), *International Firms and Modern Imperialism*, Harmondsworth, Penguin.

Palloix, C. (1976) 'The labour process: from Fordism to neo-Fordism', in Conference of Socialist Economists, *The Labour Process and Class Struggle*, London, Stage 1.

Parry, T. (1979) 'Competition and monopoly in multinational corporation relations with host countries', in R. G. Hawkins (ed.), *The Economic Effects of Multinational Corporations*, Greenwich, Conn., JAI Press.

Pearson, S. R. and Cownie, J. (1974) *Commodity Exports and African Economic Development*, Lexington, Heath.

Penrose, E. (1971) 'Monopoly and competition in the international petroleum industry', in E. Penrose, *The Growth of Firms, Middle East Oil and Other Essays*, London, Frank Cass.

Petras, J. and Rhodes, R. (1976) 'The reconsolidation of U.S. hegemony', *New Left Review*, 97.

Petras, J. and Zeitlin, M. (1968) 'Miners and agrarian radicalism', in J. Petras and M. Zeitlin (eds), *Latin America, Reform or Revolution*, Greenwich, Conn., Fawcett Publications.

Philip, G. (1976) 'The limitations of bargaining theory: a case study of the international petroleum company in Peru', *World Development*, 4, 3.

Picciotto, S. (1978) 'Firm and state in the world economy', in J. Faundez and S. Picciotto (eds), *The Nationalization of Multinationals in Peripheral Economies*, London, Macmillan.

Picciotto, S. and Radice, H. (1971) 'European integration, capital and the state', *Bulletin of the Conference of Socialist Economists*, 1, 1.

Plasschaert, S. (1985) 'Transfer pricing problems in developing countries', in A. Rugman and L. Eden (eds), *Multinationals and Transfer Pricing*, London, Croom Helm.

Poulantzas, N. (1975) 'Internationalization of capitalist relations and the nation-state', *Economy and Society*.

Quijano, A. (1974) 'The marginal pole of the economy and the marginalised labour force', *Economy and Society*, 3, 4.

Radetzki, M. (1977) 'Where should developing countries' minerals be processed?' *World Development*, 5, 4.

Radhu, G. (1973) 'Transfer of technical knowhow through multinational corporations in Pakistan, *Pakistan Development Review*, 12, 4.

Radice, H. (ed.) (1975) *International Firms and Modern Imperialism*, Harmondsworth, Penguin.

Radice, H. (1984) 'The national economy – a Keynesian myth?' *Capital and Class*, 22.

Reuber, G. L. (1973) *Private Foreign Investment in Development*, Oxford, Clarendon Press.

Reynolds, C. (1965) 'Development problems of an export economy. The case of Chile and copper', in M. Mamalakis and C. Reynolds (eds), *Essays on the Chilean Economy*, Homewood, Illinois, Richard D. Irwin.

Robbins, S. and Stobaugh, R. (1974) *Money in the Multinational Enterprise: A Study of Financial Policy*, London, Longman.

Robinson, J. (1983) *Multinationals and Political Control*, London, Gower.

Rose, S. (1977) 'Why the multinational tide is ebbing', *Fortune*, August.

Rosenberg, N. (1982) *Inside the Black Box: Technology and Economics*, Cambridge, Cambridge University Press.

Roumeliotis, P. (1981) 'Underinvoicing aluminium from Greece', in R. Murray (ed.), *Multinationals Beyond the Market*, Brighton, Harvester.

Rowthorn, B. (1975) 'Imperialism in the 1970s – Unity or Rivalry?', in H. Radice (ed.), *International Firms and Modern Imperialism*, Harmondsworth, Penguin.

Rugman, A. M. (1981) *Inside the Multinationals: The Economics of Internal Markets*, London, Croom Helm.

Rugman, A. and Eden, L. (eds) (1985) *Multinationals and Transfer Pricing*, London, Croom Helm.

Sabolo, Y. and Trajtenberg, R. (1976) *The Impact of Transnational Enterprises on Employment in the Developing Countries: preliminary results*, Geneva, ILO, WEP 2–28, WP 6.

Salama, P. (1976) *El proceso de 'subdesarrollo'*, Mexico City, Ediciones Era.

Salama, P. (1978) 'Specificites de l'internationalisation du capital en Amerique Latine', *Revue Tiers Monde*, XIX, 74.

Samuelson, H-F. (1982) *Transnational Corporations in the Export Processing Zones of Developing Countries*, United Nations Centre on Transnational Corporations, mimeo.

Sandbrook, R. and Cohen, R. (eds) (1975) *The Development of an African Working Class*, London, Longman.

Schiffer, J. (1981) 'The changing post-war pattern of development: the accumulated wisdom of Samir Amin', *World Development*, 9, 6.

Schmitz, H. (1985) *Technology and Employment Practices in Developing Countries*, London, Croom Helm.

Segall, M. (1975) *Pharmaceuticals and Health Planning in Developing Countries*, Institute of Development Studies, communication 119.

Semmler, W. (1982a) 'Competition, monopoly and differentials of profit rates: theoretical considerations and empirical evidence', *Review of Radical Political Economics*, 13, 4.

Semmler, W. (1982b) 'Theories of competition and monopoly', *Capital and Class*, 18.

Semmler, W. (1984) *Competition, Monopoly and Differential Profit Rates*, New York, Columbia University Press.

Sercovich, F. (1974) 'Dependencia Tecnologica en la Industria Argentina', *Desarrollo Economico*, 14, 53.

Serra, J. (1979) 'Three mistaken theses regarding the connection between industrialization and authoritarian regimes', in D. Collier (ed.), *The New Authoritarianism in Latin America*, Princeton University Press.

Shaikh, A. (1979) 'Political economy and capitalism: notes on Dobbs' theory of crisis', *Cambridge Journal of Economics*, 2.

Shaikh, A. (1980) 'Marxian competition versus perfect competition: further comments on the so-called choice of technique', *Cambridge Journal of Economics*, 4.

Shepherd, P. L. (1985) 'Transnational corporations and the international cigarette industry', in R. Newfarmer (ed.), *Profits, Progress, Poverty: Studies of International Industries in Latin America*, Notre Dame University Press.

Sigmund, P. (1980) *Multinationals in Latin America: The Politics of Nationalization*, Madison, University of Wisconsin Press.

Soete, L. (1981) 'Technological dependency: a critical view', in D. Seers (ed.), *Dependency Theory, a Critical Reassessment*, London, Frances Pinter.

Sourrouille, J. (1980) *El Complejo Automotor en Argentina*, Mexico City, ILET/Editorial Nueva Imagen.

Stewart, F. (1978) *Technology and Underdevelopment*, London, Macmillan.

Stewart, F. (1979) *International Technology Transfer: Issues and Policy Options*, World Bank, Staff Working Paper 344, Washington DC.

Stopford, J. (1974) 'The origins of British-based multinational manufacturing enterprises', *Business History Review*, vol. XLVIII, no. 3.

Stopford, J., Dunning, J. and Haberich, K. (1980) *The World Directory of Multinational Enterprises*, London, Macmillan.

Stopford, J. and Dunning, J. (1983) *Multinationals: Company Performance and Global Trends*, London, Macmillan.

Strassman, W. (1968) *Technological Change and Economic Development*, Ithaca, New York, Cornell University Press.

Streeten, P. (1981) *Development Perspectives*, London, Macmillan.

Sunkel, O. (1972) 'Big business and "Dependencia": a Latin American view', *Foreign Affairs*, 517–31.

Sunkel, O. (1973) 'Transnational capitalism and national disintegration in Latin America', *Social and Economic Studies*, 22, 1.

Sweezy, P. and Magdoff, H. (1969) 'Notes on the multinational corporation', *Monthly Review*, 21, 5 and 6.

Taira, K. and Standing, G. (1973) 'Labour market effects of multinational enterprises in Latin America', *Nebraska Journal of Economics and Business*, 12, Autumn.

Tanzer, M. (1980) *The Race for Resources: Continuing Struggles over Minerals and Fuels*, London, Heinemann.

Teece, D. (1977) 'Technology transfer by multinational firms: the resource cost of transferring technological knowhow', *Economic Journal*, 87.

Teece, D. (1981) 'The market for know how and the efficient international transfer of technology', *The Annals of the American Academy of Political and Social Science*, 458.

Teitel, S. (1984) 'Technology creation in semi-industrial economies', *Journal of Development Economics*, 16.

Thoburn, J. (1977) *Primary Commodity Exports and Economic Development*, London, John Wiley & Sons.

Thomson, D. and Larson, R. (1978) *Where Were You Brother? An Account of Trade Union Imperialism*, London, War on Want.

Thym, J. (1981) *Global Corporate Strategy of Aluminium Multinationals and Implications for Producer Countries*, Master's Thesis, Institute of Social Studies, The Hague, Netherlands.

TIE (Transnational Information Exchange) (December 1982–January 1983) 'Industrial Relations: A guide for trade unionists', *TIE Bulletin*, 13/14.

TIE (1985) 'Meeting the corporate challenge', *TIE Report*, 18/19.

Trajtenberg, R. (1976) *Transnational Enterprises and the Cheap Labour Force in Less Developed Countries*, Geneva, ILO, WEP 2–28, WP 15.

Trajtenberg, R. (1985) *Concentracion Global y Transnacionalizacion*, Buenos Aires, Centro de Economia Transnacional.

Turner, L. (1983) *Oil Companies in the International System*, London, George Allen & Unwin.

Turner, T. (1980) 'Iranian oilworkers in the 1978–79 Revolution', in P. Nore and T. Turner (eds), *Oil and Class Struggle*, London, Zed Books.

UN (1973) *Multinational Corporations in World Development*, New York, United Nations, Department of Economic and Social Affairs.

UNCTAD (United Nations Conference on Trade and Development) (1972) *Major Issues Arising from the Transfer of Technology to Developing Countries*, Geneva, UNCTAD, TD/B/AC, 11/10.

UNCTAD (1975) *Major Issues in Transfer of Technology to Developing Countries: A Case Study of the Pharmaceutical Industry*, Geneva, UNCTAD, TD/B/C, 6/4.

UNCTAD (1977) *Dominant Positions of Market Power of Transnational Corporations: Use of the Transfer Pricing Mechanism*, Geneva, UNCTAD, ST/MD/6.

UNCTAD (1980) *Legislation and Regulations on Technology Transfer: Empirical Analysis of their Effects in Selected Countries. The Implementation of Transfer of Technology Regulations: A Preliminary Analysis of the Experience of Latin America, India and Philippines*, Geneva, UNCTAD, TD/B/C, 6/55.

UNCTAD (1981) *Examination of the Economic, Commercial and Developmental Aspects of Industrial Property in the Transfer of Technology to Developing Countries: Review of Recent Trends in Patents in Developing Countries*, Geneva, UNCTAD, TD/B/C.6/AC.5/3.

UNCTAD (1981) *Handbook of International Trade and Development*, Geneva, UNCTAD.

UNCTAD (1984) *Handbook of International Trade and Development*, Geneva, UNCTAD.

UNCTC (United Nations Centre on Transnational Corporations)

(1978) *Transnational Corporations in World Development: A Re-examination*, New York, UN, E/C 10/38.

UNCTC (1979a) *Transnational Corporations in Advertising*, New York, UN, ST/CTC/8.

UNCTC, (1979b) *Transnational Corporations and the Pharmaceutical Industry*, New York, UN, ST/CTC/9.

UNCTC (1981a) *Transnational Corporations in the Bauxite/Aluminium Industry*, New York, UN, ST/CTC/20.

UNCTC (1981b) *Transnational Corporations in the Copper Industry*, New York, UN, ST/CTC/21.

UNCTC (1983) *Transnational Corporations in World Development Third Survey*, New York, UN, ST/CTC/46.

UNIDO (United Nations Industrial Development Organization) (1978) *Transnational Corporations and the Processing of Raw Materials: Impact on Developing Countries*, Vienna, ID/B/209.

UNIDO (1983) *Industry in a Changing World*, New York, UN.

US Senate, Committee of Finance (1973) *Implications of Multinational Firms for World Trade and Investment and for US Trade and Labour*, Washington DC.

Vaitsos, C. (1972) 'Patents revisited: their function in developing countries', in C. Cooper (ed.), *Science, Technology and Production*, London, Frank Cass.

Vaitsos, C. (1974a) *Inter-Country Income Distribution and Transnational Enterprises*, Oxford, Clarendon Press.

Vaitsos, C. (1974b) 'Employment effects of foreign direct investment in developing countries', in E. Edwards (ed.), *Employment in Developing Nations*, New York, Columbia University Press.

Vaitsos, C. (1975) 'The process of commercialization of technology in the Andean Pact', in H. Radice (ed.), *International Firms and Modern Imperialism*, Harmondsworth, Penguin.

Vaitsos, C. (1976) *Employment Problems and Transnational Enterprises in Developing Countries: Distortions and Inequality*, Geneva, International Labour Office.

Vaitsos, C. (1978) *The Role of Transnational Enterprises in Latin American Economic Integration Efforts: Who Integrates and With Whom. How and For What Benefit?* Paper presented to UNCTAD Round Table on the Role of Transnational Enterprises in the Latin American Integration Process, Lima.

Vaupel, J. and Curhan, J. (1973) *The World's Multinational Enterprises: A Source Book of Tables*, Boston, Division of Research, Harvard Business School.

Vernon, R. (1973) *Sovereignty at Bay*, Harmondsworth, Penguin.

Vernon, R. (1977) *Storm Over the Multinationals: the Real Issues*, London, Macmillan.

Vernon, R. (1981) 'Sovereignty at bay, ten years after', *International Organization*, 35, 3.

Vickery, G. (1984) 'Some aggregate measures of new forms of investment', in C. Oman, *New Forms of International Investment in Developing Countries*, Paris, OECD.

Villela, A. (1984) 'Multinationals from Brazil', in S. Lall (ed.), *The New Multinationals: The Spread of Third World Enterprises*, Chichester, John Wiley & Sons.

Warren, B. (1973) 'Imperialism and capitalist industrialization', *New Left Review*, 81.

Warren, B. (1975) 'How international is capital?', in H. Radice (ed.), *International Firms and Modern Imperialism*, Harmondsworth, Penguin.

Warren, B. (1980) *Imperialism: Pioneer of Capitalism*, London, Verso.

Waterman, P. (1975) 'The labour aristocracy in Africa: introduction to a debate', *Development and Change*, 6, 3.

Waterman, P. (ed.) (1984) *For a New Labour Internationalism*, The Hague, ILERI.

Weeks, J. (1977) 'Backwardness, foreign capital, and accumulation in the manufacturing sector of Peru, 1954–1975', *Latin American Perspectives*, issue 14, IV, 3.

Weeks, J. (1981) *Capital and Exploitation*, Princeton University Press.

Weisskopf, T. (1978) 'Imperialism and the economic development of the Third World', in R. G. Edwards, M. Reich and T. Weisskopf (eds), *The Capitalist System*, Englewood Cliffs, NJ, Prentice Hall.

Wells, L. T. (1973) 'Economic man and engineering man: choice in a low wage country', *Public Policy*, Summer.

Wells, L. T. (1983) *Third World Multinationals: The Rise of Foreign Investment from Developing Countries*, Cambridge, Mass., MIT Press.

White, E. (1981) 'The international projection of firms from Latin American countries', in K. Kumar and M. G. McLeod (eds), *Multinationals from Developing Countries*, Lexington, Lexington Books.

White, L. J. (1978) 'The evidence on appropriate factor proportions for manufacturing in less developed countries: a survey', *Economic Development and Cultural Change*, 26.

Wilkins, M. (1970) *The Emergence of Multinational Enterprise: American Business Abroad from the Colonial Era to 1914*, Cambridge, Mass., Harvard University Press.

Wilkins, M. (1974) *The Maturing of Multinational Enterprise: American*

Business Abroad from 1914 to 1970, Cambridge, Mass., Harvard University Press.

Williams, M. L. (1975) 'The extent and significance of the nationalization of foreign-owned assets in developing countries, 1956–1972', *Oxford Economic Papers*, 27, 2.

Wilson, C. (1974) 'The multinational in historical perspective', in K. Nakagawa (ed.), *Strategy and Structure of Big Business*, University of Tokyo Press.

Woods, D. (1979) 'Current price and investment trends in the world aluminium/bauxite market: their effect on the U.S. economy', in D. Denoon (ed.), *The New International Economic Order: a US Response*, New York University Press.

World Bank (1985) *World Development Report, 1985*, Washington DC, The World Bank.

World Bank (1986) *World Development Report, 1986*, Washington DC, The World Bank.

Yamin, M. and Nixson, F. (1984) *Transnational Corporations and the Control of Restrictive Business Practices: Theoretical Issues and Empirical Evidence*, revised version of a paper presented to the Development Studies Association Conference, Bradford.

Young, S. and Hood, N. (1980) 'Recent patterns of foreign direct investment by British multinational enterprises in the United States', *National Westminster Bank Quarterly Review*, May.

Index